T0329563

After Redundancy

To the men and women in Sheffield
whose story this is

After Redundancy

The Experience of Economic Insecurity

John Westergaard, Iain Noble and Alan Walker

Polity Press

Copyright © John Westergaard, Iain Noble and Alan Walker, 1989

First published 1989 by Polity Press
in association with Basil Blackwell

Editorial Office:
Polity Press, Dales Brewery, Gwydir Street,
Cambridge CB1 2LJ, UK

Basil Blackwell Ltd
108 Cowley Road, Oxford OX4 1JF, UK

Basil Blackwell Inc.
432 Park Avenue South, Suite 1503,
New York, NY10016, USA

British Library Cataloguing in Publication Data

Westergaard, John
 After redundancy : the experience of
 economic insecurity.
 1. Great Britain. Personnel. Redundancy.
 Social aspects
 I. Title II. Noble, Iain III. Walker,
 Alan, *1949*–
 306'.36
 ISBN 0-7456-0150-1

Library of Congress Cataloging-in-Publication Data

Westergaard, John H.
 After redundancy.
 Bibliography: p.
 Includes index.
 1. Unemployment – England – Sheffield.
 2. Steel industry and trade – England – Sheffield.
 3. Plant shutdowns – England – Sheffield.
 4. Economic security – England – Sheffield.
 5. Sheffield (Eng.) – Social conditions.
 I. Noble, Iain. II. Walker, Alan. III. Title
 HD5766.S48W7 1989   331.13'7942821   88–34960
 ISBN 0-7456-0151-0

Typeset in 11 on 12½ point Ehrhardt
by Hope Services, Abingdon

T. J. Press Ltd, Padstow, Cornwall

Contents

List of tables and figures   ix
Preface   xi
Introduction: the study   1

1 THE ECONOMIC AND POLITICAL CONTEXT

From social reconstruction through corporatism to
   neo-liberalism   7
Perceptions of unemployment and the unemployed   13
Labour market insecurity and class structure   18
The local context   25

2 THE COMING OF REDUNDANCY

The people who lost their jobs   30
News of the plant closure   32
Non-resistance and division of views   34
Redundancy payments and their distribution   40
Views of the payments   45

3 THE IMPACT OF REDUNDANCY
The First Search for New Work

Early initiative – and its irrelevance   49
Means to the search for jobs   53
Registration as unemployed   56

4 THE IMPACT OF REDUNDANCY
Economic Experience over Three Years

Re-employment, unemployment and discouragement   59
Class polarization of the declining labour market   62
Social differences in withdrawal from the labour market   67

Class divisions in and out of the market   68
The widening of the market gap over time   71
Incomes three years after redundancy   75

5   RE-EMPLOYMENT AND UNEMPLOYMENT

Reactions to redundancy   81
Patterns of post-redundancy experience   82
Re-employment and 'secondary redundancy'   85
Commitment to paid employment   90
The experience of unemployment   94
Partial withdrawal from the labour market and
    social life   98
Redundancy payments and their uses   100

6   RETIREMENT AND EARLY RETIREMENT

Early retirement: demand push or supply pull?   104
The impact of redundancy on employment status   105
Normal retirement: those retiring at 65   109
The decision to take early retirement   110
Pressures on older workers to take early retirement   114
Social exclusion, discouragement and early retirement   120
Attitudes towards retirement   122
Attitudes towards re-employment   125

7   VOTING AND DEFECTION FROM LABOUR

Economic experience versus political views: a disjunction? 127
Voting trends   130
Defections from Labour and socio-political division   132
Socio-economic factors in defection from Labour   136
Reasons for defection from Labour   139

8   AMBIGUITIES OF SOCIO-POLITICAL ORIENTATION

For peace in industry   147
For labour solidarity   151
Conflicts of 'conventional wisdom'   153
Ostensible inconsistencies of opinion   155
Varieties of 'inconsistency'   159
Sources of 'anti-militancy'   162
Views of British society   164

9 CONCLUSIONS

The survey as a case study 169
Unemployment and non-employment 170
Divisions of economic experience 171
The need for an employment policy 175
Trends and divisions of political opinion 180

Appendix 1 Response to the Survey 185
Appendix 2 Summary of the Interview Schedule 186

References 195
Index 203

List of tables and figures

TABLES

2.1 Average redundancy pay, by occupational level and length of
service 43
3.1 For respondents under 60 at interview: employment status at
two points of time after redundancy, by former occupational
level and time of job search start 52
4.1 Employment status soon after redundancy and at interview,
by age 60
4.2 Employment status at two points in time, by age and
occupational level with firm 64–5
4.3 Employment status at interview for respondents (A) working
and (B) unemployed at different dates after redundancy; by
occupational level with firm 72–3
4.4 Average net joint income per week in households of two or
more persons, at time of interview in 1982–3, by informant's
employment status then and his/her occupational level with
firm 76
5.1 Informants' current employment position at time of interview
by duration of current position 83
5.2 Age and former occupational class of informants by
proportion employed for 90% or more of the post-
redundancy period and average number of months in paid
employment 86
5.3 Average scores for employment commitment scale and items
by employment position at interview 92
5.4 Average number of months unemployed between
redundancy and interview by age and former occupational
class of informants 95

List of tables and figures

7.1 Votes or vote intentions, 1979 and 1983: the UK, Sheffield and the After-Redundancy study group 131

7.2 Party support and defection from Labour, by occupational level before redundancy 134

8.1 Views on issues of industrial relations, by party-political support and by occupational level before redundancy 148–9

8.2. Consistencies and inconsistencies of view on issues of industrial relations, by party-political support and by occupational level before redundancy 156–7

8.3 Ideas about British society, by occupational level before redundancy 166–7

FIGURES

6.1 Employment status of older male workers following redundancy according to age at time of redundancy 107

6.2 Employment status of younger and middle-aged male workers following redundancy according to age at time of redundancy 108

Preface

The starting point of this book was quite a while ago: in 1979, when the people whose story it is lost their jobs at a Sheffield steel company, which must still remain anonymous. We interviewed them in 1982–3, to find out what had happened to them in and out of the labour market since their redundancy; how they saw that experience; and how their views on politics and industrial affairs might have been affected. The fact that rather more than three years had passed between their redundancy and our survey was an advantage. It meant that we could piece together a record of their experience over a fairly long period: long enough, in particular, to distinguish temporary difficulties from enduring hardships; long enough also, for example, to see whether an early start on job-hunting after notice of redundancy makes any long-term difference in outcome for people who are poorly placed in a declining labour market.

Another four years and more passed between completion of the fieldwork for the study and completion of the manuscript of this book. Even allowing for the time needed for analysis, and for the fact that we have already published some of the results in article form, this was longer than we had thought and hoped. No doubt deficiencies of our own contributed to the delay; but it reflected also an intensification of the pressures in academic life since the beginning of the 1980s. Like most of our colleagues, we have had to try to keep more plates spinning with less help to do it. So writing this full account of our study proved a slow and often interrupted business.

Those pressures, of course, were as nothing to the pressures that lost our survey respondents their jobs in 1979 and kept many of them out of paid work for long or forever afterwards. Yet, ironically, the two sets of pressures had something of a common source – in the shift of economic and political climate which has marked Britain since the late 1970s. It is also that shift of climate which gives, we believe, a continued relevance to the survey reported in this book, even though the book has been rather long in the making. The record of our respondents' economic experience and political opinions covers just those years when the change set in most dramatically: from 1979 to 1983. Prime features of the change, moreover, are still with us four or five years later. As we write, in mid-1987, unemployment is still high though, in officially recorded figures at least, not fully as high as it was; and the General Election of June 1987 has repeated the 1979 and 1983 parliamentary victories of a Conservative Party dedicated to 'new right' prescriptions. Both those features of the changed landscape, economic and political, set the themes of this book.

We have a great many debts of gratitude to acknowledge. Our thanks go to the management of the now-closed firm that once employed our respondents – not least the senior staff of the Personnel Office – for approaching us in the first place and for giving us the opportunity to follow their former employees up after redundancy. We are no less grateful to the trade unions and their chief conveners in the firm, who gave their blessing to our project; and in this connection we wish to record our special thanks to Mr B. R. Knapton and Mr G. L. Turner for their help and information. Our thanks go also to the Social Science (now Economic and Social) Research Council, for providing the grant without which the work could not have been done; and to the University of Sheffield, as well as our own Department of Sociological Studies within it, for housing the project and supporting it in other ways. The professional interviewers and the student coders who did so much of the detailed work are too many to list by name: our thanks to them are no less warm for that. But we can and must name Jill Sargent and Margaret Jaram, who translated our words and numbers into typed form with outstanding and unruffled competence. We wish, moreover, to express our appreciation to Tony Giddens and Polity Press for their tolerance when completion of the book dragged out. The increased demands of work in recent years mean that we owe greater debts than usual to those whose personal support has been invaluable: on this score we want to thank, respectively, Hanne Westergaard, Sheila Robertson and Carol Walker.

Our gratitude goes above all to the men and women whose experiences and views make up the substance of this book. They gave unstintingly of their time, in long interviews that took them through a period of their lives which had been disturbing for all and enduringly hard for many. Our dedication of the book to several hundreds of unnamed people can be only a token; but it is the one way in which we can mark our deep thanks to our respondents.

J.W., I.N., A.W.
Sheffield

Introduction: The Study

In 1979 a long-established private sector steel company in Sheffield – too small to have been nationalized in 1967, but taken over in 1978 by a large multinational corporation – gave notice of the first of a series of redundancies which were to lead to closure of the firm in 1983. Of a total of some 3,700 employees, about 1,000 left in that first round; but of these around 400 were transferred to work in other local steel manufacture by arrangements negotiated between their former and their new employers. The other 600 or so were made redundant, the great majority of them on a formally voluntary basis under a union-agreed scheme which boosted their statutory redundancy pay. Most were men, mainly skilled and semi-skilled manual workers with long years of service in the firm, but including some – one in every five of those made redundant – whose work had been on the staff side of the company as supervisors and low-to-middle level managers, technical employees and salesmen. A minority, about one in eight, were women; the jobs they left had been mainly in clerical and similar routine-grade office work.

This book is an account of what happened, over the next three years, to these people who found themselves redundant in 1979, as a fairly early group among the many who have come to have first-hand experience of the drastic decline in its traditional manufacturing activity which Sheffield has seen during the last ten years or so. And Sheffield's recent history on this score has many parallels across the country, indeed throughout the western world, though the slide into slump has been notably steep in this city. More accurately the book tells the story – a good part of it anyway, as far as we could piece it together from long interviews – of what happened to just under 400 out of the total of 600: those whom we were able to trace, and who agreed to talk to our interviewers in late 1982 and early 1983, about three years after they had lost their jobs with the firm.

In answer to a mainly 'structured' interview schedule (which took an average of over two hours to go through, and which we summarize in Appendix 2), they described their experiences in the labour market over those three years: the search for new work which most had gone through after losing their old jobs, their successes and failures in that search. The many for whom this had been hard talked about their experience of unemployment, often still continuing; or about the decision a number of them had reached to pull out of the labour market – some at once, others only as their hopes of finding paid work again faded – into retirement, usually early, or into work without pay as a 'housewife'. They told our interviewers how they had felt when they heard about the redundancies which were to change their lives; or if, as over half had done some time after their redundancy, they had signed on as unemployed; or when, at different times, they had come to such terms as they could with new jobs, or lengthy unemployment, or withdrawal to retirement or housework. We found out from them about their redundancy payments and how they had used this money; and from most of them – some held back over this – about their current incomes, whether from new paid work, social security or pensions and savings. We also felt out their views on politics and other public affairs, through a wide range of questions about how they had voted and intended to vote, about trade unions and industrial relations, about policies to deal with unemployment and about the fairness or unfairness of social arrangements in Britain as they saw them.

We included a good many questions of the latter sort – on political matters in a broad sense – because it was one of our aims to find out whether the experience of redundancy, often followed by protracted personal hardship, tends to change people's political attitudes: whether, for example, it generally pushes them leftwards and prods trade union supporters towards more militancy; or at least, since ours was only a local study, whether this is a common outcome in a city like Sheffield, where there is already a tradition of labour radicalism in organised politics. This issue – how people respond in their political views, and so also perhaps in their actions, to individual experience of the kinds of economic sea-change which recession brings about – is rightly a question of much interest. But knowledge in answer to it has been, so far, more a matter of general impressions than of specific facts, despite the considerable volume of research into unemployment and related issues stimulated by the crisis of recent years. (See, however, Fraser, Marsh and Jobling, 1985.)

Ours is in any case not a study of unemployment – or rather not just of that. Many of our respondents did become employed after redundancy, whether for a short time, recurrently or continuously. Many, too, sooner or later pulled out of engagement with the world of formal paid work, and so reduced the official count of unemployment though they took a number of the problems of being unemployed with them into retirement or housework. Many others, though far fewer than would have wanted it, found jobs again, whether on a par with their former work or, as quite often, rather below that mark. It is this diversity of experience, from the common starting point of sudden redundancy, which affords a valuable opportunity for study. We can compare those whose experiences differed: to see how they differed, what made for the differences, and how their reactions and views differed according to their experience.

The opportunity to carry out a study of this kind is in fact fairly rare. Of course, samples can be drawn from among the unemployed, or at least those registered as unemployed; and even, as in one major official study (Moylan, Millar and Davies, 1983) from among those who registered at a particular time in order to follow up their later experience. Nevertheless, the story that can be told will miss out those people who, having lost their former jobs, either walk more or less straight into other paid work or, conversely, pull out of the labour market altogether. There are no official records kept of redundancies, with the names and addresses of those involved, from which a sample might be drawn in order to follow through how they all fared. But occasionally such a list can be constructed (Harris, Lee and Morris, 1985) or it comes to hand by good fortune. Our case was of the latter kind.

In the summer of 1980 – not quite a year after the round of redundancies in our study began – the management of the firm approached us with a suggestion that, from a list of names and addresses, we might trace some or all of the people made redundant in order to find out what had happened to them. The reasons for this interest were not entirely clear. It may have come from genuine concern on the part of a management – especially its Personnel Department – locally known to have maintained a tradition of paternal interest in its labour force, even through take-over of the company by a multinational corporation a couple of years earlier. It may also, perhaps, have reflected a sense that a study to follow-up a redundancy scheme involving fairly generous terms of severance might benefit the company's image and its relations with the remaining workforce, or might offer some guidance for future redundancies. Management in any case thought of the project as a modest one – a job, perhaps, for a postgraduate student looking for a thesis subject. We welcomed the proposal in principle, as a rare opportunity, for the reasons we have outlined. But just for those reasons we stressed the need for a thorough and full-scale study – of as many of the people made redundant as could be traced; with the questions to be

asked a matter for our decision in the final instance, and so almost
certainly covering a wider range than the company had in mind; and, of
course, on an understanding that respondents' anonymity and our
responsibility for data collection, analysis and publication, independent
of the firm, would be guaranteed. All this meant that we would need
financial support from a research council or foundation, and the firm's
agreement for us to apply for this.

Such agreement was delayed, and for a time seemed unlikely. This
was not, we think, because management found our 'no strings'
conditions unacceptable, or the scale of the survey we proposed
unreasonable even if it was more than they had envisaged. But the
company's financial situation steadily worsened; our link to the board via
the Personnel Department was interrupted by a change of staff and a
downgrading of that Department; and in these circumstances, interest in
the project – at least at the level from which agreement would have to
come, but probably also lower down in management – appeared to
vanish. Certainly the board had more pressing things to worry about. In
the event, however, we coupled an appeal against a provisionally
negative decision with an assurance that we would need only permission
– subject also to union agreement – to use the list of names and
addresses which, together with some supplementary information for
eventual checks on response, was already to hand. No further demands
on the company's hard-squeezed resources would be made. The board
now agreed; we secured union agreement, with the help of the
conveners who had negotiated the original redundancy scheme; and we
applied for, and obtained, a grant from the Social Science (now
Economic and Social) Research Council to allow the work to start
towards the end of 1981.

Three points follow as corollaries to this process of negotiation. The
first is of small significance, even though it calls for explanation: we
cannot name the firm. Its identity may not be hard to guess for readers
with local knowledge, and some others, from such incidental facts about
the company and the redundancies as we need to report to set the scene:
we cannot fully anonymize these. But it was part of our agreement with
the company that in no publications arising from the study would the
name of the firm be disclosed, save by permission of the board; and the
firm and the board no longer exist to give such permission.

Second, in addition to the list of names and addresses from which we
were able to trace respondents, we obtained only limited preliminary
information from management about the company, the circumstances
which led to the redundancies, and the discussions, negotiations and

decisions about these. We would have expected to obtain more, had our own negotiations for the study not stalled first; and then been resumed to positive effect but with the proviso that we would not ask for more information than we already had or needed additionally, on a minimum basis, to follow through interviews with the people who had been made redundant. This is therefore, in essence, a study only of those people *after redundancy* – and of their recollections of the time when the redundancies were notified – not of the processes which led to redundancy. We heard a little about these from management in the early phase of contact; and a little more – especially about the negotiations that led to the redundancy scheme – from the trade union conveners who had been closely involved. But this was enough only to sketch in part of the background.

We can say little or nothing, for example, about such selectivity as management may have operated in implementing the redundancy scheme. The scheme applied to one part of the firm in the first instance, the Forging Division, which was closed and its order book sold to another company, the local competitor with which the main arrangement for transfer of a number of workers was agreed. But the redundancy scheme was also, on a discretionary basis, made open to application from employees in other sections of the firm, who no doubt saw that the writing on the wall looked ominous if still not clear beyond doubt. We do not know what selectivity management may have practised, by way of encouraging or turning down such applications from outside the Forging Division, as well as in the arrangements for transfer of some workers from the Division to employment with its former competitors. Experience elsewhere (e.g. Harris, Lee and Morris, 1985) suggests that management selectivity in this stage *before* redundancy may have worked to similar effect as labour market selectivity *after* redundancy – to favour employment, continued or new, of the more skilled by comparison with the less skilled; of middle-grade 'staff' by comparison with routine-grade office workers; of younger, established employees by comparison with their elders. But any such first-stage setting of the trends we shall describe as prominent in the second stage remains, in the case of our study, a matter for speculation. The very difficulties of the company which led to the redundancies restrict our detailed information to the period after redundancy.

The third point we have to note as a consequence of the delay in approval of the study proved, in the event, a positive one. It concerns the length of the period after redundancy over which we were able to trace the experiences of respondents. It was not by our choice that the period became one of three years – in fact an average of a little more (38 months from redundancy to interview), with individual variations but none of significance between the various sub-groups of informants we came to distinguish in the analysis. This was forced on us, first by the delay in obtaining final agreement to the study; then by our need to apply for money to carry out the work and, having got it, to find and appoint the research officer in everyday charge of the project (Iain Noble); and finally, by the extensive preparations necessary for systematic tracing and interviewing of respondents. In fact, we worried that too much time might have elapsed for us to trace a sufficient number, representatively constituted, of the people made redundant, when we knew only their addresses of three years earlier. Our anxieties turned out, by and large, to be unwarranted: the response to the interview survey was good and well spread, as we explain with more technical detail later. The passage of a little over three years from redundancy to interview, moreover, meant that we could follow up the impact of job-termination over a period long enough for the differing patterns of experience to have become settled. Incidentally, it also brought us fairly close to the General Election of 1983 when we interviewed, so giving respondents' accounts of their voting intentions and attitudes a firmer substance than otherwise. Yet it was not too long for memories of the redundancies and what followed to have faded or suffered significant distortion. In this respect, our initial handicap in launching the research turned into unplanned advantage for its design.

I

The Economic and Political Context

FROM SOCIAL RECONSTRUCTION THROUGH CORPORATISM
TO NEO-LIBERALISM

The redundancies at the Sheffield firm in 1979 were, of course, only one instance of a much larger phenomenon: the end of a period, three to four decades long, in which some sort of dependable livelihood from paid work had been available to almost all men who wanted it; and to women too in increasing numbers, though with neither the dependability nor the rewards usual for men. The familiar, simple measure of this growth of job insecurity is the rise in the officially recorded rate of unemployment: from an average for the United Kingdom of under two per cent in the post-war years to the second half of the 1960s, then unevenly to between five and six per cent by the end of the 1970s, and to nearly 14 per cent by early 1986. Thereafter, from about mid-1986, the official count began to show some fall. By mid-1987 the rate stood at about 12 per cent, by the mode of percentage calculation previously used; but this was still twice as high as the corresponding rate from the public record of eight years earlier.

With this shift in an essential parameter of the economic climate, moreover, have gone shifts in the climate of policy and public debate about employment and unemployment, whether as cause or effect or a combination of the two. Like many other western countries, Britain emerged from the Second World War with a politically agreed commitment to high and stable levels of employment – by contrast with the inter-war period – and to the use of Keynesian prescriptions for macro-economic demand management to that end. True, the degree of consensus about both the end and the means was rather less than now often imagined in retrospect. It remained a widespread view in policy circles for some years after the war that keeping inflation at bay would require, on a regular long-run basis, a good deal more unemployment

than was actually experienced. And it was not until the early 1950s that
the wartime coalition's imprecise commitment in the 1944 White Paper
on *Employment Policy* came to be translated into a target of 'full
employment' involving an unemployment rate of no more than two or
three per cent (Deacon, 1981). Yet for most of the next two decades this
limit held in practice; and until late in this period doubts about it were
rarely aired in public, while the political parties seemed agreed that any
significant rise above it would spell electoral disaster for the government
in office. The conditions of economic growth and buoyant demand for
labour that kept unemployment low were commonly taken to help both
business profits and wage-or-salary incomes; and so also to maintain the
social stability which had been the aim of the political settlement in the
1940s, a package for 'social reconstruction' considerably extending
public welfare services as well as promising high employment.

Agreement in these terms – 'Butskellism' as it came to be called from
the names of two of its main Conservative and Labour spokesmen,
Butler and Gaitskell – began to evaporate from the second half of the
1960s. Among the several factors responsible for the change two were
central.

First the general maintenance of economic growth and buoyant
demand, despite fluctuations from 'go' to 'stop', had placed organized
labour in a sellers' market; and by the 1960s trade unions, more
especially an informal network of shopfloor organization stimulated into
rapid growth by boom conditions, had begun to pull muscle in that
market more visibly than before. The signs and effects of this – a rising
incidence of industrial action and a shift of it into growing industries
previously regarded as the vanguard of peaceful labour relations,
mounting wage claims and an upward 'wages drift' beyond the terms of
nationally negotiated agreements – were commonly overstated as
evidence of an imminent threat of 'anarchy'. But such overstatement was
significant because it pointed the way to new doubts and controversies
over the 1940s settlement and its labour market provisions not least.

Second, there were signs from about the middle 1960s which
suggested an incipient slackening of the international post-war boom;
and this appeared all the more ominous for Britain because, despite
continuing expansion, economic growth remained slower here than in
many other industrial countries and the share of British business in
world trade had been steadily sliding down.

Review of policy and associated assumptions and attitudes therefore
centred on two issues: how to devise new controls for labour relations,
and how to 'modernize' or 'restructure' the economy for enhanced
growth. In relation to both these issues, moreover, a third was seen as

crucial also: how to cut back rising inflation. Inflation was then regarded conventionally as the outcome of excessive wage claims; or less fashionably as yet as the outcome of excessive government creation of money to meet unrealistically rising expectations of public largesse among an electorate now used to competitive bribery by the political parties. On either view, inflation was seen as a threat to British business prospects in the international economy, and the Achilles heel of the post-war political settlement.

In essence two alternative lines of solution seemed possible – if, of course the solution were to be sought within a continuing framework of essentially capitalist economic arrangements, whatever the particular mix of private and public enterprise; and only the left wing of the labour movement questioned that assumption. One line was to combine some form of 'indicative planning' for co-ordinated modernization of production with measures to restrain labour demands adopted in co-operation between government, employers and above all trade unions. Such tripartite 'corporatism', with counter-inflationary incomes policies as their centre-piece, involved government in offering inducements to business and labour to ensure their co-operation. The carrots held out in common to both were promises of sustained demand and growth, as well as representation at the tables around which public economic policy was worked out. Business in addition was offered the hope of improved labour discipline, negotiated curbs on the pressure from trade unions and shopfloor organization; and more help towards investment as well as more protection from market insecurity. Labour in addition might be offered promises of income redistribution down the scale – whether as an ingredient of policies to restrain pay rises or through new tax and social security measures – and enhancement of union rights in collective bargaining. (Among the extensive literature on 'corporatist' policy see e.g. Crouch, 1977; Middlemas, 1979; Panitch, 1980, 1981; Westergaard, 1977; Winkler, 1975, 1976, 1977.)

Whereas this approach was designed to keep essential features of the 1940s settlement intact – and to hold back any rise in unemployment, even if not to keep it within the earlier 'full employment' limit – the alternative was to challenge the very premises of the settlement. This was to cut back state activities in the economic field: to reduce public expenditure and the inflationary pressures seen, from this perspective especially, to be generated by its steady increase hitherto; in that process, to re-educate the electorate and all manner of interest groups into greater self-reliance, to wean them away from continuously rising expectations of 'something for nothing'; to redirect economic activity from the public sector to private enterprise which, to many supporters of

this line, was the only source of true wealth; to free market forces for
unsubsidized competition, in which economic reconstruction would
follow as the weak went to the wall; and to discipline labour through that
release of market forces in conjunction with direct measures to break the
allegedly monopolistic and so market-inhibiting powers of trade unions.
This line of policy involved the use of sticks more than carrots:
withdrawal of government aid to business; forced restriction of trade
union autonomy, activities and legal 'immunities'; heightened selectivity
in public provision of welfare services; sharpened uncertainty of profits
for business and of employment and wages for labour as, with market
forces freed to impose their own disciplines, unviable enterprise would
be weeded out and at least transitional unemployment rise; and – rather
paradoxically for a set of economic prescriptions in direct line of descent
from nineteenth-century liberalism – a strong assertion of authority on
the part of the state, to enforce measures for its own reduction and to
maintain order against the social unrest that might follow. But there
were carrots on offer too: the promise of tax reductions and of freer play
for market incentives; of enhanced consumer choice, though within the
constraints of incomes likely to be more unequal than before; of the
longer-run economic regeneration which adherents of this approach
claimed for it as its achievable goal. (For cogent presentations and
discussions of the 'social market' alternative see, e.g., Brittan, 1977,
1978; and Gamble, 1979, 1981.)

Public policy emphasized the first alternative until the end of the
1970s. Versions of this 'corporatist' solution were adopted by Conservative
governments from about 1960 to 1964 and again, following a brief
counter-experiment, from about 1972 to 1974; in more explicit form by
Labour governments from 1964 to 1970 and again from 1974 to 1979.
True, neither these policy packages nor those in the alternative mode
conformed fully to the respective blueprints we have just outlined.
Already under the Wilson government from 1964 to 1970, for example,
the assumption began to creep in that some rise in unemployment – in
fact now visible – would have to be accepted to keep labour demands
and inflationary pressures in check; and the same government toyed
with ideas for legislation to restrict union powers, if only at the margin,
though it did not follow them through. Even in its 'corporatist' phase,
the Heath government kept alive the counter-union Industrial Relations
Act which it had passed in 1971, and so helped to nullify its own late
efforts to secure co-operation from organized labour. After the middle-
1970s the Callaghan government, despite an explicit 'social contact' with
the trade unions, adopted some of the 'monetarist' curbs on public

expenditure ideal – typically associated with the 'social market' solution; and recorded unemployment rose under that government's auspices to five per cent, a trend which its opponents were quick to underline as evidence that the way forward inescapably led through new market stringency. Conversely, the governments committed to free-market prescriptions – Heath 'Mark 1' from 1970 to about 1972, and Thatcher from 1979 – never stayed long in practice with their theoretical preference for withdrawal of all aid from business, their own prime constituency. Despite new restrictions and new selectivity in services for social security, moreover, even the Thatcher government held back from radical 'privatising' reconstruction of welfare provision – though education did become a target of new initiatives, announced in 1987, which might prove partly to that effect and which were associated with a running battle against local authorities. Finally, the Thatcher government's efforts to cut public expenditure failed, if only because reductions on many counts were counterbalanced by upward drift on others, most notably the public costs of steeply increased unemployment (see, e.g. Hills, 1987).

So the shift in the climate of policy and debate about the labour market cannot be simply equated with changes in government composition, or neatly periodized to fit in with those changes. Yet, by and large, the first choice made between the two blueprints favoured 'corporatist' prescriptions, and so only hesitantly accepted some limited deviation from 'full employment'. Indeed, free-market prescriptions hardly came onto the agenda for serious debate until the late 1960s. This is not surprising. By contrast with its alternative, the 'corporatist' way represented much less of a breach with the post-war political settlement and the economic practices surrounding it. It involved a reformulation of the relations between business and labour encapsulated in that settlement. Yet it offered general continuity of compromise, instead of sharpened conflict, at a time of still prevalent growth when labour as yet had market weight to sustain it in militancy, and business as yet had sound market reasons to shy away from confrontation. Indeed, 'corporatist' measures were a common response to incipient crisis in the 1960s in many western countries, those especially with a well-entrenched trade union movement.

That this solution gave way in Britain (or more dramatically here than anywhere else) to the alternative of free-market experimentation, can perhaps be explained in large part on two counts. First, when economic recession eventually broke on the world, the economy of this country proved especially vulnerable; in consequence both of the circumstances which had long held growth back at a relatively slow pace, and of the ties of dependence linking British business into the international economy. All this gave economic policy a particular salience in public debate; and it set a high pass mark for the tests to be met by any set of prescriptions to cure 'the British disease', the syndrome of economic weaknesses for which a good deal of blame was now assigned, in conventional opinion of most shades, to organized labour and the workings of the labour market. Second, the 'corporatist' prescriptions visibly failed those tests. Not only did recession eventually come and begin to bite hard; but also, and even before that, the co-operation of labour and business with government which 'corporatism' required had proved shaky.

This form of tripartite economic management is arguably by its nature liable to instability. Both business and labour pay a price – summarily, through acceptance of regulation and self-limitation of autonomy – for their participation; and either or both may withdraw if the returns do not seem to match the price. In Britain the trade unions twice took an overt initiative to pull out in this way, by repudiating incomes policies that had required them to discipline their own members in return for rewards – by way of dependable economic growth, redistribution or firmer bargaining rights – which appeared increasingly uncertain or illusory. They did so once at the tail end of the 1960s; the second time in the strike-ridden 'winter of discontent' of 1978–9. On both occasions they were in dispute with governments of 'their own colour', and the following General Elections brought free-market oriented governments into office – Heath 'Mark I' and Thatcher. But though it was the unions which thus visibly opted out, business in any case had divided, on the whole diminishing interests in maintaining tripartite regulation: divided interests, because different sectors and firms varied in their capacity to cope unaided with market uncertainties and labour pressures; diminishing interests, on the whole, when 'corporatist' policies in fact failed to give the promised relief from labour pressures while rising recession looked as if it would crack the whip and do the trick instead.

So, as tripartism crumbled from its own internal tensions, the way was cleared for the alternative of free-market prescriptions to come seriously onto the policy agenda. True, the first Conservative government experiment with them was half-hearted and short-lived, from 1970 to 1972 at most. But the second, from 1979, proved far more tenacious. By then – with the international oil crisis earlier in the 1970s as one trigger for recession – recorded unemployment had already risen above 1.3 million for the UK as a whole, though the trend turned down in the year of election. During the next six years or so, and very sharply at first, it grew to well over three millions: in consequence largely, if not wholly, of policies which both replaced the old commitment to high employment by other priorities and, indeed, sought to use job shortage and labour hardship as a means to socio-economic renewal.

The sheer scale and persistence of unemployment at its new level almost certainly exceeded government intentions. But the induction of a sharp rise was deliberate, as an essential weapon in the armoury of 'social market' policy; and this reflected not just a change of government and of internal groupings within the now governing party, but also a longer preceding shift in policy-influential thinking. Already, from the 1960s some economists had re-activated the notion of a 'natural' level of unemployment, sufficient both to accommodate labour mobility – everyday job changes as well as 'shake-out' from declining to growing sectors of the economy – and to keep wage rises within or below increases in productivity. The re-activation of that notion went hand in hand with arguments that this 'natural' rate, to be sought for economic health, was above the low level associated with 'full employment' and likely to be rising still further above it: actual unemployment ought therefore to be increased. In one version, moreover, arguments to this effect came to form part of a larger revision of economic theory, critical of the forms of Keynesianism which had fed into government economic policies in most western countries since the war. Often labelled 'monetarism' from one important strand within it, this exercise in revision in fact involved an updated return to classical economic theory and its celebration of free markets. (See Showler, 1981, for a succinct non-technical account of these developments in economic theory.) Contested though it was and still is by many economists, politically linked though it is in hard form only to the 'new right', some of the assumptions of this line of interpretation seeped into the thinking of governments – whatever the party or infra-party group in control – well before the electoral watershed of 1979. Moreover, as the notion of a 'natural' – and so proper – level of unemployment significantly higher than the two or three per cent effective post-war limit gained official acceptability, so images of the conditions of unemployment and market insecurity for labour began to change.

If viewed as a harsh means to a good end, acceptance of the postulated national need for higher unemployment might have been coupled with attitudes of support for the unemployed as innocent victims of change in the public interest; and with measures, accordingly, to spread the costs away from them. Some steps taken could be seen in this light. Mobility allowances, introduced for a time in the early 1960s, were intended to help those made workless in one place to cope with the costs of taking jobs elsewhere. From the mid-1960s, provision for statutory redundancy payments gave some lump-sum compensation to those who lost previously regular employment; and basic unemployment benefit was later boosted for some by a six-months supplement related to previous job-earnings, though this provision was phased out again in the early 1980s. Measures of this sort did reflect an official concern somewhat to spread the costs of economic transition beyond the ranks of those who otherwise immediately had to pay them, even if generally they gave least help to people among the unemployed – the unskilled from previously irregular and low-paid work – whose needs were most acute. And the variety of schemes for training or re-training of those without work, which entered the policy catalogue from the 1970s onward, were also in part intended to support individual adjustment to change for general public benefit, even though critics came to see other intentions to such schemes as well – that in particular of lowering both wages and the formal count of unemployment. By and large, however, official attitudes in Britain to the condition of unemployment and labour market insecurity hardened as larger numbers came to experience it and as, more or less apace, the notion of its necessity took firmer hold.

In fact, it proved a short step from the argument that the rate of unemployment ought 'naturally' to rise well above the levels familiar from the 1940s, 1950s and 1960s, to the inference that many of those then employed but now without work, or at risk of losing it, were 'unemployable' – unemployable at least, so this conclusion ran, in any but artificially induced and economically pernicious inflationary circumstances. A second inference, increasingly voiced, was that the growing numbers of unemployed people on the register included, not only these many who *could* not work, but also many who *would* not work – people who joined the recorded dole queues in order to draw social security benefit, whereas at lower benefit levels or with more stringent controls they would either have found work or have been content with unpaid domestic activity as housewives or retired people. If these assumptions were right, measures against the former category – typically seen as able-bodied men engaged in benefit fraud which might be compounded by illicit earnings from 'black economy' work – would need to include sharp checks and loud publicity to weed out 'scrounging'. Measures against the latter category – married women and elderly people – would need to include at least exhortation for wives to stay at home, and encouragement of early retirement. Except that new government discouragement of job-market participation on the part of married women has been only verbal and low-key, measures of just this sort have in fact followed in recent years; and the picture implied of the unemployed and their condition has changed to add more social stigma to their economic hardships.

The assumptions involved were nevertheless highly contestable. Take, for example, the re-description of many unemployed as un-employable – a conceptual slide familiar from the inter-war years. About the only truths behind this are the points that employers can be more choosy when they have more job applicants to choose from, and that long unemployment gives people poor credentials and experience for finding work again and little hope to sustain them in their search for it. There were notable flaws, too, in the assertion that 'high' benefits were tempting increasing numbers of others to prefer voluntary unemploy-ment to paid work. For most – except only those in low-paid corners of the labour market with many children – the gap between earnings in work and state support out of work remained wide, as intended. And though this gap had narrowed somewhat on one score (in respect of insurance-based benefit conditionally available during the first year of unemployment) over the years up to 1970, it widened again thereafter just when unemployment began to rise more sharply. (Showler, 1981, pp. 42–5; see also e.g. Sinfield, 1981a, pp. 106–18.) Personal accounts of the experience of unemployment (e.g. Marsden, 1982) and psychological survey evidence (Warr, 1985) squared poorly with the claim that workers who lost their jobs lacked commitment to work. Indeed, in a contrasting strain of fashionable commentary, prophets of a new age of information technology expressed anxieties that adaptation to prospects of more 'leisure' might be hindered by the very persistence of a widespread adherence to the 'work ethic'. Speculative postulates that opportunities for 'moonlighting' work were increasingly available to ameliorate registered unemployment, and to encourage 'scrounging', have proven shaky after evidence that such opportunities in general are limited, even when local circumstances seem favourable, and are so in particular for the sort of people who are most vulnerable in the formal labour market (Pahl, 1984, pp. 91ff, 216ff, 247ff). Finally, suggestions that many nominally unemployed married women and elderly people were content with domestic activity ran counter to indications that the official record of unemployment set the figures low, rather than high, by failing to count considerable numbers who, while not registered, would take paid work if they could find it in suitable form (e.g. Sinfield, 1981a, pp. 11 and 84).

We shall have a good many points of fact to feed into these controversies, from the records and accounts of our Sheffield respondents after redundancy. For the moment, however, our emphasis is on the ways in which the conditions of unemployment and labour market insecurity – once fairly commonly agreed to be preventable evils – became the subject of contested interpretations as they grew; and in one line of increasingly vocal interpretation, with official support, came to be seen as simultaneously unavoidable, beneficial and over-stated. We add 'over-stated' because, as we have already begun to point out, the rising controversies about the social character and economic role of unemployment were also, of necessity, controversies about the numbers of people affected.

In 1980, for example – not long after the redundancies in Sheffield which we follow up in this book – the registration count of the unemployed in the United Kingdom rose to a total of about two million. An estimate from a source committed to free-market ideas put the 'true' figure as only half of that – one million – by discounting various subgroups within the registered total school-leavers; people registered for less than four weeks, on the assumption that these were merely jobchangers; people with occupational pensions to support them; and guessed numbers of others to be regarded as either unemployable or too choosy in the demands they set for a new job. By contrast alternative estimates, from sources of different persuasion, put the 'true' figure for the same time at nearly three million, principally by adding to the registered numbers the many people – married women especially – who, while not having signed on, could be calculated from the official General Household Survey to be without paid work but willing to take it up if it was suitably available; or even at 3.5 million, if to this were added an allowance for recession-induced short-time work among those still in jobs. (Sinfield, 1981a, pp. 11–13).

The registration figures have been challenged not only in these ways, for alleged regular 'over-count' or 'under-count', but also because they have been affected by changes over time which, whatever their other implications, put question marks against their use to measure year-by-year trends. The direction of those changes, with notable near-consistency, has been to lower the figures recorded. Some have come from alterations in the methods and sources drawn upon to compile the record. More have come from the introduction of a variety of new measures for handling benefit claims and making provision for claimants. Recent tightening of the tests of claimants' statements of 'availability for work' is a prime example of the former. Most important among the latter have been government schemes for training or special work opportunities, which remove the recipients at least temporarily from the unemployment register; and inducements, by way mainly of enhanced welfare benefits, for men aged 60 and over to take themselves out of the labour market rather than stay in it on the dole. A summary review (Unemployment Unit, 1986) put the number of such changes of all kinds at a total of 15 between October 1979 and March 1986. Two more were then in the pipeline, including an immediately imminent statistical innovation which, by enlarging the denominator for ·the calculation, would reduce the recorded percentage rate of unemployment – as distinct from the absolute numbers – by one to 1.5 percentage points. As estimated in the same source (Statistical Supplement), without these 15 changes the official count of unemployment for the United Kingdom in Spring 1986 would have been some 450,000 more than it was – a total of nearly 3.8 million (including school-leavers without jobs) instead of the little more than 3.3 million then recorded. Another and later review brought about the number of changes affecting the official record to some 19 between 1979 and early 1987, and estimated the resulting gross 'under-count' comprehensively on all scores as upward of one million (Taylor, 1987).

Much of this may seem a bewildering numbers game, confirming the cynical adage that all statistics are lies. To accept this would be to dismiss the serious underlying issues far too glibly. So would it be to adopt an indiscriminate, one-directional formula in response to every point in the dispute about the figures – to assume, for example, that any adjustment or change made with the effect of lowering the count is just another instance of government-friendly manipulation designed to veil the size of the problem. Nevertheless, from all the evidence taken together we have no doubt that, on balance, the official record of unemployment significantly understates the full shortage of regular paid work for people who need and want it. We shall not pursue the argument further now, though our own findings to come will have a good deal to say about the situations and experiences of 'silently jobless' people who have been pressed by redundancy and its aftermath to withdraw from the labour market, and so are off the register of the unemployed while yet willing to take paid work if it were there to be taken.

In any case, regardless of its precise magnitude, the drastically steep rise in unemployment over the last ten years or so, and especially since 1979, is well beyond dispute. The fact that the magnitude has been continuously disputed over the same period is, as we have tried to emphasize, a striking illustration of the concomitant surge of conflicting interpretations about the nature, causes and effects of the new insecurity of labour markets. The lead in these controversies has come from commentators and politicians on the whole newly wed to free-market ideas, who have first applauded the stringent tightening of job opportunities as an essential means to economic discipline for future advance and then – in a paradox frequently unnoticed because it has become so familiar – denied that it extends nearly so far as it seems or causes nearly so much hardship as previous convention assumes. This denial *is* a paradox, because it seems to leave the whip of labour market discipline without the sting otherwise claimed for it. But it follows past practice in the innuendoes of recession, by putting a good deal of the blame on the victims. That is the stigmatizing implication of arguments which make out many of the unemployed to be unfit for paid work; or better left to stay quietly at home; or 'scroungers'; or people with ideas above their station about pay and conditions in any new job. But in the same line of thinking – that associated with the revival of free-market ideas – the latter charge is also made against very many who are still employed. Blame on the immediate victims of recession is here complemented by blame on those who escape its impact, but are said to do much to cause it by union-sponsored pressure for exorbitant wages and preservation of restrictive practices.

LABOUR MARKET INSECURITY AND CLASS STRUCTURE

This assignment of significant responsibility for rising unemployment to unionized workers is one thread in a larger and long-standing bundle of arguments that economic growth has been impeded above all by obstruction from labour. In its commonly one-sided form, the thesis is unconvincing for both historical and present-day application. The complex of factors likely to have caused the protracted decline of the British economy from nineteenth-century international hegemony plausibly includes worker-organization and attitudes only in a rather subsidiary role (see e.g. Gamble, 1981, chapters 1 and 2; Nichols, 1986; Wiener, 1981). If wage pressures at times from the 1960s onwards have exceeded the capacity of productivity growth to meet them within a broadly unchanged pattern of income distribution, the low ceilings set on such increases in productivity stem at least as much from features of capital composition, enterprise organization and managerial practice as from labour resistance. In the very recent past, moreover, unit labour costs generally fell over just those years when unemployment rose most steeply (Taylor, 1985). Yet the postulate has one notable implication which cannot be so readily set aside. This is the possibility that, as labour market insecurity has grown – and especially if it continues to grow, in the form of semi-employment as well as unemployment –

divisions of circumstances and interest will widen more and more between those with and those without dependable livelihood from paid work. The structure of class may then be set to change.

Evidence accumulated about unemployment and recruitment to it seems, at first sight, to give a good deal of support for that supposition. To be involuntarily jobless for more than a brief spell is, for most people who experience it, a condition that sets them apart from others, in both material and social terms. It is a misfortune, moreover, to which those are especially liable who had poor jobs, pay and conditions when they were at work. (Among sources for the summary elaboration of these points that follows, see especially Colledge and Bartholomew, 1980; Daniel, 1974; Moylan, Millar and Davies, 1983; Showler and Sinfield, 1981, including in particular Sinfield, 1981b; Sinfield, 1981a; Townsend, 1979; Walker, 1985; Warr, 1985; as well as the official statistical data regularly reported or reproduced in *The Department of Employment Gazette, Social Trends*, the reports of the *General Household Survey*, and the *Unemployment Bulletin*, published by the independent Unemployment Unit.)

Poverty in Britain no longer usually involves the extreme deprivation that it did 100 or even 50 years ago. But defined by present-day standards, it is a frequent consequence of unemployment: the great majority of those who are unemployed for more than a year have no effective income other than from state benefit, at a level of livelihood which has come to be conventionally regarded as a minimum definition of poverty today. Reciprocally – much as once shown in the classic urban surveys around the turn of the century and in the inter-war years – unemployment has again become a major cause of poverty, after three decades in which its contribution had been small. It is also a condition which, now as before, commonly diminishes individual and family contact with others; which leads often to loss of hope as the search for work becomes harder, and of self-confidence as the jobless take on board the disrespect that seems to be shown them by others; which carries a high risk of mental stress if not, at least with any certainty of evidence, also of physical ill-health.

All this, by and large, becomes more probable the longer the period of unemployment; and as recession has bitten more deeply, unemployment over long periods has grown steeply in both relative and absolute terms. For example, in 1980 – shortly after our Sheffield respondents were made redundant – altogether about 40 per cent of the people registered as unemployed in the UK had been out of work for at least six months, just under 25 per cent for at least a year. By early 1987 the corresponding ratios were over 60 per cent and 40 per cent respectively

– close on 2 million people with at least six months' experience of continuous unemployment; 1.3 million of them jobless for a year or more; and these numbers without allowance for those, especially married women and elderly people, who would by then have converted earlier inability to find paid work into 'housewifery' or premature retirement. When unemployment rises high and then persists, its average duration lengthens in cumulative fashion; and in similarly cumulative fashion, the individual consequences of deprivation and loss of hope become more deeply entrenched.

If the tendency of all this is to set the long-term jobless apart, they have in any case often been distinct by disadvantage before they lost such footholds as they had in the labour market. Unemployment is very unevenly spread. It hits especially hard the young who have not yet entered regular work, and workers of late middle-age and over. Even leaving Northern Ireland aside, it is higher by about two thirds or more in the northern regions of the country, now also in the Black Country, than it is in the south-east; and these well-known broad regional variations conceal sharp local variations within them, between particular towns and districts, often between 'inner' and 'outer' city areas. In fact this pattern of territorial concentration is in considerable measure the result of another, and more significant, pattern of concentration: by class. From several sets of data over recent years, the risk of losing employment looks about twice as high for men in manual work as for men in non-manual work. The risk remains small among the latter if they are in career employment as professionals or managers; higher, though still well below the skilled manual rate, if they are in more routine white-collar work. It reaches a peak for blue-collar workers in jobs not designated as skilled, where the liability to unemployment appears to be around twice as high as for skilled manual jobs. So the flow into the ranks of the unemployed is made up disproportionately of people with the most adverse previous experience of the labour market and the poorest resources from the past. Moreover, as joblessness has reached very high levels in recent years and come to last longer for many of its victims, the flow back from unemployment into paid work has dwindled by comparison with the contrary flow; and the poorest chances of a return to regular employment prove again to be those for the people with the slimmest resources of credentials and money. They have come, then, to make up the ranks of the long-term unemployed in doubly disproportionate numbers.

It is no new phenomenon that a prime effect of recession is to accentuate pre-existing patterns of inequality; and the basic contours of the class structure might, at least on this score alone, remain unchanged if recession were again to give way to economic growth combined with a more or less full revival of market demand for labour. But many commentators have argued that, even with a renewal of expansion, labour demand will not be regenerated on the scale and in the forms familiar from the post-war period. This line of argument suggests that, among Western countries, Britain in particular is undergoing a drastic transformation of economic organization. Rising unemployment has been only one sign of this. Another is 'de-industrialization': a recent acceleration of the long-term shift away from materially productive activities to service provision, so sharp now as to be eroding the previous manufacturing base of the economy. By the early 1980s, for example, little more than 25 per cent of the employed population were engaged in mining and manufacture, compared with over 40 per cent a decade before; and that downward trend continues. With rising productivity, of course, the same output has needed fewer workers to produce it; but even by 1985, after some very recent recovery, total output from manufacturing industry remained below the level of ten years earlier. (Department of Employment and United Kingdom National Accounts.) The more pessimistic scenarios add that the growth of micro-processor information technology may spread displacement of labour from the materially productive industries to a range of service activities, even if Britain keeps up with applications of the new wizardry; and will still further undermine the economy's capacity to compete internationally, if she does not.

Above all, this strain of commentary continues, employers and the government are responding to these new times by effectively restructuring the labour market and the pattern of industrial relations in ways that will increase insecurity for many and durably sharpen inequalities. New jobs which have made up for some of the loss of old ones include many part-time jobs; low-paid and routine in character; often with a high turnover of labour encouraged or expected by employers; and in workplaces – especially in service activities – where trade union organization is weak or absent. Work of this sort recruits women not least and, by meeting the conventional time-table needs of 'housewives' better than much other employment, can be seen as expanding female opportunity; but this then is at the cost of low rewards and little protection. Relatively large companies appear increasingly to be farming out some of their work to small sub-contracting firms or even individuals who are then nominally self-employed: in these circumstances, again, workers' security and support from collective bargaining are at risk. A series of government measures, moreover, have been deliberately aimed to foster develop-ments of this kind: to reduce trade union influence, to encourage small business and free it from previous labour-protective restrictions. (For a valuable review of these and related recent trends, see Craig et al., 1985; and for discussion of their link with the free-marketeering swing against 'corporatism', see Goldthorpe, 1985.)

All the tendencies here seem to go towards increased segmentation of labour markets – towards sharper distinction between a 'primary' labour market, on the one hand, where employees remain selectively secure in their jobs with firm support still from well-established union organization and/or, in Japanese corporation style, with protection as 'core staff'; and, on the other hand, a 'secondary' labour market (or several such subordinate markets), where employment is by comparison ill-paid, unprotected and irregular, with a continuous sizeable shuttle of people into and out of work. Coupled with the possibility of a lasting shrinkage of aggregate demand for labour, these signs of accentuated 'dualism' in the organization of the markets for labour have encouraged forecasts in turn which, despite many differences of genesis and thrust between them, have in common the postulate of an emergent new division of class.

Increasingly, so it is argued, this will separate employees of the 'primary' labour market from a growing under-group of people – especially women, members of ethnic minorities, the non-skilled in general – at best insecurely engaged in the 'secondary' labour market and often without employment and other income than from public welfare provision. (See e.g. Bauman, 1982; Gorz, 1982.) This new axis of class will turn more on the distinction between work and non-work than on distinctions arising from within work. Both the words 'new' and 'class' in this summary characterization need qualification. There are several echoes here of old Marxist references to 'labour aristocracy', 'reserve army of labour' and even 'lumpen proletariat'; but there are versions of the thesis which see the likely outcome, when coupled with other contemporary developments, as a dissolution rather than a re-formation of class structure. Yet the effect in any case is to prophesy a split into two worlds (or more) of what had perhaps previously become essentially one, the world of wage-earning labour.

These are speculative arguments based on still questionable assumptions. They assume, first, a future in which aggregate demand for labour is much and permanently reduced, and access to regular employment as the prime source of income is at least as sharply unequal as it is today. The latter indeed seems plausible without a radical transformation of basic economic institutions (see e.g. Walker, 1985). But the former – the prospect of a continuing steep downward slide of overall employment – is, very arguably, open to counter-action through public economic policy. This would certainly require a change of political climate, but not of necessity a conversion of capitalism in fairly familiar 'mixed economy' form into socialism in some mould-breaking form.

Second, the scenarios of fundamental new division in the lower reaches of the class structure assume that the visible contrast of circumstances between the state of regular secure employment and the state of semi-employment, unemployment or non-employment becomes a cleavage between generally distinct groups of people. The bridges will be few and narrow, so it is implied, between the world of skilled and credentialled attachment to the 'primary' labour market and the world characterized by at best insecure association with subordinate labour markets. There will be only quite limited movement of individuals between one and the other, and relatively little straddling of the two by households with members in both. Life chances, and so the logical bases for formation of economic and political interests, will be at least as much counterposed between the two as has been the case hitherto around other divisions further up the class scale – the division, for example, between capital and labour at large, or the division between people confined to employment in subordinate 'jobs' and those whose lives are shaped by 'careers' that progress over time. While it is conceivable that things may go this way, there are also good factual reasons for doubt on these scores. We shall come to some of them when we present and discuss our findings.

There have of course been many other arguments to the effect that the class structure is in process of fundamental change or even dissolution. Indeed, in one version or another the postulate has for so long been a favourite theme of both academic and lay social commentary that, against evidence of much continuity in inequality, it is tempting to regard every new claim to the same effect as merely another false cry of 'wolf'. We do not need to review the whole of this persistent debate even summarily; but we should briefly pick out one or two further strands from it, to round off our sketch of the larger context in which the after-redundancy study was set.

Time and time again it has been said that class, in the sense of cleavages of collective interest arising from differences of economic role and circumstance, was or is giving way to a set of more subtle distinctions and fine gradations unlikely to form the main ground for socio-political conflict. That was the thrust, for example, of arguments starting shortly after World War II that common citizenship of all in a 'welfare state' was displacing class division (see especially Marshall, 1950); and of a chorus of commentary, too extensive to list here, that with steady economic growth 'affluence' was turning the working class middle-class. This tide of optimism subsided during the 1960s when signs of increasing conflict, in considerable part of a class character, breathed political life into dry evidence of continuing inequality. But in new versions, and often now without the earlier gloss of complacent optimism, something like the same idea has re-emerged from about the middle-1970s. True, disparity of life chances and work circumstances between economically distinct groups of the population diminished little in relative terms between the 1950s and the 1970s; and thereafter, as growing 'affluence' turned into deepening recession, it tended to widen. (E.g. Byrne, 1987; Goldthorpe, 1980; Halsey, 1978; Halsey, Heath and Ridge, 1980; Urry, 1985; Westergaard, 1983; Westergaard and Resler, 1975.) But for all the tenacity of inequality, so a common line of commentary suggests, its cutting edge in making for class conflict is being blunted. This, the argument runs, is for several reasons: for example, because there are differences within 'classes' which divide interests, and inequalities of gender and ethnic origin which cut across those of class (e.g. Parkin, 1979); or because, without thereby turning 'middle-class', 'working-class' people nevertheless increasingly try to lead their lives privately with less reliance on collective organization and pressure than before, this whether in circumstances of general 'affluence' (Goldthorpe, Lockwood et al., 1968–9) or of the unevenly spread recession which has followed in the wake of boom (e.g. Newby et al., 1985).

Of course, political events have added much steam to interpretations of this sort. The shift in policy-influential circles towards free-market ideas can, as we suggested earlier, be in large part explained by the collapse of 'corporatist' prescriptions for economic management under the strain of their internal tensions. But it was a shift in patterns of popular voting that brought a government to office in 1979 committed to promotion of those ideas, in a package incongruously presented in authoritarian wrapping; and which confirmed this government's tenure in 1983 as again in 1987. No doubt special factors helped to account for the distinctive triumph of 'Thatcherite' Conservatism in 1983: a strain of popular jingoism brought alive by the Falklands War; the secession from Labour of part of its right wing to form the Social Democratic Party in alliance with the Liberals; a protracted bout of factional in-fighting within Labour which, whether or not through amplification by the media, reduced the credibility of the party as one 'fit to govern'. But none of this was sufficient by itself to explain an accumulation of signs that the Labour Party's hold on its actual past and potential future class-constituencies had been slipping away.

An apparent increase in political 'volatility' among voters during the

1970s had come to damage Labour more than its rivals (e.g. Sarlvik and Crewe, 1983). Taken together, the General Elections of 1979 and 1983 saw a significant defection of manual workers from the party – especially of skilled workers, or at least foremen, technicians and independent craftsmen of the sort conventionally counted among the skilled; and of workers who owned rather than rented their homes (e.g. Dunleavy and Husbands, 1985; Heath, Jowell and Curtice, 1985). Moreover, Labour had been unable to make any new compensating advance in appeal to wage-earners of routine non-manual level. Even if some of this should prove temporary – as opinion surveys over the next inter-election period could suggest (e.g. Curtice, 1986) but the election results of 1987 seemed to tell against – there was clearly more to it than the long-running fall in numbers of those blue-collar workers, in manufacture and mining especially, who had formed the historical core of support for Labour. (For left-wing debate on this and related issues, see e.g. Curran, 1984; and Hobsbawm et al., 1981.) The years 1979–83 marked some sort of electoral watershed in Britain, whatever may happen over a longer period ahead. It was about their economic experiences and political responses during these years of the crucial change of tide that our respondents in Sheffield talked to our interviewers.

THE LOCAL CONTEXT

As we have explained, we planned neither the opportunity for the after-redundancy study nor its location in Sheffield. But the fact that this city was the research site had distinctive advantages for exploring a number of the issues we have outlined in setting the scene. In summary, these special local features were two-fold. First, Sheffield's recent experience of recession and industrial decline, while in many respects illustrative of wider trends, has been abrupt as well as harsh: 'working-class affluence' evaporated quite suddenly here. Second, the culture of organized politics in and around the city is infused with a tradition of labour radicalism, which has set local 'public ideology' in overt opposition to that of central government since the year in which our informants found themselves redundant. On both counts the research project gained something of the character of a 'test-case' study.

Sheffield's economic base for long, until its very recent erosion, has been steel: the manufacture of steel itself and of steel products, including tools and cutlery, with a range of engineering activities linked to this. Production and employment grew rapidly in the nineteenth-century, especially from the 1850s and 1860s when the introduction of the Bessemer and Siemens processes for mass-manufacture of steel began to give large companies the leading role in the local economy. (On Sheffield's economic and associated socio-political history, see Pollard, 1959; Pollard and Holmes, 1976; Smith, 1982. The process of recent industrial decline is outlined in Walker, 1981, which we have updated on a few points from official data including information from the City Council.) For well over 100 years following the mid-nineteenth-century boom, Sheffield remained in essence a manufacturing city – a city of manual industrial labour – and steel the core of its manufacturing activity. Here, as elsewhere, service employment came later to grow fast – in the public sector especially, with expansion of local government, education and healthcare, and with relocation of the Manpower Services Commission to the city in the 1970s. But even by the mid-1970s manufacture altogether still accounted for about 40 per cent of all people employed, and the production of metal and metal goods for some two in every three of these in turn.

Decline of the manufacturing base set in seriously only from then onwards, and particularly from the tail end of the 1970s. By the census of 1981 already, employment in manufacture had fallen to less than one in three of all in paid work. A total of nearly 50,000 jobs in manufacture had disappeared since the previous census ten years earlier, mainly during the second half of the period; and over the next five years to 1986 more than 30,000 further redundancies in this sector were officially confirmed. An estimate for 1986 put the number of jobs then remaining in manufacture in the city at around 60,000, in contrast to nearly 140,000 15 years before. Steel and related activities were the prime victims: plants associated with the British Steel Corporation, for example, employed over 11,500 people in 1981, but little more than half that number four years later. Some continuing growth of service employment, moreover, was quite insufficient to make up for this process of rapid 'de-industrialization'.

Unemployment therefore grew apace. It had risen, in Sheffield as in the country at large, already from the late 1960s. But by later standards the increase then was still quite moderate; and – by contrast with most other areas of South Yorkshire, especially the long declining industrial and mining districts of the Dearne Valley – the rates of unemployment recorded in the city remained below the national average until the end of the 1970s. Sheffield's strength in the production of 'special steels' helped for a time to keep the impact of rationalization and the general run-down of British steel manufacture a little at arm's length, and so to maintain the city's record of relative 'affluence' rather longer than would have been the case otherwise. But with sharp overall deflation of the economy, mounting foreign competition and the spread of recession in the markets also for 'special steels' – not least domestic motor car manufacture – this small measure of protection came to an end. From rates of under five per cent in 1979 and around six per cent in 1980 (still below the rising national average), unemployment in Sheffield shot up to over 12 per cent in 1981. This was a doubling in only one year. It brought the rate recorded for the city suddenly to a level about two percentage points above that for the country as a whole; and this new gap to Sheffield's disadvantage maintained itself as joblessness spread still further during the following years, here as elsewhere. By early 1986, the official count gave a local unemployment rate of 16 per cent, by comparison with rather less than 14 per cent for the United Kingdom overall; and though the rates recorded for the city and the country as a whole began to fall later that year, unemployment in Sheffield stayed above the national average. Out of a total population of about 500,000, and a working population of about 250,000, more than 40,000 people in Sheffield were registered as unemployed in early 1986. Proportionately, moreover, long-term unemployment had set in still more deeply there than in the country as a whole: getting on for half (45 per cent) of the city's registered unemployed had now been on the books for at least a year, compared with just under 40 per cent in the UK as a whole at the same time; 29 per cent for two years or more. It was in this abrupt change of local economic fortunes that our respondents were caught up. Redundancy in 1979 came to them earlier than to many others; but during the three years for which we followed up their subsequent experiences, the job market around them was crumbling fast.

The sudden onset of the slide into recession thus marks the city's economy off from those of many (by no means all) other areas of high labour market insecurity, where tendencies to depression and decline have been of longer standing and where undertones of poverty and distress continued to grumble even in the decades of 'full employment'. This might perhaps make for some distinctiveness in response – say more 'militancy', to use a crude shorthand term – on the part of people in Sheffield in face-to-face experience of the new slump; and the city's history of labour radicalism could be thought to point in much the same direction. A tradition of tough-minded working-class organization has long local roots. It pre-dates the mid-nineteenth century conversion of the steel-based economy from workshop production to mass manufacture led by large companies. But it was maintained in new forms through that transformation; and it was historically shaped and given force both by the relative homogeneity of the city's industrial structure, and by the comparatively small role played in politics and public affairs by 'middle-

class' businessmen and professionals, as bridge-builders or mediators
between local working-class pressure groups and an old aristocratic elite
which dominated land ownership in and around Sheffield but oriented
itself above all to the concerns and networks of national rule. (See
especially Smith, 1982.) The spirit of labour collectivism in this
Victorian Sheffield mould was self-reliant and assertive, stubborn in
expression of both working-class independence and local autonomy,
sceptical of the national establishment and hostile to central intervention.

This is still true of organized politics in the city today, coloured as the
twentieth-century scene has been by Labour Party predominance in
alliance with the trade unions. To jump to the period of the present
study, even the landslide General Election of 1983 left five of the six
Sheffield parliamentary constituencies in Labour hands, as before: the
familiar odd-one-out remained the single constituency covering the
prosperous gentry districts which nestle against the foothills of the
Pennines on the western side of this classically class-segregated city.
True, a mere constituency count is misleading by itself. Not quite 45 per
cent of all Sheffield votes in 1983 – the year when our survey was
completed – went to Labour, nearly 30 per cent to the Conservatives
and not many fewer (26 per cent) to the new Alliance of Social
Democrats and Liberals. Precise comparisons over time are hindered by
boundary changes; but clearly support for Labour had then slipped
substantially, by about nine percentage points since 1979 and altogether
11 or 12 since 1974. Nevertheless, the party was to regain a fair amount
of local ground in 1987 when, with a swing of about six percentage
points in its favour across the city (as against 4 in the country at large) its
share of the aggregate Sheffield vote recovered to a little over 50 per
cent. Moreover, even at the time of the deep 1983 dip in its national
standing, Labour remained by far the largest single party on the
Sheffield scene; and the politics of the city and the metropolitan county
continued to carry its imprint.

Local government has for long, brief aberrations apart, been
controlled by Labour; and in recent years its leading orientations have
earned for Sheffield a reputation as the metropolitan centre of 'the
socialist republic of South Yorkshire'. Whether used by opponents or –
as often – by admirers, the label has a tongue-in-cheek character. There
is necessarily more rhetoric than substance to it: all else besides,
constraints from central government and the workings of the national
and international economy ensure that. But this reputation reflects not
least dogged resistance to just such constraints. City council opposition
to Conservative government measures for local budget reduction, and for
abolition of metropolitan county organization, have been well publicized

examples of this, however unsuccessful and tactically tortuous those campaigns ultimately were. Policies which give some more positive substance to the claim of leftward pioneering have included the city's long post-war track record of council-house provision, and its achievements in control of air pollution. More recently there have been its dedicated promotion of cheap fares for public transport, until central government removed the means for this; and, in face of rapidly spreading recession, a series of local initiatives to alleviate unemployment. These latter, the responsibility of a fairly recently established employment department within the City council, have ranged from training and recreational support for the unemployed, through work on product innovation as well as research and organizational support for employment creation, to promotion of labour-intensive council services and help to small firms and producer co-operatives.

However tight the limitations to distinctive local achievement on these scores, measures of this sort and the set of explanations and justifications which have gone with them underline Sheffield's character as a centre of open opposition to recent national trends in public affairs. Especially given its long historical roots, the culture of organized politics in the city might be thought to set a tone for individual response to recession, 'at the grassroots', in more radical or militant fashion than elsewhere. Our informants' material experiences of redundancy and its aftermath were unlikely to differ much from those of people made redundant in other places where the employment market was similarly crumbling around them. But because the change in economic circumstances had been so abrupt in Sheffield, and because the local labour movement's tradition of class-conscious self-assertion seemed to loom so large, their political interpretations of what happened to them in and after redundancy might prove to go against the national grain at the time. It was in order to explore this possibility, not least, that we spent a good deal of our time in interviews feeling out our respondents' political views.

2

The Coming of Redundancy

'We were stunned. It was as though the carpet had been pulled away from us under our feet.' Recollections to similar effect were common when, rather more than three years after the event, our interviewers asked respondents how they and their colleagues had felt when they first heard about the impending redundancies. Widespread though this was as an immediate reaction, it seems often to have been less an expression of total surprise than of disbelief that 'it could actually happen to us'; and of worry about the future after many years of stable employment in one place: 'A lot of us had worked there so long and put in so much, we thought we were set up for life.' The man who said this – a skilled production fitter who was to find only one fairly short-lived job, as a labourer, over the next three years – was 57 years old when the axe fell. He had been in steel all his working life, the last 30 years with this company, and had never been unemployed before. There were many like him in the group we followed up.

Nearly half of them had been in unbroken service with the firm for 20 years or more, altogether some two in every three for at least 10 years. The skilled blue-collar workers had particularly long records of service there, about 60 per cent for over 20 years or more; and the great majority of these men had received their training or apprenticeship in the company. But of the four broad categories which we distinguished by occupational level at the firm (non-skilled manual, skilled manual, routine non-manual, higher non-manual) only the routine-grade office workers, mainly women, were distinctly less 'tied' to the company in terms of their employment records. Two thirds of these had been there for less than 10 years before redundancy; but their jobs, too, had been full-time, and they generally shared the sense of shock and anxiety remembered by so many others as their first reaction to the news. True, the non-skilled – mostly 'semi-skilled' – blue-collar workers in the group had rather shorter records of employment with the company than either their skilled mates or 'staff' above the routine level of non-manual work, especially when comparisons are made age for age. Even irrespective of age, moreover, the traditionally looser labour-market foothold of non-skilled workers was evident from their more frequent previous experience of redundancy. One in four of them had been made redundant at least once before in their working lives, as against one in six overall and only one in every fourteen of the skilled manual workers. But still the big majority among the non-skilled had not been forced out of a job earlier; and when the redundancies now came here, over 65 per cent of them had at least 10 years continuous service with the company behind them, more than 40 per cent service of at least 20 years.

Because so many in the group had been with the firm for long, the people whom we followed up showed of course a fairly high age profile. Fewer than a quarter were under 40 by the time we interviewed them (and they included hardly any apprentices, for whom the company had generally made special arrangements for training to continue elsewhere); nearly 45 per cent were then 60 or more; and almost 20 per cent were between 50 and 60 (these figures are for the interview date, some three years after redundancy). While our study therefore has nothing to say directly in the continuing debate about 'youth unemployment', it has a fair amount to offer on a subject which by comparison has attracted less attention than it warrants: the situation of middle-aged and older workers in circumstances of a crumbling labour market.

The profiles of age and length of service were in fact slightly higher for the group interviewed than, so far as we could estimate, for all those made redundant by the firm in 1979. Of approximately 600 people on the list given us by the firm, just under 75 proved unavailable for inclusion in the main survey: some because they had died or were too ill; others because the addresses given for them were untraceable or they had moved far away; others again because we had tested drafts of the interview schedule on them in advance, before we finalized it. (For these and other details of the response, see Appendix 1.) This left us with about 530 names. Their addresses, of course, were over three years out of date; and that – the inevitable fact that many people had since moved, and quite a number of these proved untraceable despite our best efforts – was to be the main cause of shortfall in response. Refusals came to only ten per cent, and failure to contact people whom we were able to trace to still less. In the event, we interviewed just under 380 respondents (although the numbers recorded in tables in the book will usually be rather lower because – especially when informants were in poor health – a small number of the interviews were too incomplete for consistent use). The overall effective response rate of more than 70 per cent was very satisfactory, in our view, given that the address list was well out of date.

Moreover, the firm had provided details, for everyone on the list, of their age, gender, length of service and job in the company at the time of redundancy. Using this information to check the composition of our interviewed 'sample' against that of the full group 'in scope' for inclusion in the survey, we found a good match between the two. Only in respect of length of service coupled with age was there any response bias worth noting: this to the effect that young and middle-aged people with less than five years service were under-represented among respondents (with response rates of around 50 per cent, as against the average of rather more than 70 per cent). But the under-represented sub-groups made up only a limited fraction of the total – 18 per cent of the population 'in scope', 13 per cent of actual informants. Although we might have 're-weighted' our results to compensate for this particular shortfall (one which no doubt reflected rather greater mobility, and so 'untraceability', on the part of younger people with only short records of work for the firm), we decided not to run the risks of this debatable procedure, especially since a set of tests showed that to do so would have a negligible effect on the results in any case. Overall, therefore, our respondents were well representative.

NEWS OF THE PLANT CLOSURE

First news of the decision to close the Forging Division and of the redundancies to follow was bound to come as a shock to so well-established a labour force. For many of these people, however, news of trouble ahead in some fairly drastic form was not a surprise. The firm had been quite widely known to be running into difficulties for some time; and British steel manufacture generally – even now the production of special steels, on which the industry in Sheffield and this company too concentrated – was visibly set on a downward path. Over half our respondents said in retrospect that they had expected the closure. Office staff in particular – whether managerial and technical or merely routine-grade – seem to have been better forewarned than the manual-worker majority. Two in every three of the office staff said they had felt no surprise on hearing the news, compared with rather fewer than half the manual workers. Even rank-and-file clerical workers may, through their everyday work locations, have been a little more in the picture about the company's prospects than their blue-collar colleagues on the production floor; and some certainly had the news confirmed earlier: 'My boss told me before the notices were put out', said a secretary, for example. A main channel of information for the shopfloor, apart from the official statements sent to all in April 1979, was of course the trade union network – the conveners and union meetings; and the great majority were members of a union (95 per cent of manual workers were members, compared to 80 per cent of the non-manual people, with about 30 per cent of the routine-level office workers outside any union). But active involvement in union affairs – as a present or past convener/ steward or as a fairly regular attender – does not on the whole seem to have led to special foreknowledge of the redundancies. Some 45 per cent of union members – activists and others more or less alike, and rather more than among the predominantly office-bound non-unionist minority – said that the news had come to them as a surprise.

But if this may suggest imperfection of the union grapevine, as well as a familiar division between shopfloor and office – and a few blue-collar workers complained that the first they had heard of the closure was through the local press or radio – too much should not be made of it. Union representatives – in particular the conveners for the main union, the Engineering Workers' Union – were closely involved in negotiating the compensation deal which accompanied the redundancies; we shall come to this. The 'surprise' which a good many said they had felt in any case often seemed to reflect something more complex than just ignorance of where the wind was blowing: 'There'd been gossip for a long time, and we guessed that something would have to go. But we'd not been put in the picture about which plants would be hit.' So some of the surprise was that 'it was *us* who were for the push' – and also that, whatever the rumours and guesswork beforehand, the crunch had now actually come. The prospects that came with it of drastic changes of circumstance may well have seemed especially stark for the manual-worker majority, who remembered 'surprise' as an immediate reaction more than the others: for the skilled because their tenure with the firm had generally been very long, even though they might be able to cope better in the labour market after redundancy; for the non-skilled because they could have particular cause – good cause as it proved – to fear for their futures in that market.

On top of this, the take-over of the company by a multinational corporation a year before or less, had helped to confuse the situation, at least in the eyes of ordinary employees who were not well 'in the picture'. Most, it is true, said they had felt no effect of the take-over on their everyday working lives in the firm. A few noted some change 'for the better', for example greater management concern with rationalization and efficiency. Rather more, though still only a small number, detected some change 'for the worse' – the reverse of the same coin, it seems, as a matter of increased pressure on workers and the beginnings of a management withdrawal from the fairly 'easy' labour relations of the past into concentration on 'money-making'. At least one trade union convener commented scathingly, from his negotiating experience, on the transfer of ultimate control to 'people in London who know nothing about steel'. But the great majority – 80 per cent, with little variation between union activists, members and others, or according to job level, length of service, general political views or even subsequent economic experience after redundancy – remembered the effect of the take-over on their everyday lives at work as leaving things 'much the same' as they had been before. Of course, there had been less than a year for any changes to make themselves felt, before the terminal change of redundancy.

Yet the take-over had set off new speculations about the future of the firm: if the prospects really were as bleak as quite a lot of talk had it, why should the multinational have wanted to come in? For some of our respondents at least, answers to this question had suggested a healthier state of affairs than assumed, or new investment to follow the take-over. For many others the signals were obscure, if it was even worth bothering to try to read them; and survival of the firm in some shape might in any case be made to go with a significant 'slimming-down' of jobs. All in all, transfer of the company to multinational ownership probably muddied the waters of conjecture so far as its ordinary employees were concerned, and gave an extra twist to the impact of the news – anticipated or not – that the Forging Division was to close down with a large shake-out of workers and associated staff.

NON-RESISTANCE AND DIVISION OF VIEWS

There may seem to have been much in the situation to make for militant resistance, by the shopfloor workforce at least. They faced ostensibly common prospects of insecurity and hardship after long years of work together. They had a fair amount of foreknowledge of crisis to come in some form – even if this was unevenly spread – and so a base for preparation in advance. Despite 'easy' management-labour relations earlier (as we shall say a little more about soon), there was at least incipient distrust among them of the new and remote bosses above the local management. And a high level of union membership was reinforced by the fact that more than 25 per cent of members claimed to have been actively involved in union affairs.

In fact, the unions took no action by way of strike or go-slow to protest against or stop the redundancies (though one union, representing some of the white-collar workers, challenged the terms of the redundancy arrangements on the grounds that it had been insufficiently consulted). Nor was there unofficial action from the floor without union or convener sanction. There was, so one of the chief conveners of the Engineering Workers' Union told us, pressure or encouragement from full-time union officials outside the firm for some form of action to be taken. But the union leaders on the spot ignored this, just as they kept negotiations with management about the terms of compensation in their own hands, with as little involvement of outside union officials as possible. They argued that the workforce would not have backed them if they had called for action against the redundancies.

They seem to have been right in this assessment, judging by our respondents' later comments on the situation. Of course we cannot be sure how far those comments may have had an element to them of retrospective apology for inaction; or whether, at the crucial time, a militant lead from conveners and stewards might have been able to galvanize the hesitant. But hindsight might also cut the other way, to elicit subsequent support for a strong stand from some respondents who had themselves held back when it all actually happened. In fact, only about a quarter of all the people interviewed three years later then said that the workforce 'could have put up more of a fight'; and among trade union members, again only the same proportion felt that their own union should have done something more – or something else – in response to the closure. What 'more' and what 'else' was usually left fairly open; but though answers included occasional suggestions for earlier negotiations with the firm, or a bid for EEC funds to boost the eventual compensation deal, the overall tenor of such comments was for some form of overt action or demonstration.

They were voiced most often by skilled manual workers, trade union 'activists', and those who scored high on an index of 'labour solidarity' which we constructed from respondents' views on matters of industrial relations. This, by and large, is what one might expect – although, perhaps curiously, managerial and technical 'staff' showed almost as strong minority support in retrospect for firmer action as did skilled shopfloor workers; and although (as a point worth bearing in mind for our later discussion of general socio-political attitudes and their complexities) suspicion or hostility to labour militancy expressed in

answer to abstractly formulated questions – to the effect of a low score
on the 'solidarity index' – did not preclude some support in hindsight
for 'more of a fight' in the particular circumstances of the redundancies.

The point remains that this was minority support. Even in the 'front
line' groups which we have just mentioned – the skilled men, the union
activists, the people in principle most committed to labour solidarity –
majorities of 60–70 per cent thought that the workforce and the unions
could have done no more than they did or, occasionally, were too
uncertain to venture a view. True, it may seem from this evidence that
the balance within the long-established skilled workforce on the
production floor was sufficiently fine for their 'militants' (if that is what
they were) to have given a lead into organized confrontation or at least
protest; and this even with a degree of sympathy from among local
managerial staff. But to do so with effect would have been quite a hard
job – to talk round into support, not only the many 'reluctants' on their
own side of the skill-line, but also the still more numerous 'passivists'
among the non-skilled production workers. Well after the event,
anyway, 75 per cent or more of these felt that no more could have been
done than was done. This, plainly, was not because the non-skilled were
to fare well after redundancy – on the contrary, as we shall see; but it
may have been because, with somewhat shorter records of employment
with the firm than their skilled mates, they were also rather less firmly
'tied into' the workforce from which any collective action would have
had to come. Be that as it may, no such action came; and our
respondents' further accounts of the situation as they saw it gave some
idea of why not.

It is tempting at first to explain the peaceful settlement of the issue
largely by reference to an inherited climate of 'easy' labour relations in
the company. The firm had a long record free of significant disputes,
management had a reputation for paternal interest in their employees,
and the workforce had no experience of tough action against them. With
a high level of membership, the trade unions – the Engineers in leading
place – were well recognized and closely involved in the running of day-
to-day affairs. Indeed, some of the 'militants' who would have wanted to
see action against the redundancies thought that the unions had become
too close to management: 'The conveners weren't in touch with the
shopfloor. You get these chaps who take big jobs on, and the first thing
management do is to talk them into taking their side – give them an
office – allow them to come in dressed up instead of being on the
shopfloor with the men.' But this again seems to have been a minority
view. To go by most of our respondents' comments, the unions generally
enjoyed the support of their members in their long-standing involve-

ment with management; and the firm as a place to work was the better for it, so the common view ran.

Echoes of a 'paternalist' atmosphere were certainly strong when we asked people to describe how they had felt about their working lives there. 'It was like a big family, all good mates together': remarks to that effect abound in the interview records. Yet, widespread and genuine as such feelings undoubtedly were, some pinch of salt has to be taken to this as the main explanation for the lack of militant action in response to the closure. The long climate of 'good relations all round' may have tipped the initial odds against such action; but hardly to decisive effect by itself. It was, for one thing, a climate of bonhomie among workmates above all, and between shopfloor and immediate supervisors. 'I had a friendly lot of fellows to work with.' 'We were all pals where I was. And the foremen were really good – they'd go out of their way to help.' The overriding emphasis in most of these reminiscences was on the immediate workgroup. Not that higher management had been a target of suspicion: 'It was a friendly workforce – and there was no trouble with management.' But higher management's virtue, as described or implied in the typical accounts we got, was that they intervened little. The days were past – though recalled with nostalgia by a few with very long service – when the Managing Director would make a regular point of going round departments and talking to the workers. But while there was now more distance between shop and top – even before the take-over by the multinational – everyday relations remained easy-going because 'they just left us to get on with it. You could do a good job, with nobody bothering you.' It was of course also a steady job – and, as quite a lot felt, a job that paid good wages by local standards.

So much of the 'family atmosphere' – and such inertia as this may have made for against a militant response to redundancy – seems to have turned on a tradition of 'tolerant distance' on the part of senior management, as well as on the sheer stability of employment on fair or acceptable monetary terms. Closure itself, of course, disrupted the latter precondition; and already before this, the former could be seen as at risk because the multinational had moved into control. It is true that, judging by our evidence, only a 20 per cent minority of the employees had yet felt any significant effect of consequent reorganization on their own situations at work – whether their assessments of new pressures for efficiency and increased tempo were negative or positive. But it could not have been hard to foresee more of the same to come, if the firm were to survive at all. And though we cannot equate hindsight with foresight, the take-over had probably begun to erode the old basis of trust and mutual tolerance between labour and top management in the run-up to the redundancies. In retrospect, certainly, very many respondents took a jaundiced view of the shift to control by a large corporation.

Over two in every three thought the general trend towards control by big metropolitan-based companies with many shareholders 'bad', by contrast with ownership and direction by local people. Only the 'staff' group were a little more – and then just a little more – inclined to see some advantage to it, by way of improved commercial sense, as against the common diagnosis that the shift made for board ignorance of production processes, insensitivity to local needs and labour relations, and concern only with profit. 'Big companies have their fingers in so many pies, all they care about is making money'. Moreover, when asked about their views of the causes of the closure and redundancies, about half thought that the take-over by the multinational had had 'something to do with it'. The most usual explanation was that 'they came in just to make some quick money' – some added by selling off the sites – though so bare an account is hard to square with the probability that, on balance, the multinational lost money on a transaction which ended with the closure of the entire firm a few years later and difficulties in disposing of the land. Others took account of this and referred, for example, to a rumour they had heard that the multinational had somehow been misled into thinking the firm's prospects better than they were, '. . . and when they found out, they decided not to put any more money into the business'.

We are not concerned with the plausibility of these accounts. Nor did the multinational corporation figure so prominently in the explanations of the closure which our respondents gave first in answer to a general question about why it all happened. References to the take-over usually came in response to a prompt about the possible role of the multinational, while before this most people had talked about longer-term factors. They had said that there was a world recession; that the steel industry as a whole was set for decline; that foreign competition, and subsidies in other countries to boost it, were knocking out the industry; and quite often also that the firm itself was long 'run down', with inadequate updating of plant and poor or indifferent physical working conditions. But though most of the people interviewed did not put first blame for their redundancy on the new top management, they were plainly no longer on such secure terms with 'the boss' as to rule out a harder stance from the workforce when the crunch came. And when we talked to them about the way their colleagues and the unions had responded, very few explained their 'passivity' by reference to the old climate of tolerant labour relations. They gave, in essence, two reasons –

simple, but arguably persuasive and significant for an understanding of the industrial scene in recession.

First, they often said, there was not really anything they could do: 'There weren't enough orders coming in', and 'When a firm runs out of money, there's an end to it'. There was no point in resistance to a *fait accompli*: it would not have saved jobs. What the unions could do was to try to negotiate the best terms of redundancy possible; and this, by and large, the majority thought the conveners had done. Comments to this effect did not, of course, generally signify 'approval' of the redundancies; or acceptance that, nominally 'voluntary' as almost all were, they were also genuinely voluntary; or emotional indifference to them. Nearly 40 per cent of our respondents insisted on describing their break with the firm as enforced, although they had had to 'volunteer' in order to obtain the advantages of the compensation scheme agreed between conveners and management. Only among those who retired, either immediately or later, or who otherwise pulled out of the labour market at once and stayed out, did a large majority accept the term 'voluntary' without blinking; and even here one in every six or so rejected the formal description. So, too, well over half the people we talked to described themselves as 'angry' or 'upset' (rather mild terms in relation to the words of some of the detailed comments on this point); and again the main differences were between those who then withdrew into retirement or domestic activity, and those who stayed in the labour market whether or not they succeeded in finding regular work again. But while resentment and anxiety were one thing, resistance was another: 'It was unfair after so many years. But the firm was going to the dogs, there was no way to stop it.'

Second, but of no less importance it seems, views were divided. Anger, worry, rejection of the notion that the redundancies were truly voluntary – these were certainly widespread reactions. But they were, as some of the points we have just made indicate, in no way universal. And the workforce were well aware of this, those who would have liked to see some kind of firmer stance rather more so than others. Our respondents split more or less equally three ways when we asked them whether news of the closure had 'united or divided' the workforce. That 'response split' is hardly by itself evidence of divided views at the time; but the comments which came with it are. The third who said that the news brought people together usually had in mind an increased attendance at union meetings, and the common talk about what was to follow. The third who said that the news made for division (and a good many of the third who gave mixed answers to the question) generally emphasized, by contrast, the differences in assessment of individual prospects which came to the fore with notification of the redundancy scheme. 'There was a lot of worry about the future. But many weren't bothered because they thought they would do all right with the money.' The scheme, as we shall explain, gave most to the people with the longest previous service as well as the highest previous pay; and an extra bonus to those who, if close to retirement anyway, were willing to take it immediately rather than look around for other employment. So one potent source of divided views was calculation of the different individual economic balance-sheets – potent especially, perhaps, because many had never before had a four-figure capital sum to hand; and because the labour market then, in April 1979, had not yet turned down so decisively as it was to do a little later. 'It was the money angle that split the workers – those who reckoned they'd get a few thousand pounds they'd never had before.'

The way 'the money angle' came out seems to have varied, moreover, from one part of the works to another, according to the composition of the particular work-team. 'In one shop they'd stand to get a lot, but maybe not in the next one.' Age was commonly seen to play a main part in the division of views: in part because, coupled with length of service, it was important for the size of the individual 'hand-outs'; but not only for that reason. 'A lot of the older ones were not really bothered – they'd done their bit and were quite pleased to get out.' Many of our older respondents, as we have already indicated, themselves confirmed this: 'I felt I needed a good rest. I'd done my service, and it's great to be able to relax.' We shall describe later how such a sense of relief at the prospect of freedom from long and hard work could be – or could come to be – mixed with worry about the financial implications. For example, the man we have just quoted, 63 years old when the redundancies came, looked unsuccessfully for other work for 18 months thereafter before he eventually retired – 'I needed the money, the pension's not good enough to live on as you want it' – and he said at the interview that he would still take a part-time job to help out, if only he could find one. But these were mixed feelings which came into play as time went by, rather than immediately; and they were at most mixed, with no head of steam for action or protest against the closure.

REDUNDANCY PAYMENTS AND THEIR DISTRIBUTION

Trade union activity therefore centred on negotiations, conducted mainly by the senior conveners of the Engineers' Union, over the terms of severance. The agreement reached for compensation in return for 'voluntary' acceptance of redundancy went a good way beyond the legal minimum. It added two elements to statutory redundancy pay. The first was a tax-free lump sum representing pay 'in lieu of notice'. This varied, of course, with the level of normal pay and the period of notice allowed for; and, on the latter score, it deferred entitlement to unemployment benefit for many who looked for other work without finding it. The second element was a further sum related to length of service as well as to previous wage or salary. For most people this comprised one week's pay for every year of employment with the firm; for those nearing statutory retirement age and willing to retire early (up to four years before 'their time', at 61 or over for men, at 56 or over for women), it was boosted to one and a half weeks' pay for every year of service.

Finally, a number of people were able on their redundancy, if they so wished, to draw out some or all of the contributions which they had made earlier to the firm's internal pension scheme – of course with corresponding loss of eventual pension rights. Just over half our respondents took an extra sum with them on this account, to add to their redundancy money proper. But though this provision was outside the general compensation package, we thought it impracticable to ask for details of the sums involved under the contributions-repayment heading as distinct from the total amounts received under all headings – totals received either in one go or in a few instalments over a short period, without uniform difference on this score between those whose take-away money included a pension refund and those for whom it did not. Most of what we shall say about 'redundancy pay' and the uses to which people put it will, therefore, relate to all the money they took with them from the firm on losing their jobs, without this distinction by source.

A very small number of informants, mainly people who had been with the firm only quite briefly, said they had received no money from the firm when they left it. But some others held back on information about the sums they received, or reported them to our interviewers in terms too broad for use in analysis. Some 15 per cent of the respondents for whom we otherwise have more or less fully completed interview data are, therefore, omitted from our account of redundancy pay. The effect may be somewhat to overstate the sums involved. We were thus told by management at an early stage of our contact with the firm, that the average paid out had been somewhere around £3,000 – this apparently excluding such refunds of earlier pension contributions as were added. From the interview data, the average for those of our respondents who received no pension refund (a group of much the same composition as those who did, in terms of length of service and occupational level in the firm) was rather higher, some £3,600. But the figure given us by management was a rough, off-the-cuff one (which the history of the project and the firm prevented us from checking later); and, on balance, the 15 per cent or so of our respondents whom we were unable to include in our account of redundancy pay seem unlikely to have received much less than the majority who did give us details. They included proportionately rather more people in the categories likely to get the smallest pay-offs – short-service employees and routine-grade office workers; but as against these they included also proportionately rather more in the categories eligible for most money – very long-service employees and staff in the higher non-manual grades. Some overstatement probably remains because, as we noted earlier, our 'sample' overall missed out a little among the youngest people who lost their jobs after relatively short periods of employment with the firm. But with that proviso, we can take the figures reported by our informants as tolerably representative; and we can be confident that they do not err on the low side (for example, through a retrospective expression of grudges against the company).

Payments varied greatly – far more than is shown in Table 2.1, which presents only the averages for broad categories of informants. They ranged from trivial sums of a few hundred pounds for the lowest paid with short service, to packages for some managerial staff ranging up to over £19,000. What mattered, in addition to length of employment with the firm, was the level of normal pay, which in turn depended broadly on the nature of the work and the occupational grade. Consistently by duration of service, the routine-grade office workers – mainly women – took least money with them; and generally the non-skilled manual workers – overwhelmingly men – came next lowest in the league table. The skilled workers did a good deal better, both step for step on the ladder of length of service; and overall, because so many of them could add to their occupational premium a premium for long years of employment with the firm. The deal for non-manual staff above routine-grade work was more mixed (and the averages for them set out in Table 2.1 conceal wide variations) because this sub-group itself was a mixed lot, comprising technical employees and sales staff as well as 'managers' of differing levels, from juniors and supervisors to the middling range of local plant management. It is not, therefore, so surprising as it may seem at first sight that relatively short-service staff from this group – many quite new in the firm – on average received somewhat less on leaving than did the non-skilled with under 10 years' employment; or that even in the middle length-of-service bracket, the staff average fell below that for the skilled shopfloor workers. But the seniors on the staff side – those who had been with the company for at

Table 2.1 Average redundancy pay, by occupational level and length of service

Length of service with firm	Occupational level in firm on redundancy				All reporting redundancy pay
	Manual		Non-manual		
	Non-skilled	Skilled	Routine	Higher	
Under 10 years	£1422 (33)	£1851 (26)	£1162 (23)	£1357 (17)	£1436 (102)
10–19 years	£3318 (23)	£4258 (14)	£1534 (7)	£3714 (14)	£3386 (60)
20 years or more	£5047 (42)	£7381 (55)	£4317 (6)	£9560 (27)	£6916 (132)
All reporting redundancy pay	£3407 (101)	£5407 (95)	£1760 (36)	£5745 (58)	£4302 (297)

Notes.

'Redundancy pay' includes refund of pension contribution (see text).

Included in the totals for 'all reporting redundancy pay' are figures for a few informants for whom information on occupational level and/or length of service was insufficient for their classification in these respects.

The figures in brackets show the number of respondents from whose reports the average sum in each category has been calculated.

least 20 years – took the largest sums of all: on average about twice as much as their non-skilled and clerical counterparts. And it was among them that the highest individual payments were made, up to more than £19,000, – 'handshakes' rather than 'hand-outs', though still very far below the 'golden' variety common in higher business circles.

The general pattern was of a kind to sharpen rather than soften those divisions of a hardening labour market which were to become prominent after redundancy. This was not, of course, by direct and deliberate design. The criteria adopted for the size of redundancy pay merely followed the usual conventions; and for people who took an immediate decision to retire early, the special incentive in the scheme to do so provided extra cash to bridge the gap before state pension and perhaps occupational superannuation would come into play. But even that bonus was highest for those who had been best off while still at work and who were to cope best with retirement – former managerial staff in particular. And among the many who either could not or did not retire, by and large the bigger amounts of compensation for redundancy went to those who were to prove better able to find new work.

Except among people nearing retirement, formal job credentials mattered far more than age in the search for new employment after redundancy. As we shall show in more detail later, the middle-aged, commonly with longer service behind them and so on average more cash in hand from their pay-off, were not much handicapped by comparison with younger people just because of their age. But those who had little by way of job qualifications or credentials from their work with the firm were. Below the age of 55 or 60, the people who fared distinctly best in the labour market were the skilled workers and former members of the 'staff'; yet it was also they who had generally received the more money from their redundancy. By contrast, the people who drew the shorter straws from the severance pay package were just those, on the whole, who were to draw very much the shorter straws in the labour market after redundancy: the non-skilled blue-collar workers and the routine-grade clerks.

Abstractly considered, redundancy payments may be thought of as resources to mitigate individual hardship after job loss; and in loose terms they do offer some mitigation of this sort. But their actual distribution – certainly in this instance, almost certainly in the common run – acts to blunt the implied effect. Usually geared to step up the money the higher the previous pay and the longer the previous service, redundancy compensation schemes generally offer the least help to those people whose past pay was the lowest and whose past footholds in employment were the loosest. But these are just the ones whose needs are the greatest, because their future footholds in the labour market are also the most at risk.

Illustration of this point from our evidence might seem to lack full force because, for convenience, we have included pension contribution refunds in our figures of redundancy pay, even though such refunds are arguably distinct from severance compensation. And if we compare the sums which included a refund with the sums that did not – a reasonable if rough measure of the 'refund effect', as we noted earlier – past pension contributions do seem to have given a special boost to the overall payments received by 'staff': an extra £2,500 on average for all managers and the like who got a refund, an extra £4,000 or more for those of them with very long service, by contrast with much smaller amounts for ordinary wage-earners. Whatever this may suggest about the terms of the internal pension scheme for staff compared with others, nevertheless the broad pattern of inequality in pay-off, by past job-level as well as by past service, was much the same whether a refund was included or not. In any case the practical reality remains that the groups who were to prove most vulnerable in the labour market after redundancy – the non-skilled and the routine-grade office workers – were also those who generally came to it with least cash in hand from the firm, whatever its source.

They came to it, moreover, with fewer material resources of other kinds: with smaller savings, no doubt, though we know this only patchily from spontaneous comments rather than from systematic questioning; and commonly without ownership or part-ownership of their homes. Overall, a little under half our respondents were owner-occupiers (whether now free of their mortgages or still paying them off); while almost all the rest were council tenants. But home-owners were fewest, by occupational level, among the non-skilled (29 per cent); few too, by subsequent labour-market experience, among those who were still without a job but looking for one over three years after redundancy (31 per cent); and fewer still among those who combined lack of recognized skill with continuing unemployment (23 per cent). To note this is not to regard owner-occupation as an unmixed benefit: home-owners could, and quite often did, get into difficulties after redundancy in keeping up still outstanding mortgage payments if they were out of work for any length of time. Yet even their incomplete and now risky ownership constituted something of an asset to carry with them into harder circumstances: both a small deposit, and a sign, of past savings which had been less within the reach of the people whom redundancy was to hit the hardest.

VIEWS OF THE PAYMENTS

All this might be thought to have given the hardest hit special grounds for thinking their redundancy pay inadequate – if not perhaps immediately, then over time as the hardships really began to bite. But our data show no trends of the sort that this would imply. They show neither widespread discontent about the size of the pay-off among those who came to experience long unemployment; nor *more* discontent among these (among the non-skilled blue-collar workers and the clerks, among those who took away the smallest sums – all these groups in overlap with each other) than among the better-placed. Just about 25 per cent of the entire 'sample' said that they had been dissatisfied with what they got, whether at the time of their redundancy or at some time later: a sizeable minority, it is true, but leaving the great majority apparently satisfied. And though the 'malcontents' had drawn a little less money on average than the rest, that difference of a few hundred pounds seems an accidental accompaniment of other things making for discontent or its opposite, rather than a straight reflection of some special sense of hardship. What did make for discontent with the pay-off – for more than average discontent, that is – was the combination of long service in the firm with the need or the preference to stay in work; and this more or less equally, whether the people concerned actually found new work or had to join the dole queue.

About one in every three of these respondents – still committed to work after long service – expressed dissatisfaction with the money they had got, even though their long years of employment with the company had helped to give them more money to go with than many others. 'It wasn't enough when you think of all the time and work I'd put in for them,' said a skilled man who, after 40 years service with the firm, took away some £10,000 in severance pay and pension refund. But aged 59 when he lost his job, he was still committed to work – at least to the income it would bring. And although he in fact never found work again, and wore down much of his redundancy money simply on living expenses in the following years, it was the indignity of being made redundant after so long, and while still able-bodied and willing, that appeared to irk him especially about his compensation package. Such a sense of grievance over effective dismissal – a sense that after all the money was not enough to make up for unfair rejection, never mind where the blame lay – seems to have played a good part in making long-service employees who were still committed to work more critical of their pay-off than others.

By contrast with the one in three of these people who were dissatisfied, only one in five of those who decided to retire from work at some point after redundancy gave voice to discontent over the money they got. This was the case even though they, too, of course often had long service behind them. Generally, they thought their own package good enough, and a fair help towards the new life outside work which for most of them would have come a few years hence anyway, even without redundancy. Not that they had wanted to pull out already, before the plant closure was announced; nor that they were to find life without work financially easy, even with the redundancy pay to help: far from it, in many cases. But they had no longer the same comitment to carrying on work as their fellows who tried doggedly to keep a foot in the labour market; and so also, it seems, not the same sense of unwarranted and undignified dismissal which inclined more of those others to complain about their redundancy pay.

When in general most people did not complain – even those who might be thought to have had good cause to do so, because they came to face particular difficulties after redundancy with relatively little help from their compensation money – this may have been because they got as much as they expected or more; and more, too, than they had perhaps had cash-in-hand in their lives before. 'It seemed a lot of money at the time,' said a middle-aged crane driver about his £1,000 or so, including some weeks' wages in lieu of notice. And although it proved not to be such a lot – 'it all just went on bills and living' during his long unemployment thereafter – he bore no grudge over that; only a mild regret that he and his family had not spent a chunk of the money instead 'on a good holiday before things became hard – we would have had something to look back to'. But while many others had similar stories to tell about how their money went, if their search for new work had proved difficult, they also usually said little or nothing directly about why they felt satisfied with the money they got on redundancy. For one thing, there may have seemed to them no need to look the gift horse in the mouth.

For another, their opportunities for invidious comparison – of a kind that might have sparked resentment among those who drew the shorter straws in terms of both redundancy compensation and later fate in the labour market – were probably quite limited. All, of course, knew the terms of the scheme on paper. But few may have bothered to work out, or have heard outside a small circle of workmates, just what these meant when translated into different packages for different people. Moreover, by the time those who were to founder in the search for work after redundancy could fully recognize their plight, they had generally lost touch with former colleagues anyway. Comparisons were occasionally brought into critical comments on the redundancy money; but this by way of claims that workers at British Steel had got a better deal, because that Corporation, unlike their own firm, had drawn on the EEC help to top up redundancy pay. When our respondents made any 'internal' comparisons in their comments on the compensation scheme, they usually referred only to the length-of-service provisions, and then to positive or neutral effect: they felt that it was fair in itself to reward long service, and to help the older people especially – even if that served to rule out any collective protest against it by dividing workmates' reactions to the closure. Comparisons critical of the disparities according to past pay (so according to job-level and in turn, effectively though not by intention, in perverse relation to labour market survival chances) hardly ever figured in what our informants had to say about the arrangements for redundancy pay. Occupational differentials may be so taken for granted as to be rarely questioned in practice, even by 'left-wingers' in our respondent group who were otherwise much concerned about current inequalities. In any case, the mismatch between the distribution of take-away pay and the distribution of post-redundancy need, which we have underlined, is not so readily visible to those who themselves are its individual victims.

How people spent their redundancy money – after usually depositing it in a building society or other savings account, though quite a few put it on current account without interest – has already been a subject of brief comment. In the case of many who could not find work again for long after they had lost their jobs with the firm, much of it went 'just on trying to manage'; and more of it might have gone that way had they realized, in advance, how hard 'managing' would prove to be. For others, there was often a real element of a 'nest egg' or 'windfall' to the money. But so much depended on the diversity of individual circumstances which followed the closure, that a further account belongs to the story of people's experiences over the months and years after their redundancy.

3

The Impact of Redundancy:
The First Search for New Work

In our initial contacts with management and trade union conveners, we heard a story that seems to have circulated at the time of the closure: that many of the people affected took their prospects after redundancy sufficiently on trust to go on holiday first, before worrying too much about what to do later. We have heard much the same thing rumoured in impressionistic accounts of redundancies elsewhere in the country during that period – the late 1970s and early 1980s – when workplace closures were on a fast rising curve, but the stubborn persistence of high subsequent unemployment had still to become fully clear. Yet to go by our respondents' later recollections at least, the story had something to it of the character of the inter-war myth that council tenants commonly stored coal in their baths: more folklore than fact. Asked about their immediate intentions after losing their jobs, some of our Sheffield informants did indeed say that they had planned a holiday first. But they were a small minority – about 11 per cent – and their holiday plans were not necessarily a sign of assurance about the future: some were explicit that they had felt in need of 'a rest', or of 'a good break' to look back on, *before* the new uncertainties and now that they had a pot of cash in hand.

Yet there is this to the story, factually off-target though it was, that the peak of recession *was* still to come. So individual prospects, in any case very variable, might often have looked better at the time than they were to prove in due course. There are hints of just that in our respondents' accounts – of rather less initial anxiety about the risk of not finding a job again than one might perhaps have expected with hindsight. Roughly 70 per cent intended to find other paid work when they lost their jobs with the firm. This included the vast majority of people still at least some years away from normal retirement age, though among them those from non-manual work – routine-grade clerks especially – were rather less committed to steady continuation in employment than the blue-collar workers, skilled and non-skilled alike. And it included more than 40 per cent even of the elderly who, aged 60 years or over at the time of our interviews three years later, were getting fairly close to retirement when they became redundant.

Of all these people who wanted paid work again, one in three had actually managed to find a job before they left their old firm. We asked the other two thirds whether it had worried them not to have a job lined up for them to walk into immediately on redundancy. Just over half said they had been worried then. But by the same token, almost as many had *not* been; and worries about job prospects and their consequences had apparently been no more common – if anything a little less common, overall – among the people who later proved to have the greatest difficulties in the labour market than among those who in fact were to manage quite well. There were plenty of anxieties to come for the former. But prospects were evidently quite hard to predict in a local economic situation still at an early stage of sharp decline; and they were perhaps especially hard to predict for people short on the know-how, as well as the credentials, which helped others to find footholds again in the crumbling market for employment.

However these uncertainties appeared at the time, very many of the men and women due for redundancy did in fact start searching for new work even while they were still with their old firm. This was not the rule among the older people who, tempted by the monetary incentive built into the redundancy scheme, were often inclined to take retirement at once, or were unsure whether to do so. Nevertheless, about half the older people whose hope then was still to find some alternative paid work started looking for it already before their jobs actually ended. Far more did so among their younger colleagues (those under 60 at the time of the interview, and so no more than at most 56 or 57 when redundancy came). Almost all of these wanted to find steady work again, with some wavering only among non-manual employees; and about 70 per cent began the search for new employment while they were still with their old firm – they started to ask around, looked in the newspapers, and quite often put in for jobs already then.

Those who started the search early in this way were, moreover, quite often successful. About two thirds of them either had a job to walk into immediately they left the old one, or they found one within some weeks. This compared with only one in six or seven of their colleagues who put off looking for new work until after actual redundancy. More tellingly, it may seem, nearly 80 per cent of them had paid work six months after redundancy (a point of time that was to prove important for later labour market experience) and over 70 per cent were still in employment over three years after redundancy. By contrast, for the minority who had deferred the start of their search until after they had left the firm, the corresponding figures were just under 50 per cent at both the same dates.

It is no doubt tempting to make a simple causal inference from this: to take it as proof that 'the early bird catches the worm'. And a related point may appear to encourage further moralizing about the importance of individual initiative. The qualified or 'credentialled' people in the redundant workforce were a great deal more inclined than others to make an early start on job hunting. Over 80 per cent of the skilled blue-collar workers and the mixed group of 'staff' (under 60 years old at interview) began to look around for new paid work before actual redundancy, while little more than 50 per cent of the non-skilled and the routine-grade office workers made so early a start. Might it not be, then, that the latter 'brought upon themselves' the particular hardships which – as we shall show in more detail – they were to face in the labour market over the following years? And if these people were to blame in this sense for making a slow start, might not their 'lack of initiative' be seen in turn as a sign of long-enduring personal characteristics which could help to explain why they had not acquired skills or credentials earlier in their lives? Conclusions of this sort would certainly be well in tune with the line of contemporary social commentary that sees economic inequality as a necessary reflection of individual – even if perhaps culturally reinforced – differences in personal competence; and whose prescriptions for recession have been epitomized in the catchphrase injunction to the jobless to 'get on your bikes'.

In fact, conclusions to this effect do not stand up to closer examination of our material. The early birds did *not* catch and hold the worm after all – not, in the longer run, if they lacked the skills or credentials which proved to help others. By the time of our interviews, three years and more after the closure, it made no difference for the relatively unqualified group (the non-skilled shopfloor workers and the routine-grade office clerks) whether they had begun to look for other work before they actually lost their old jobs, or they had left the start till afterwards. In either case, only about 40 per cent of them now had paid work; and in either case, virtually just as many were on the dole – an unemployment rate of nearly 50 per cent by the conventional measure (which leaves out of account those who have 'voluntarily' withdrawn from the labour market, even though they often do so just because jobs are so hard to get). The story on this score is summarized in Table 3.1,

Table 3.1 For respondents under 60 at interview, employment status at two points of time after redundancy, by former occupational level and time of job search start

Employment status	Non-skilled manual and routine manual		Skilled manual and 'higher' non-manual		All respondents under 60 at interview	
	Started job search		Started job search		Started job search	
	Before redun-dancy %	At or after redun-dancy %	Before redun-dancy %	At or after redun-dancy %	Before redun-dancy %	At or after redun-dancy %
6 months after redundancy						
In paid work	63	46	87	53	79	48
Unemployed	28	41	12	23	17	35
Out of labour market	9	13	1	24	4	17
At interview						
In paid work	42	40	88	64	72	48
Unemployed	40	38	8	18	19	32
Out of labour market	18	22	4	18	9	20
Total (= 100%)	43	37	78	17	130	54

Notes

The table is confined to respondents under 60 years old at the interview (three years plus after redundancy) for whom information about job search start and employment status at both dates is available. The totals for all such respondents exceed the subtotals for the two broad occupational categories distinguished here by including a few informants who could not be classified by occupational level at the firm.

'Unemployed' are those registered as such *and* wanting to work. 'Out of labour market', in the case of these respondents still under 60 when interviewed, included only one who had 'retired' and so indicated permanent withdrawal from 'economic activity'.

where the figures in the bottom-left part are those first relevant to the point.

Making an early start on the search for work does seem to have helped people in this group to find employment at first – during the initial six months after redundancy – though even so it helped them a good deal less than their more qualified colleagues. And among the latter – skilled shopfloor workers and non-manual 'staff' – the early starters continued to keep a firmer foothold in work than the minority of late starters throughout the full three-year period. This was in part (as the figures here hint, and respondents' more detailed accounts confirm) because the late starters from this 'qualified' category included a few managers and the like who felt no strong need to continue in work on a regular basis: enough to tip the scales in a sub-group with absolute numbers too small for very solid conclusions to be drawn anyway.

What is very plain, however – and has a basis of considerably firmer numbers – is the hardship of the labour market as it was encountered by men and women without special skills or credentials. By contrast with their more qualified counterparts, their situation got worse over time. A number of them, who had managed to find jobs of a kind six months after the closure, lost them again as recession struck deeper. With that, such limited advantage as the early job-starters among them had found at first now vanished. Their hold in the employment market was then, after three years, every bit as insecure as that of their occupational peers who had left job-hunting rather late – and a good deal more insecure than that even of the late starters among their better qualified former colleagues. An early start on the search for new work may or may not have reflected commendable personal determination and initiative. But in aggregate, and beyond the quite short run, it played no part in what happened to the people who came to redundancy without particular marketable qualifications or credentials. What proved to matter for them was simply the lack of demand for their labour. As the overall labour market tightened, its segmentation also became more pronounced: it was their parts of it that came to be squeezed most.

MEANS TO THE SEARCH FOR JOBS

We shall look more closely later at these 'class conditioned' divergences of experience over the full period after redundancy and we shall then also bring into the picture the experience of older workers – 60 years or over when interviewed – whom we have so far mainly left out. Before that, however, it is worth saying a little more about the first search for work

of those – the great majority of our informants – who were committed somehow to finding it again if they could. Why, despite their commitment, did
quite a number of them not start looking for alternative employment until at
least the formal date of their redundancy? And why were these late starters,
though a minority overall, fairly numerous among the less qualified?

We asked no questions explicitly about this. Nor did we find room, in
an already long interview schedule, to ask about the precise date when
each respondent left the firm. Had we done so, we could have checked
on the possibility that the late starters – including the less qualified, in
particular – may have had a shorter time to begin job-hunting between
the general notification of closure and their own varying specific dates of
departure. It is quite plausible that this could be part of the story; but it
is unlikely, from what we can otherwise piece together, that it is the
whole of it. Differences of situation and prospects in an uncertain and
divided labour market look as if they also played some part; and these
again reflect 'class-tied' inequalities of resources.

Some people volunteered reasons why they had put off looking for
other work until after their redundancy – commonly that they had
wanted time to think about where and how to look for a job which would
last, or pay a fair wage, or be nearer home; occasionally with reference to
private or idiosyncratic reasons, such as illness in the family, or a faint
hope that redundancy might not come after all. Most of the people in
question, however, offered no direct explanation. But their postpone-
ment of the job search seems often to have meant, in effect, that they
waited until they signed on as unemployed – which could be many weeks
after they left, if their terms of notice debarred them from immediate
registration. This in turn may have reflected a decision – or just an
assumption that it would be natural – to try official channels first in the
search for new work: to begin with advice from the Unemployment
Benefit Office and then the Job Centre.

We cannot be sure just how often use of these official channels in fact
led to a job. Though we asked our respondents to tell us in general
terms about how (as well as when) they looked for new work, we did not
ask them – job for job – how they had got it if they did. But 'unofficial'
channels loom large in the accounts given by those who managed to get
back into paid work fairly quickly: personal contacts and hear-say from
family or friends; searches through the small ad columns of the
newspapers; a lot of just 'looking and asking around'; and direct
applications either in consequence or merely 'on the off-chance'. When
advice in connection with unemployment registration or from a Job
Centre comes into respondents' reports (whether from those who did
find work or from those who did not) it is rarely described in positive

terms. 'They had nothing to offer', 'I was just told I'd have to change my trade', 'All they could say was there were no jobs going in steel – and at my age. . .', 'They did send me off to a couple of jobs, but they'd gone long ago' – these were typical comments; and reports of success through this means were infrequent.

This is in line with evidence from other research (e.g. Jenkins, 1985) showing the weight which 'unofficial' channels have in the hunt for work. To note it is not to charge the staff of the public agencies with indifference or incompetence. The local economy had indeed then set into decline. When there were job vacancies, they may often have been filled – and through the grapevine, if not indeed by internal recruitment – before they could go on the Job Centre's books. Moreover, the minority of people who postponed their work-search till after redundancy, and in doing so tended to rely first on guidance from the authorities, were predominantly 'unqualified'. They were therefore the harder to help as the bottom – their potential job opportunities in particular – slid out of the labour market.

Why so relatively many of these waited until they could register – leaving even a visit to the Job Centre till then – still calls for some explanation. To repeat, it was not, at least in the case of men from manual shopfloor jobs with the firm, for lack of commitment to finding work again. The non-skilled all in all were as little inclined as the skilled to pull out of work which was their prime source of income, as well as of some personal dignity and independence. And though anxiety on the score still had not fully developed, they worried no less often than the skilled if they had not yet got a new job on hand immediately after redundancy. But an early start on the search for alternative employment probably took rather more than just general will or worry. It usually involved use of a variety of means for 'looking and asking around', informal channels especially. And effective use of these requires, or at least is helped by, a degree of know-how as well as of confidence; of contacts and 'feel' for the market, harder to pin down than formal credentials but important alongside them.

Respondents who told us how 'I heard about this job from a mate', or 'My wife worked in a place that still seemed to be going quite strong, so I went along and had a word with the foreman', were referring to real if intangible resources. Such resources are unevenly spread. The opportunities to acquire and develop them differ according to long-term economic and social experience; and the formally less qualified are, by and large, also the less likely to have these aids to hand. Moreover, in so far as the non-skilled among our respondents could assess their prospects realistically (not all could, or more would have been anxious from the outset) then they were also less likely to have such confidence as it may take to pitch straight into job-hunting without guidance. For other than in the quite short run, as we have shown, neither will and worry nor early initiative were in fact to help them climb over the obstacles set against them by the fall in demand for their labour. These people in particular were often caught in a trap. They had been thrown into finding work again with the slimmest of resources, material and otherwise, to help them through. So they were the more dependent than others on support from public sources. Yet help and advice from these sources were the more impotent in their case just because, in falling generally, the labour market was closing off employment opportunities for them above all.

<h2 style="text-align:center">REGISTRATION AS UNEMPLOYED</h2>

There was of course no guarantee for anyone – regardless of qualifications, know-how, confidence or early initiative – that they would find work again, let alone a job to walk into straight after redundancy. In fact, the great majority of our informants did *not* have new employment lined up when they left: about 75 per cent overall, over 65 per cent of those who were committed to finding work again. Very many, therefore, registered as unemployed at least for a time – an experience that was generally new, and quite often disconcerting, to these people when set against their common record of steady and usually long employment in a single place.

   Not that everyone without a job to go to immediately did sign on. For one thing, as we have noted earlier, the severance package for many included pay 'in lieu of notice' in such a way as to preclude their registration for sometimes a long period. Indeed, of all those who signed on the dole following their redundancy, fewer than a third did so within a fortnight; fully one half waited for at least a month, in particular cases up to three months or more. Some of the people ineligible to register more or less immediately on redundancy actually found work again before their period of notice on severance pay ran out, and so never registered. Some others seem not to have bothered to sign on, even if they were eligible, because they had a prospect of employment soon in hand; and a few others again did not register because their contribution records were inadequate (for example through recurrent past sickness) to entitle them to unemployment benefit. Altogether, some one in seven of those who were without a job for a time following their redundancy – while not, or not yet, having pulled wholly out of the labour market –

never signed on then as unemployed, for one or other of these reasons. Though their period without work at that time was often fairly short, they nevertheless represent an 'under-count' of the full impact of redundancy.

Secondly, there were those who withdrew from 'economic activity' altogether as soon as they left the firm – either into early retirement, or just into domestic life at least for the time being – and who put this in a sense on record by not registering as unemployed. They were rather few, however: about one in eight of all the people who had no job to go to immediately on redundancy. The decision to pull out of the labour market altogether was often, as we shall describe later, a hard one; to take it at once, and so firmly as to rule out any claim to unemployment benefit, was still harder. So most people who were leaning in this direction (some 60 per cent even of those who were close enough to the decision to retire or withdraw within a month or two of their redundancy) did first sign on as unemployed, though only for a short time. Whether or not they signed on, the dilemmas facing these people defy any simple, let alone precise, enumeration towards resolution of the controversies about 'under-count' and 'over-count'. But after not very long, they were all out of the official record of unemployment anyway. Since many remained in two minds about their new status as 'economically inactive', by then in gross aggregate they weighed down the scales on the side of 'under-count'.

When three in every four of the people without a job to go to at once – over half the entire respondent group, all told – did sign themselves onto the unemployment register some time during the first weeks or months after their redundancy, this was a novel experience for most; and a worrying one for many. It put into stark relief the abrupt change in their fortunes; and some respondents turned the stigma which they associated with the dole queue against themselves: 'I hadn't thought I'd ever come to that. I felt disgusted with myself – it took the heart out of me.' The submergence of individuality in the mass routines of registration could be traumatic. 'All those people queuing to sign on, it was like a cattle market, I felt degraded,' said a middle-aged skilled craftsman and one-time shop steward. 'And when you then got to the desk in the end, it was all just a formality. They got your facts on a card, and that was it.'

There were a good many comments of this sort when we asked people about their memories of registration. But reactions were far from uniformly to that effect. About one third had favourable recollections, and remembered the staff as friendly and helpful. This was more true of the older and the middle-aged than of the younger people; and more of those who were already well inclined to pull out of work. 'They were

very fair in the end,' said a former stockman, then close to retirement. 'I
was apprehensive, never having been to the Unemployment before. But
it was alright when it came to the interview. She just said "You're 63,
aren't you? So don't you bother too much." She knew I wasn't keen on
looking around for another job at my age, and there wouldn't have been
any work going.' Another quarter or so were non-committal. With the
older workers again rather to the fore, they remembered nothing
especially good or bad about the business of signing on, but took it just
as it came: as a necessary sequel to redundancy, unfamiliar though the
experience usually was.

However when others (just short of 40 per cent) said they had
unfavourable memories of registration, this was in part for reasons of the
kind we have already pointed to: lining up to sign on could underscore a
sense of loss of dignity and independence, of reduction to a number on a
mass record and a set of data on a card. But the complaints made were,
above all else, an expression of frustration or resentment that there was
little help to be gained from the process – either at registration or from
later consultation – for what mattered most: to find paid work again.

It was those who stayed 'economically active' that were more often
dissatisfied with their experience of signing on and what followed – this
with little difference between people who in fact found employment
later, usually through 'unofficial' channels, and people who did not; with
little difference either, by the same token, according to job-level in their
former firm. But it was, in particular, the people who had been through
two or more interviews following registration who were most often
dissatisfied: as many, in fact, as 60 per cent of them. Their concern,
especially, was not in the end with their own pride; or commonly with
any rudeness or high-handedness attributed to staff. Complaints on the
latter score were fairly rare; more often staff were acknowledged to be
doing what they could, if in an impersonal manner. It was simply that
staff had very little to offer: 'They just checked over my details, and
nothing came of it.' The interviews, critics commonly said, were
'useless', 'a waste of time', 'a routine'. To go through several with no
better result plainly increased their exasperation and, often, the sense
that they themselves had been found useless for all their years of honest
work: 'The most they could say was change yourself and get ready to go
somewhere. But that was pointless. All this hanging about but no work at
the end of it.' In fact, as many acknowledged one way or another, the
interviewers no less than the interviewees were caught up in circumstances
well beyond their own control: 'There just wasn't anything they could do
to help.'

4

The Impact of Redundancy: Economic Experience over Three Years

RE-EMPLOYMENT, UNEMPLOYMENT AND DISCOURAGEMENT

A single statistic can be taken for first sharp summary of the long-run impact of this instance of workplace closure at the turn of the 1970s into the 1980s. Every man and woman whom we followed up had been in regular full-time work up to the day of their redundancy. When we met them, rather more than three years later, almost 60 per cent were now without paid work.

Closer analysis adds some qualification to that stark statistic; but not very much. The qualification concerns those who withdrew, over these 38 months or so, from officially recognized 'economic activity': whether they did so by taking retirement, or by just staying at home without registering as unemployed and available for work. On the one hand, of course, there were many older people in the redundant workforce; and many of these (more than 50 per cent of the men and women who had reached the age of 60 or over by the time of the interview) declared themselves 'retired' on, or at some point after, redundancy (see Table 4.1). Yet it was the redundancy that had often precipitated their retirement. The great majority of the people who retired did so 'early', before the normal age of 65 for men and 60 for women; and of these in turn a similarly large majority – some 75 per cent – said that they had previously entertained no thought of retiring early, at least until redundancy came onto the agenda or until they found new work impossible to get thereafter.

On the other hand, there were people who disengaged from 'economic activity' without calling this retirement – 16 per cent of respondents overall after three years, rather more among the older than the younger ones. But their withdrawal, too, had often been precipitated by redundancy and its aftermath. When new paid work proved hard to find, pulling out of the labour market into unpaid work at home was one way –

Table 4.1   Employment status soon after redundancy and at interview, by age

Employment status (at R or I)	Age at interview (3 years plus after redundancy)						All respondents	
	Under 40		40–59		60 and over			
	R %	I %	R %	I %	R %	I %	R %	I %
In paid work	64	69	41	62	11	13	34	41
Unemployed	31	18	51	27	38	15	41	20
Retired								
early	—	—	—	—	27	43	11	17
normal	—	—	—	—	4	12	1	6
Other	5	13	8	11	20	17	13	16
Total no. (= 100%)	82		113		155		350	
% 'economically active'	95	87	92	89	49	28	75	61
Conventional unemployment rate (%)	33	20	55	30	76	53	54	31

Notes

This table is confined to respondents for whom all relevant information is available.

Date of employment status: *R* = within a few weeks of redundancy; *I* = at interview.

Employment status: 'in paid work' includes respondents (only about 3 per cent) now in part-time work; 'unemployed' = registered and wanting work; 'retired – early/normal' = before versus at or after 65 for men, 60 for women; 'other' = withdrawn from 'economic activity' without reporting this as retirement, e.g. through illness or into unpaid domestic work only or non-employment otherwise without registration as unemployed.

The 'economically active' are the subtotal of those 'in paid work' and those 'unemployed'. The 'conventional unemployment rate' gives the percentage of this subtotal who were 'unemployed'.

for a number of women especially – of maintaining self-respect and avoiding the stigma of formal unemployment. Nursing a condition of ill health, which had not prevented full-time employment before the works closed, was another way of doing much the same thing. So, just as the numbers of people taking early retirement rose as time went on, the numbers otherwise withdrawing from engagement in the employment market also rose over the three years – even though these people kept the door open for possible future return by not thinking of themselves as 'retired'.

It was not, we must add, that they had instead taken up work in 'the black economy'. Very few altogether – in or out of work in the formal economy – said they had even occasional odd jobs on the side; and of the small number who did, most got too little money from it to make any odds. Here as elsewhere, 'the black economy' is generally least within reach of the people who are most at risk in the formal one (cf. Pahl, 1984); and in Sheffield, it seems, neither past regular employment in industry nor residence in the manufacturing districts and working-class suburbs offers much opportunity for 'moonlighting'.

In short, both retirement and withdrawal from the labour market in other guises were frequently a response to the same pressures in the local economy as were making for high registered unemployment. True, both could still be individually welcome on a number of scores, in a sense that formal unemployment could not: for the personal dignity they allowed by contrast with 'life on the dole'; for more positive use, then, of the time and energy spared from the often hard grind of everyday employment; and, also, so far as many of the retired were concerned, for a monetary bonus in return for retiring early that came with the redundancy package and/or from a change in the social security system to encourage older men to take themselves permanently out of the competition for jobs. Yet relief on these scores was, as we shall show later, not uncommonly mixed with regret – regret at the loss of regular pay, not least.

In real terms, then, the line between registered unemployment and officially unrecorded non-employment is hard to draw; and it becomes harder to draw the deeper recession bites and the more its victims, therefore, may sign themselves off the register while still hankering for paid work if it were to be found. Even by the conventional measure of unemployment (the percentage which the registered unemployed make up in the total of people still formally 'economically active'), the long-run impact of this instance of redundancy was sharp enough: overall a 31 per cent rate of unemployment for the entire group some three years after the closure (at a time when the Sheffield average was 14 per cent); and 20 per cent even among the younger of them, still under 40 at the time of the interview (see again Table 4.1). But the real rate of wholly or partly enforced 'worklessness' was a good deal higher still.

Exactly how much higher is hard to say, because it requires an estimate of how many among those who retired or otherwise pulled out of the labour market would have stayed 'economically active', if they had not found it too hard to do so in the new circumstances; and, as we have pointed out, when in fact they took themselves out of the competition for jobs, for good or for the time being, their feelings were often mixed and therefore uncertain as pointers to their responses to a hypothetical improvement of the economic climate. But from piecing their comments together, it is clear that at least some 35 per cent – quite possibly up to 50 per cent or more – would not have withdrawn from 'economic activity' by the three-year point of our record, if they had not first found themselves suddenly redundant and then come up against a crumbling market for re-employment together, in the case of older people, with active discouragement from economic activity in ways that we discuss in more detail later (Chapter 6). Adding these people to both sides of the account – as wanting paid work, yet in fact without it – the real rate of enforced exclusion from work and pay was then between 45 and 50 per cent: this by contrast with the just over 30 per cent rate of unemployment shown by conventional calculation.

In that one set of figures is a measure of two points: first, of the crushing impact of the redundancies which had come to this workforce some 38 months earlier; second, of the understatement of that impact if attention is paid only to registered unemployment. The latter point needs particular emphasis. It is no quirk of our survey but well in line with the general results of other research (e.g. Corrigan et al, 1987). There remains room for some dispute about precise figures, but there can be no dispute that to count only the registered unemployed as pressed out of paid work by the hardening of the labour market in recent years involves a significant neglect of realities.

CLASS POLARIZATION OF THE DECLINING LABOUR MARKET

Age plainly played a part in shaping the economic experience of these men and women after redundancy. The older people had the option of retirement and used it often, as we have just said, as a less stressful alternative to battling on in the labour market. They also, more often than others, chose the half-way house of pulling out without calling this retirement; and for some of the older women, indeed, self-labelling as retired might have little meaning, if it did not bring with it an entitlement to pension for them in their own right.

Only in the case of these older people, however, was age by itself an important influence on post-redundancy experience. True, Table 4.1 gives a first impression to the contrary. It shows that the under-40s were quicker off the mark in finding jobs again than the middle-aged: well over 60 per cent of the former had paid work once more within some weeks of their redundancy, by contrast with just above 40 per cent of the latter. Yet this was not to have lasting effect. As we noted in the previous chapter, getting off to an early start in fact mattered little in the end. And so here, too: by the time over three years had passed, the early gap between the younger and the middle-aged people had dwindled to quite a small difference. More in both age-groups now had paid work – around 65 per cent in total – but only a marginally higher proportion of the young than of the middle-aged. Moreover, that small remaining difference – together with a higher ratio of registered unemployment among the middle-aged, as distinct from officially unrecorded 'non-employment' – proved by and large to be only fortuitously associated with age. What mattered far more was job-level before redundancy. Just as, in the long run, an early start on the search for work could do little to counter the handicap of low qualifications or credentials, so again relative youth did not help much by the end of the day.

This can be seen in Table 4.2. That takes as its starting point for tracing respondents' labour market experience not as before a time just after redundancy, but a date six months later. This was in at least two senses a crucial time. For one thing, the overall number of people in paid work grew quite fast over the first six months – from 34 per cent to 46 per cent of the entire group regardless of age; it had then very nearly reached its peak, and began to fall again from a year after redundancy. People's experience later was to hang a good deal on how they had fared by then. Though there was still to be individual movement into and out of work thereafter – more out than in – over 75 per cent of those who had paid work at the six-months point, for example, were in work also when we interviewed them more than three years after redundancy; by contrast, this was true for less than 25 per cent of those who were registered as unemployed at the six-months time. Putting the point differently, more than 80 per cent of the men and women who had a job 'at the end' (when interviewed some 38 months after the closure) had in fact found work already by the time the six months had passed.

For another thing, however, the more qualified and the less qualified came to be still more clearly set on different paths in the labour market from this time onwards. Overall, among the skilled workers and 'staff' under 60, the numbers in paid work actually grew a little still from the six-months point to the time of the interview – from 81 per cent to 84 per cent. But among their counterparts from non-skilled and routine clerical jobs with the firm, the numbers in work fell sizeably over the same period: from 56 per cent to 41 per cent. So the 'class gap' in

Table 4.2 Employment status at two points in time, by age and occupational level with firm

Employment status	Age under 40 at interview					Age 40–59 at interview					Age 60 or more at interview				
	Former occup. level					Former occup. level					Former occup. level				
	OM %	RNM %	SM %	HNM %	All <40 %	OM %	RNM %	SM %	HNM %	All 40–59 %	OM %	RNM %	SM %	HNM %	All 60+ %
6 months after redundancy															
In paid work	60	56	73	91	73	51	64	88	74	66	16	14	27	3	17
Unemployed	40	13	27	9	20	40	22	6	16	25	29	14	45	33	34
Out of lab. mkt.	—	31	—	—	7	9	14	6	10	9	55	72	28	64	49
Total: %	100	100	100	100	100	100	100	100	100	100	100	100	100	100	100
(No.)	(10)	(16)	(26)	(21)	(82)	(47)	(14)	(30)	(20)	(113)	(55)	(14)	(49)	(31)	(155)

At interview (3+ years after redundancy)

In paid work	50	44	88	73	69	40	36	84	95	62	13	7	31	—	13
Unemployed	40	12	12	13	18	45	36	13	—	27	17	7	18	16	15
Out of lab. mkt.	10	44	—	14	13	15	28	3	5	11	70	86	51	84	72
Total: %	100	100	100	100	100	100	100	100	100	100	100	100	100	100	100
(No.)	(10)	(16)	(26)	(21)	(82)	(47)	(14)	(30)	(20)	(113)	(55)	(14)	(49)	(31)	(155)

Conventional unemployment rates: per cent unemployed among those still 'in labour market'

6 months after redundancy	40	18	27	9	22	44	25	7	18	27	64	50	63	91	67
At interview	45	22	12	16	20	52	50	14	—	30	56	50	37	100	53

Notes

The occupational levels distinguished are: OM, non-skilled manual; RNM, routine-grade non-manual; SM, skilled manual; HNM, higher non-manual (above routine-grade).

The numbers of all respondents, age by age, exceed the summed numbers of respondents in the different occupational categories because they include a few who could not be classified by occupational level.

For other notes, see table 4.1.

experience after redundancy widened as time passed; and the six-months date was a signal point in this forking of the ways.

That increasing divergence of labour market experience is one of the features to be seen from Table 4.2. True, in calling attention to it a moment ago we summed, for simplicity, figures that are shown separately in the table. We put together the middle-aged and the young, without reference to this difference of age. We also contrasted the 'better credentialled' with the 'less credentialled', without reference to the distinction on either side between manual and non-manual workers: a conventional line of contrast which Table 4.2 does take into account. One main purpose of the table is precisely to show – rather than to leave the point to be taken on trust – that such summing up makes sense.

So far as the people under 60 were concerned, it was in fact 'class' much more than age – middle-age versus relative youth – that mattered for how they fared after redundancy. And the difference of 'class' that mattered was not between manual and non-manual workers *per se*: it was between the non-skilled shopfloor workers and routine-grade office workers on the one hand, the skilled workers and 'staff proper' on the other.

Here and elsewhere we refer, for convenience, to this distinction as one between the less and the more 'qualified' or 'credentialled', or by other words to similar effect. The shorthand, of course, is rather crude: the degree of training is mixed on either side of the line. Skilled manual workers, for example, were so designated by their last job with the firm, and not all had served a craft apprenticeship; routine-grade office workers ranged from low-level clerks to secretaries with typing, shorthand and even *de facto* some everyday managerial skills; higher-grade 'staff' had employment 'credentials' from their status in the firm, but not necessarily former training or education to match. The distinction nevertheless is overwhelmingly clear from its effects on post-redundancy experience.

For both the two 'less credentialled' groups the percentage at work six months after redundancy was in the range from 50 per cent to a little over 60 per cent, more or less regardless of age; by contrast, for both the two 'more credentialled' groups it reached from around 75 per cent to as high as 90 per cent, again without regular distinction by age under 60. Three years and more after redundancy, it had fallen for the former to a range around 40–5 per cent; but it had stayed high, around the 80–5 per cent mark or above, for the latter. Summarily, the long-term divergence of destiny between the less and the more 'qualified' came to be of the order of two to one.

There were, it is true, differences in precise detail of experience between various sub-categories of the two 'classes'. But these can be seen to arise mainly as differences of percentage calculation based on small absolute numbers; they are not consistent in direction; and, above all, they are trivial when set against the over-arching contrast in fortunes between the less and the more 'qualified'. Even as the local labour market spun into further decline, most of the people under 60 who had craft skills or staff credentials to back them managed to find and hang onto paid work in some form – not all of them, but so large a majority as to hold the unemployment rate among them, three years after redundancy, to a little less overall than the Sheffield average of 14 per cent at the time. It was their former colleagues without corresponding marketable credentials who had to face the full force of recession. As the market contracted, their employment opportunities slipped from bad to worse. By the time three years had passed, registered unemployment among the non-skilled workers and routine-grade clerks under 60 had reached a level of almost 50 per cent all-in-all; and including those who had pulled out, often in deep discouragement, a full 60 per cent were now without work. As the labour market declined, so it had also become sharply polarized.

SOCIAL DIFFERENCES IN WITHDRAWAL FROM THE LABOUR MARKET

A further nuance should be noted. In the hard-hit group especially, the people who came from office jobs within the firm were more inclined to pull out of the market than to sign on as unemployed: they included many women, for whom the option of being a 'housewife' could have the attraction at least of some conventional dignity. And for the older people, of course, withdrawal from 'economic activity' – especially formal retirement – was similarly an option with some advantages over unemployment certified by official registration. Among the people over 60 in fact, Table 4.2 shows 'class' differences in labour market experience after redundancy to be very much less marked than those, among the young and middle-aged, on which we have focussed so far; and when they do come into play, they follow quite a different pattern.

In the case of the older people, so it will be seen, manual workers (especially the skilled) were a good deal more inclined to cling on in the labour market than their former colleagues from office or staff jobs. Fewer had pulled out even after three years; and among those who had, fewer had come to that decision as early as six months after redundancy. Much the same pattern comes to light in a closer analysis of the paths taken by older people into disengagement from the world of paid work.

Among all those who had formally retired by the time they were interviewed, for example, nearly 75 per cent of the men and women from non-manual work with the firm did so almost immediately after their redundancy; and hardly any waited even as long as 18 months. By contrast, fewer than 50 per cent of the blue-collar workers who eventually retired took their retirement more or less on redundancy; and nearly 35 per cent deferred their decision at least till after 18 months had gone by.

Deferment of retirement for so long commonly meant hard experience of unemployment beforehand: virtually none of the people who sooner or later took retirement managed to get work again once they had left the firm; and over 70 per cent of the many among them who held back from retiring more or less immediately, went through a period of registered unemployment before they decided that enough was enough. But this was far more a 'blue-collar' than a 'white-collar' or 'white blouse' experience – not because the older people from office and staff work found it much easier to get jobs again than their manual age-fellows; but because they generally decided on retirement a good deal earlier, and so much less often exposed themselves to the risk of unemployment in the official sense.

All this points to a marked reluctance on the part of the older shopfloor workers – and the skilled among them still more than the non-skilled – to take the definitive step of excluding themselves for good from the world of paid work. So does the fact that quite a number of them – but few of their non-manual counterparts – went through a period of officially unrecorded 'non-employment' (as well as, or instead of, registered unemployment) before deciding to retire; while others, again overwhelmingly former manual workers, were still in that state of limbo – in fact workless, but neither on the dole register nor yet formally retired – when we interviewed them more than three years after closure.

CLASS DIVISIONS IN AND OUT OF THE MARKET

There may seem to be an oddity to the social divisions of post-redundancy experience we have now highlighted. The cleavage of 'class' that mattered for the under-60s – and rode high over any differences between the middle-aged and the younger people – was that between the less and the more 'qualified', with people from manual and non-manual work on both sides of the line. But among those aged 60 or more (a rough indicator of proximity to retirement age) it was rather a difference between former manual and former non-manual employees that came into play: conventional notions of 'class' here seemed to re-assert themselves. It is certainly important to note the point; but it is a good deal less puzzling than it may seem at first sight. Though the explanation needs more factual elaboration later, a summary in advance is worthwhile.

Provided they still had more than just a short span of working life left, skilled manual workers plainly came to redundancy with advantages that put their chances of re-employment in some form pretty well on a par with the premium, familiar enough, enjoyed by people from managerial and other 'staff' work. This, in a generally downward-spiralling market, placed them well ahead of their colleagues from routine and non-skilled jobs, whether office or shopfloor. Their advantages were not just craft skills in themselves; probably not even mainly those, given the overall rundown of the local steel industry in which they had learned and practised their former trades. They surely included the benefits not least – though we cannot measure these – of more cachet in the eyes of potential employers; of assumptions to their credit that they would prove dependable employees; of better access on their own part to hear-say about such job vacancies as did crop up; of more self-confidence in turn, and less cumulative despair, just because they did, on the whole, manage to make their way. On all these scores, as gaps in the labour market widened, they were more likely to find places in it which could still offer paid employment in some regular form.

While this gave the skilled a good boost in the search for new work of one kind or another, it was no guarantee of re-employment with the same status or pay as before. As we shall show, those who found work again not infrequently slid down the job-scale in the process. Specialist craft skill is not a secure market commodity, readily transferable from job to job when overall demand for labour is falling. At least as importantly, it carries little or no weight into retirement. The skilled, it is true, left the firm with more cash in hand from the redundancy deal than others, except senior people from the staff side; so with more to tide them over for a time. But their longer-term money prospects were hardly better than those of their non-skilled and routine-grade former colleagues, if and when they came to leave the world of work for good. They could expect at best only slightly higher pensions on retirement, from state funds and sometimes with a bit of extra from the firm's superannuation scheme. On average indeed, as suggested by figures we give a little later (Table 4.4), once retired the skilled were left with incomes no different from the retirement incomes of the non-skilled –

and a good deal lower than the earnings which they might otherwise have had from work.

So, in the upshot, the monetary premium for skill is liable to dwindle to little or nothing in retirement. Of course protracted unemployment, too, tends to level out 'class' distinctions in these reaches of the socio-economic scale (among people normally dependent for their livelihood on wage-earning jobs), but it comes to people from skilled work much less often than to the non-skilled. Retirement, by contrast, comes to nearly all at some time; and for those who have spent their working lives in 'jobs' rather than 'careers', it carries both a risk of poverty or hardship, and a blurring of previous differences in income. Circumstances change a good deal less on retirement in the case of people who have been on 'career' tracks during much of their working lives. Rather modest though their former employment status had been, the experience of the older managerial staff in our group conformed to a well-known model. Not only did they take fair-sized sums – 'capital' rather than 'cash' – with them from redundancy; they also reported incomes, in retirement, which were distinctly higher than the small figures from pensions and supplementary sources reported, more or less in common, by those who had retired after wage-earning work of whatever level.

To summarize, therefore, the labour market in decline shows increasing segmentation: a far sharper restriction of employment opportunities for some of the people newly placed at risk than for others. The line of division in the first instance, from our evidence, is between people who carry from their former work recognized credentials of manual skill *or* staff experience (people of a kind who in any case were probably less liable to redundancy at the outset, though our own data cannot show this), and on the other hand those without credentials of this sort. Doors in the market are closing to the latter especially. Even so, the more favoured are not guaranteed new paid work in protected places of the market. A good many of the men from skilled blue-collar jobs, for example, pay for their re-employment by down-grading, and so become liable to lose out further, some time in the future. Moreover, once out of the labour market – especially in retirement – the first line of division fades; and another, between the many who just had *jobs* and the fewer who had *careers*, becomes more prominent. So, in money terms, retirement comes harder to people who move to it from a job-life than from a career-life, for all the greater strains on health and physical energy of the former. It comes, relatively speaking, especially hard to wage-earners from skilled jobs because – although in some ways they are likely to have more resources behind them than the non-skilled, such as owner-occupation of their homes – their drop in income is likely to be steeper.

This is very visible from our figures – and the detailed interview accounts behind them – showing the particular reluctance of the older manual workers, and the skilled among them especially, to take themselves out of the world of work for good. One might have expected the same to be true of the older people made redundant from routine-grade office jobs, wage-earning work in our sense no less than manual jobs. But they were mainly women – for some of whom the old conventions, that women's earnings count for less than men's and that unpaid work as a housewife has its own propriety, made withdrawal from the job-world easier. Yet they too, with their households, lost out in quite sharp financial terms, by comparison with the money that would have come in if there had been paid work readily at hand for them. Only the older people from higher-level manual work came to retirement with a measure of monetary comfort. It is not surprising that they, by and large, were fairly ready to opt out, while so many of a similar age from the shopfloor were not.

THE WIDENING OF THE MARKET GAP OVER TIME

We need to flesh out these and other financial consequences of the redundancies and their aftermath. But before we do so, it is worth briefly returning to the record of people's experience in the labour market: in particular to the way in which divisions in the market hardened over time. Table 4.3 shows some more detail of that process.

It was, as we noted earlier, the time from around six months up to a year after the redundancies that proved crucial. During the first six months the overall number of people in paid work again grew sizeably; only very few more were added to the total over the following six months; and then the number began to turn down (Table 4.3A, bottom row). To be unemployed in the immediate wake of the plant closure was not decisive for what happened later (Table 4.3B, first set of three columns). True, the risk of being unemployed – and registered as such – by the time that we conducted our interviews, proved about three times as high for the people who were unemployed at the outset as for those who had paid work again so early on (38 per cent as against 12 per cent). Yet just over 40 per cent of the 'early unemployed' were in jobs again three years later. Not so, however, in the case of the men and women who were still unemployed six months after being made redundant

Table 4.3 Employment status at interview for respondents (A) working and (B) unemployed at different dates after redundancy; by occupational level with firm

A. RESPONDENTS IN PAID WORK AT DIFFERENT DATES

| Employment status at interview | In paid work | | | | | | | | | | | |
| | Soon after redundancy | | | 6 months after redundancy | | | 12 months after redundancy | | | 18 months after redundancy | | |
(3 years + after redundancy)	OM & RNM %	SM & HNM %	All %	OM & RNM %	SM & HNM %	All %	OM & RNM %	SM & HNM %	All %	OM & RNM %	SM & HNM %	All %
In paid work	64	82	74	66	83	77	69	88	81	74	91	85
Unemployed	14	8	12	24	10	14	20	7	11	17	5	8
Withdrawn but not retired	19	8	12	8	6	8	9	5	7	7	4	6
Retired	3	2	2	2	1	1	2	—	1	2	—	1
Total: % (No.)	100 (36)	100 (72)	100 (116)	100 (59)	100 (93)	100 (160)	100 (59)	100 (97)	100 (164)	100 (54)	100 (99)	100 (160)

B. RESPONDENTS UNEMPLOYED AT DIFFERENT DATES

Employment status at interview (3 years + after redundancy)	Unemployed											
	Soon after redundancy			6 months after redundancy			12 months after redundancy			18 months after redundancy		
	OM & RNM %	SM & HNM %	All %	OM & RNM %	SM & HNM %	All %	OM & RNM %	SM & HNM %	All %	OM & RNM %	SM & HNM %	All %
In paid work	27	53	41	11	41	24	6	29	16	9	23	14
Unemployed	53	25	38	59	30	46	63	40	54	72	61	66
Withdrawn but not retired	6	6	7	11	7	11	11	12	12	4	10	10
Retired	14	16	14	19	22	19	20	19	18	15	6	10
Total: %	100	100	100	100	100	100	100	100	100	100	100	100
(No.)	(70)	(68)	(140)	(46)	(46)	(94)	(46)	(42)	(90)	(46)	(31)	(80)

Notes

Employment status and former occupational level are categorized as in previous tables, but the four occupation level categories are here combined into two: the 'less qualified' OM and RNM vis à vis the 'more qualified' SM and HNM.

The total numbers in the columns for 'all' respondents slightly exceed the sums of the numbers in the corresponding occupational level groups because they include a few respondents who could not be classified by former occupational level.

(Table 4.3B, second set of three columns) – a smaller number in all now, but a 'harder core'. Barely 25 per cent of these were in paid work at the time of the interview (compared with more than 75 per cent of their colleagues who had managed to find jobs again by the six-months point); upwards of 50 per cent were still registered as jobless; and 30 per cent had pulled out of the job world altogether, often in discouragement. As might be expected, this hardening of the market increased thereafter, as recession took still firmer hold. Very few indeed of the people unemployed a year or 18 months after the closure were to find work later; and the gap in fortunes between them and those in work at the same times widened as the months and years passed.

Above all, 'class' divisions in the labour market were sharp throughout and became more pronounced over time. Whatever the date taken in Table 4.3 from which to follow up people's later experience, the less qualified fared worse than the more qualified. If they had managed to find work by a given time, they were more at risk of losing it again than their former colleagues with better market credentials; if they were unemployed at a given time, their chances of recovering from that state were again consistently worse. On the latter score, moreover, the 'class' gap tended to become wider (Table 4.3B). Among the men and women registered as unemployed at the outset, twice as many of the 'qualified' as of the 'non-qualified' were to be in paid work three years later (53 per cent as against 27 per cent); among those still unemployed at the six-months point, the corresponding ratio was nearly four to one (41 per cent as against 11 per cent); and it rose to almost five to one in respect of people still on the dole a year after the plant closure (29 per cent as against six per cent), though narrowing a little thereafter.

In summary, the longer people were out of work after redundancy, the more likely it became that they would stay workless – whether they then continued to sign on or pulled out of the job market altogether. This was true across the board. But it had the sharpest impact on the men and women who had come to redundancy, at a time of increasing recession, short on marketable skills or credentials. This was on two counts. First, they had the hardest task in finding work at any single point of time. Second, even if they did find it, they faced the greater risk of losing it again; and if they did not, they had a still smaller chance of finding it later. Moreover, none of that was for lack of personal commitment or initiative – at least among the under-60s, for whom early retirement was no real option. As we have already underlined, the non-skilled in these circumstances were no less concerned than the skilled to keep their arm in; and whether the people without particular credentials took the initiative of an early start on job-hunting or not, it made no shred of difference to them in the end (Table 3.1). The fall in the labour market had set too hard against them.

INCOMES THREE YEARS AFTER REDUNDANCY

One long-term effect of the redundancies was, of course, a fall of real income widespread among the people who lost their jobs in 1979. This followed inevitably from high subsequent unemployment, substantial withdrawal from the labour market, and a degree of downgrading among those who found work again. Certainly, most respondents felt that they had lost out in financial terms. Some 65 per cent said that they and their households were worse off than they had been before the closure over three years earlier; only about 15 per cent thought their circumstances had improved. Obvious though the point is, it needs emphasis: for the majority, rising 'affluence' had become a thing of the past.

We made no attempt, it is true, to check such general comments by obtaining detailed information about incomes as they had been before redundancy: this would have been impracticable. But we did ask a series of questions, in precise terms, about incomes as they were at the time of the interview – the incomes of both informant and spouse (if any), from all sources, net of income tax and other immediate deductions. The response, expectedly, was a little lower than on other subjects, but good for all that. Overall we obtained full reports of 'net joint income' in this sense, and its make-up, from 300 respondents: only some 15 per cent short of the number for whom we otherwise have sufficiently complete information for more or less consistent inclusion in our analyses. There was, moreover, relatively little variation in response on this score between relevant major categories of the 'sample'. Such as it was, response variation was to the effect of rather lighter coverage of people likely to be among the best off (the shortfalls on information about incomes came up to about 20 per cent in the case of former managerial staff and respondents in paid work when interviewed); and the coverage was correspondingly higher for people likely to be worst off (with shortfalls of 10 per cent or less in the case of informants without work, including the retired, and men and women from relatively low-skilled jobs with the firm). The effect of this in turn would be somewhat to understate incomes overall, if we were to lump them all together. But such crude averaging would in any case make very little sense. Incomes at the time of the interviews, of course, varied widely – according to labour market experience after redundancy, and the factors that had fed into that – and it is with just those variations that we are concerned.

Table 4.4 Average net joint income per week in households of two or more persons, at time of interview in 1982–3, by informant's employment status then and his/her occupational level with firm

Informant's employment status at interview	Informant's previous occupational level		
	Non-skilled manual and routine non-manual	Skilled manual	Higher non-manual
In paid work	£99 (37)	£115 (55)	£133 (28)
Unemployed	£50 (34)	£52 (17)	£53 (6)
Withdrawn but not retired	£57 (30)	£57 (6)	£43 (7)
Retired	£67 (32)	£62 (9)	£92 (16)

Notes

Average net joint weekly incomes (for informant and spouse) in each category are rounded to the nearest £. The numbers in brackets show the total number of informants for whom information was obtained in sufficient detail for inclusion in the analysis.

We have excluded respondents living on their own from the table, as the concept of 'joint income' is irrelevant in their case. These numbered only 22 (approx. 7 per cent of all respondents from whom full income information was obtained), including 12 retired people.

In the classification by previous occupational level, we have combined the figures for non-skilled manual and routine non-manual, because the numbers of informants in the latter group were consistently very small. Average incomes in this latter group tended to be below the combined averages shown in the first column (except among the unemployed), the averages for non-skilled manual workers therefore on the whole a few pounds higher than the combined averages shown here.

The contrasts in income shown in Table 4.4 between people in paid work when interviewed and those out of it give a blunt impression of the slide down the money ladder which so many experienced as a prime consequence of redundancy. On average, the unemployed had joint incomes amounting to only half of those of the worst-off group among people who had managed to find employment again (the low-skilled). The gap widened up the occupational scale according to previous job-status, because earned incomes (as to be expected) were higher for each step up this scale, while registered unemployment meant more or less equal misery regardless of work-level before redundancy. People who had pulled out of the labour market without formally retiring (the smaller of the two categories of 'unregistered non-employed') were little better off than the officially unemployed. By contrast, those who had been willing and able to retire, usually 'before their time', *were* rather better off. Pensions, generally including at least a bit of extra money from the firm's superannuation scheme, lifted the retired somewhat above the low level of state-benefit living common to others without work. Even so, only former managerial and technical staff got a very sizeable retirement boost from pensions by comparison with other incomes in 'non-employment'.

There are wobbles to the picture set out in Table 4.4 which arise inevitably from variations in individual household circumstances, when the absolute numbers on which the cell averages are calculated are small. These do not need to hold us up; but there are some other features, blurred by the broad brush used for the table, that warrant comment. One concerns the fact that the incomes recorded are 'joint': the combined incomes of the respondent and his wife or her husband. Respondents who had been routine non-manual workers with the firm were mainly women. In their case the full income reported often included the earnings of a husband; and on average about half or more of the total income here came from the spouse rather than the informant. Despite that, incomes in this group were generally the lowest of all. When women respondents had found work again, it was usually very low-paid and sometimes only part-time. When the husbands had jobs, these too were often poorly paid jobs by 'male standards'. The numbers involved here are too small for further exploration; but it is clear that the adversities which so many of the women clerks came to face in the labour market after their redundancy were often matched by adversities affecting their husbands, if by way of low pay more than high unemployment.

Such household sharing of circumstances was more widespread. As has been found in other research, for example, the unemployed were more likely than the employed to have marriage partners who themselves were jobless, whether so registered or not (see e.g. Pahl and Wallace, 1984; McKee and Bell, 1985). There was a tendency this way, even when only informants of the same previous occupational level are considered. In the case of those from non-skilled manual jobs with the firm, for instance, nearly 50 per cent of the wives of men at work again when interviewed also had paid work of some sort, compared with barely 35 per cent of the wives of the unemployed among them. But the tendency was all the stronger because the wives of men with relatively good occupational credentials in the labour market were in any case themselves more likely to have jobs than other wives, irrespective of their husbands' current status in the market. Leaving aside retired informants and others who had pulled out of formal economic activity, the 'job rate' for wives at the time of interview was thus 40 per cent in the case of non-skilled men, 50 per cent in the case of the skilled, and more than 60 per cent in the case of former managerial and technical staff. Full explanation of these variations may entail more complexity than our material allows; but one prime reason is, without doubt, that marriage partners share much in the socio-economic contexts of their lives. When the market is adverse for men, it is adverse often also for their wives; and, as we have seen, vice versa.

One corollary is that the differences in joint income according to former job-level, among informants in paid work at the time of the interview, were larger than they would have been without a differential contribution from the earnings of 'spouses' (overwhelmingly wives, except in the case of former routine-grade office workers). If we look only at the earnings of employed respondents themselves, excluding money coming in from their wives or husbands, the averages in 1982–3 ranged from £60 a week for the worst-paid group, the women (as they mainly were) from low-level non-manual work; through £76 for the non-skilled manual workers; to £90 and £95 respectively for the skilled and for former 'staff proper'. The gap was wide still between the two broad groups of the less and the more 'credentialled', and the premium for manual skill at least as high as suggested by the 'joint income' figures in the first horizontal rows of Table 4.4. When total incomes in the disadvantaged group nevertheless came to an average of just under £100 per week, it was for reasons that differed between its two constituents: non-skilled manual workers gained little extra from wives' earnings, but more from state benefits of various kinds; routine-grade clerks often had husbands' earnings to add in, even though at low pay rates by market standards for men. But the differential between skilled manual workers and former staff was small – £90 versus £95 – when account is taken of respondents' income only.

It follows from this that spouses' (here almost exclusively wives') earnings added a good deal more to the joint household incomes of re-employed members of the staff than to those of their skilled blue-collar counterparts. That and earlier points to the effect that class differences tend to become more, rather than less, visible when account is taken of the economic circumstances of both marriage partners, is worth notice at least as a footnote to recent debate about the significance of gender and household relations for class (e.g. Crompton and Mann, 1986; Goldthorpe, 1983, and following debate; Pahl, 1984; Bonney, 1987–8).

It may still seem puzzling that when former managers and supervisors found employment again, they did so with little of a premium in individual pay over re-employed skilled manual workers.

In fact this is less surprising than it may seem at first sight. Our analysis so far has focused on occupational inequalities according to previous work-level, the status of the respondent in his or her employment with the firm just before redundancy. But many of those who did find work again slid down the occupational scale in the process. From as near an assessment as we can make, probably as many as half of the non-skilled manual workers went from 'semi-skilled' into 'unskilled' work, though this is a difficult distinction to make; a third of the skilled blue-collar workers went into non-skilled jobs; and again a large number of people from 'staff-level' work (usually of modest rank only in the managerial order) went into lower-grade employment, as many as 50 per cent if we regard a shift to skilled but non-supervisory manual work as 'downgrading' in their case. Very few from any level 'moved up' on re-employment; and only among the small number of routine-grade office workers who found jobs again was there no general 'downward' shift.

At least two points of general importance follow. First, pay differentials at the upper end of the scale are likely to have been compressed in the process since, for all their advantages in just finding work of some kind again, former members of 'staff' seem to have been particularly liable to pay for that by loss of status. Second, as we have underlined earlier, formal qualifications and credentials are not labour market commodities of fixed value: they can help greatly in the search for work when it is scarce; but they are in no way a passport to re-employment on as good terms as before. Social division of the labour market comes to stand out sharply in recession. But status in its more protected parts is not fixed. As the market contracts overall, people from its lowest reaches tend to be squeezed out; people from the reaches further up tend to be squeezed down.

This seemed at least as true in our story for 'staff' as for skilled shopfloor workers. But in other respects the former had distinct advantages over the latter. If they were senior at least, they came to redundancy with better material resources from the past to help them through; and they received, as we have shown, considerably larger sums in compensation, on the scale of small capital rather than just good cash-in-hand. Moreover, if they retired they had not only this premium in redundancy payment to ease their way, but also the prospect of substantially better regular income. On average, as can be seen from Table 4.4, retired 'staff' reported joint incomes at the interview about

50 per cent higher than those of people who had retired from essentially wage-earning work, manual or white-blouse, skilled or non-skilled. The difference arose in part from a 'staff boost' built into the firm's superannuation scheme to supplement state pensions: retired 'staff' drew an average of well over £20 a week from this source, others only about £3. It came also as interest on investments, a source of extra money too small to make much difference for pensioners whose previous work had been in subordinate jobs. 'Staff' retirement incomes were still far from grand sums. The people who drew them generally came from quite low places in the managerial hierarchy. But they found at least modest comfort and security on retiring; while all other pensioners – those who came from below the line between 'jobs' and 'careers' – were now much on a par with each other, at a level of living well below the staff norm. For the majority whose working lives had centred on wage-earning, differences of skill and market credentials had lost in retirement the material significance they once had.

The purpose of this chapter has been to give an overview of the economic impact of redundancy, over the following three years, on the people who lost their jobs in 1979; and to identify, in broad outline, the divergences of their experience after the plant closure. We shall trace their different paths – our respondents' experiences of re-employment, unemployment and withdrawal from the labour market, their reactions to new stresses, their means of coping with them – in more detail in the next two chapters.

5

Re-employment and Unemployment

Many of those we interviewed, when asked for their impressions of the effect on their former colleagues of the redundancy announcement, responded in ways little different from this comment from a 37-year-old machinist: 'Everyone was looking after themselves . . . the people in their fifties and the younger married men wondered if they would ever get another job but the older men were satisfied. It was like a bonus for them'. Many of these older men agreed: 'In my age group we welcomed it, we could retire earlier and have some money behind us . . . most of my age group felt at one about going – it was right for them' (retired machinist, aged 65).

Redundancy signifies a crucial change in social identity for those who experience it, and one which exposes them to powerful pressures. As Harris has pointed out (Harris, 1987) it involves not simply a change from a secure position of regular employment, with relatively confident expectations about the future, to one of insecurity and uncertainty; but also an exit from an organization, where the daily routine is of collective shared experience with those working alongside, to a highly individualized place in the labour market where the general rule is competition with other unemployed individuals for scarce employment. Redundancy occurs as a *public* event but is, inevitably, experienced *privately*. A factory is closed but, unless the closure takes place in a community largely dependent on this one employer, it is an event experienced separately by a number of individual employees and their immediate households. Individuals tend to evaluate its implications not as a public event but rather in terms of the possibilities or threats to themselves and their families: they look to their own individual interest. Subsequently, the redundant worker is isolated in several important ways. The routine of work, the activity which may have structured the organization of life for over 40 years, is abruptly removed, he or she now has to organize and fill that time themself. Secondly, along with loss of simple routine goes a loss of regular and sustained social contact of a complex and varied nature, reinforced by the reduction in socializing forced by a drop in income. Attempts to cope with these effects are inevitably within the confined social space of the household, precisely because the redundant person's access to more public realms has been restricted or removed altogether.

In addition, two of the most important effects of economic insecurity cannot but be private atomizing phenomena – the struggles to make ends meet, and the attempt to find work. The first focuses attention on personal expenditure and income to a degree that the secure employed find rare: habits formerly taken for granted, and the small amounts of money they imply, become important as never before, and choice is restricted to what to give up or, at least, cut down on. The competition with the other unemployed for scarce employment focuses attention on the redundant workers' personal characteristics: their former occupation and all that implies in terms of class, their age, gender, ethnicity, previous experience, training and qualifications, among others. These characteristics may lead to someone being rejected for a particular job and suffering long-term unemployment, and often achieve greater salience during periods of heightened competition for scarce employment when they are used by employers as initial filters to reduce the numbers of applications for detailed consideration; but they are likely to be outside individuals' capacity to control or change. This reinforces the feelings of helplessness and resignation which many of our informants reported as their reaction to the redundancy announcement. As one informant said, when asked why he was not applying for jobs as much as previously: 'I've just given up. They're not bothered about what I can do, only about how old I am. What's the point in applying when they don't take you seriously? Waste of both our times.'

PATTERNS OF POST-REDUNDANCY EXPERIENCE

The reactions to redundancy quoted above not only epitomize the widespread and justified evaluation of the redundancy in personal terms. In many ways, the division of reaction between older workers and the others prefigured a major division of subsequent experience between those who stayed in the labour market (either in or looking for paid employment) and those who became economically inactive. Over a quarter (26 per cent) of all those made redundant became 'inactive' immediately following redundancy, half of them describing themselves as 'retired' or 'early retired'; and they were augmented steadily. Three years later, nearly 40 per cent of our informants were inactive. It is clear that this pattern of what has been called 'structured extrusion' (Lee, 1987), whereby older workers and women are pushed out of the labour market altogether while male 'prime age' workers remain there with a much higher risk of unemployment than previously, has been characteristic of post-redundancy careers during the recent recession, especially in Britain. The majority, however, remained economically active after redundancy and continued to be so. At the time of interview two-thirds of this group, just over 40 per cent of the whole sample, were in paid employment (nearly all of them full-time) while the remaining 20 per cent of informants were unemployed.

As we have stressed earlier, for many of our informants their fate was sealed relatively early in the post-redundancy period. When we asked people how long they had been in their current employment position, some 75 per cent had been so for two years or more, only 11 per cent for less than a year. There was, as can be seen from Table 5.1, little difference in most respects between different employment statuses (although part-time jobs, too few to be shown separately, were of more recent origin, reflecting both their tendency to shorter length and the rapid increase in part-time employment throughout the economy in the early 1980s). For the majority of our informants, the first year after redundancy was clearly the key period.

Table 5.1 Informants' current employment position by duration of current position

	Working Full-time %	Working Part-time %	Unemployed %	Retired %	Other Non-working %	All %
Under 1 year	11	—	8	13	4	11
Between 1 and 2 years	9	—	18	13	24	14
2 years or more	79	—	74	74	72	75
All	100	—	100	100	100	100
(n)	(140)	(10)	(72)	(78)	(46)	(346)

On average 38 months elapsed between our informants being made redundant and our interview with them. For the average informant, this 38 months broke down into 16 months of paid employment, nine months of unemployment and 13 months of economic inactivity. The averages here are, however, more than usually misleading for two reasons. Firstly, our informants were polarized between those who left the labour force immediately after redundancy and never returned (24 per cent) and those who remained either employed or unemployed throughout (60 per cent). For example, the 66 manual workers aged under 50 had an *aggregate* amount of economic inactivity of only 17 months, an average of just over one week per person, while routine clerical workers in the same age range, who were in the main women, averaged just under 14 months *each*. Secondly, as noted already, movement between different economic statuses was the exception rather than the norm, especially after the first six months following redundancy. Nearly half (45 per cent) stayed in the same economic position they had immediately following redundancy (25 per cent economicaly active – either working or unemployed – and 20 per cent economically inactive), while another 31 per cent had only one change (18 per cent from unemployment to employment or vice versa, 10 per cent from economic activity to inactivity, and 3 per cent within inactivity – usually from long-term sickness to premature retirement). Only just over half (56 per cent) ever worked again after redundancy. Our informants tended to spend the major part of their time after redundancy either employed, unemployed or outside the labour force altogether rather than moving between these activities. Over two-thirds of them spent more than 90 per cent of the time after redundancy in only one of these activity statuses, and over 80 per cent of them more than three-quarters of the time.

Earlier research on the aftermath of redundancies from a bulk-steel plant in the nationalized sector had shown that the largest group here were those with 'chequered' careers consisting of series of spells of employment and unemployment, rather than either securely employed or long-term unemployed (Harris, 1987). This group had essentially become a peripheral workforce centred around their former employer and working usually on short-term fixed-length contracts. Thus a large proportion of the work formerly carried out at the plant continued to be done but now by a workforce organized on more 'flexible' lines and with lower wages than previously (Fevre, 1987). We found little if any evidence of similar phenomena in our study; less than 10 per cent of our informants had four or more economic activity statuses over the three years. As we have noted earlier, the likelihood of being in paid employment at the time of interview was skewed by a combination of former occupation and age, particularly for men.

In summary, whatever the redundant person's age the possession of marketable qualifications gave considerable advantages, closely tied to the previous occupation. Those previously employed in either skilled manual occupations or supervisory and technical non-manual posts were markedly more successful than the non-skilled and routine non-manual workers in securing further employment. This division of class-related chances is partly responsible for the creation of the two distinct groups among our informants – the long-term employed and the long-term unemployed.

For older workers, however, there was an interaction between age and class. All our informants had much reduced chances of getting further employment if they were aged over 55, and particularly if they were over 60. The significantly higher levels of occupational pensions and redundancy payments available to former higher non-manual employees gave them much greater choice in how to respond to this. They were able to opt for an (often immediate) early retirement with some security. Older manual workers, however, felt forced to remain in the labour market to a much greater extent, especially the skilled among them, who might still expect better chances of re-employment and better pay when it was achieved, even if both were less than those they had enjoyed when younger. If older manual workers took early retirement, it tended to be less the result of a positive choice, and more the acceptance of the inevitable after the experience of a high level of discouragement, a discouragement that they often felt in distressing personal terms.

RE-EMPLOYMENT AND 'SECONDARY REDUNDANCY'

The paid employment side of the time after redundancy is summarized in Table 5.2, which shows both the proportion of class and age groups who spent 90 per cent or more of their time between redundancy and interview in paid employment, and also the average length of that time (in months). Thus, on average, a skilled manual worker aged under 40 had 32 months in paid employment between redundancy and interview; a non-skilled worker of the same age had 22 months on average; a skilled worker over 60 at the time of interview only 10 months. These differences were due almost completely to age and, above all, a class differential in the difficulty of *obtaining* employment in the first instance, rather than to differences of security in the job once obtained. When we looked at the average length of each spell of employment there was no significant difference between the different types of manual workers, or between them and higher non-manual employees (all had average job lengths of approximately 25 months).

Table 5.2 Age and former occupational class of informants by proportion employed for 90% or more of the post-redundancy period and average number of months in paid employment

	Under 40	40 to 60	60 and over	All
Skilled Manual	72% (26) 32	70% (30) 30	10% (50) 11	42% (106) 22
Non-skilled Manual	50% (10) 23	28% (47) 18	11% (56) 5	21% (113) 12
Higher Non-manual	41% (22) 29	65% (20) 31	— (31) 1	30% (73) 18
Routine Non-manual	35% (17) 13	29% (14) 17	14% (14) 5	27% (45) 13
All	52% (75) 27	46% (111) 24	9% (151) 6	31% (337) 16

Note

In the above table the percentage figure is the proportion of that group (e.g. skilled manual workers under 40) who were in paid employment for 90 per cent or more of the time between redundancy and interview; the bracketed figure is the base for that percentage and the figure underneath is the average number of months in paid employment between redundancy and interview for the members of that group.

Economic insecurity implied other things besides difficulty in obtaining further employment. Among these was the continued risk of redundancy from any new job. Just under a quarter (24 per cent) of those who worked at all after redundancy were subsequently made redundant once more. This was more likely to affect those whose post-redundancy employment was in the steel industry (either metal manufacture or engineering), where the 'secondary redundancy rate' was 27 per cent, than those employed in other industries, where it was 21 per cent. In fact, 49 per cent of all those securing work after redundancy, did so within the steel industry – although the proportion was slightly higher (53 per cent) for those entering another job immediately or almost immediately after becoming redundant than for those who obtained work subsequently. This should not be taken, however, simply as evidence of enhanced insecurity for those who remained in steel rather than found work elsewhere in the local economy. The data underline rather the enhanced insecurity of all who found jobs again, whether this was in steel or in other industries. The steel industry in Sheffield suffered major contraction in the three years following the redundancy (with more than 70 per cent of the 20,000-plus statutory redundancies recorded in the Sheffield travel-to-work area in the years 1980 to 1983); it fared markedly worse than other local industries. At the same time those of our informants who took employment outside steel had a much greater likelihood of being made redundant (in their case for a second time) than those workers already employed in the industries they entered. There is an enhanced insecurity in subsequent employment acquired simply from being made redundant, regardless of the industry in which the first redundancy occurs or the industry entered subsequently. The extra insecurity acquired through finding work again specifically in steel was much smaller.

Another aspect of economic insecurity that is often thought to follow redundancy is downward mobility or occupational downgrading; that is to say that employment obtained after redundancy from stable employment may often be much less desirable (as measured by composite scales using income, other benefits and social standing) than the previous job. The greatest danger of such downgrading may lie, however, in the weakened labour market position it implies for the employee. A recent study of long-term unemployment (White, 1983) found that occupational downgrading of a major kind had occurred to 40 per cent of those long-term unemployed who had previously had a distinct longest employment (rather than a number of essentially short-term jobs), and that there was a characteristic pattern of redundancy from stable employment in a declining industry (iron and steel are notable examples) which is followed by short-term downgraded employment outside that industry and then by long-term unemployment. We were unable to estimate downgrading in the same way as White, who used the Hope-Goldthorpe scale (Goldthorpe, 1974), but we did employ a substitute measure, which counted as downgrading moves such as those from skilled to semi-skilled manual work, from semi-skilled to unskilled, from supervisory to routine clerical work, as well as a number of others. We found clear evidence of downgrading: in all, 39 per cent of those who had been employed after redundancy had been so in a lower grade job than the one held before (56 per cent did not downgrade significantly, 5 per cent upgraded). This trend was particularly pronounced for those previously in jobs described as 'semi-skilled' work (but who lacked formal apprenticeship qualifications and are therefore usually grouped in our tables with those described as unskilled), 54 per cent of whom had been downgraded, as might be expected, the description 'semi-skilled' often being applied to jobs which require experience with the particular employer rather than a generally recognized achieved qualification, something which is much less easy to trade on in the labour market. More surprisingly, an almost equal proportion of higher non-manual workers (53 per cent) had also been downgraded (although their downgraded 'finishing positions' were almost invariably in a higher position than the starting points of the non-skilled manual workers).

We were interested to see whether or not the characteristic employment history profile found in the earlier national study applied here. Contradictory patterns seemed to emerge when we looked at people who had found employment for a time after redundancy but who were, at the time of interview, long-term unemployed, that is unemployed for a year or more. Certainly a change of industry seemed to have at least some adverse effect: only 9 per cent of those who had stayed in steel were now long term unemployed, compared to 13 per cent of those who had changed industries. A more interesting pattern seemed to emerge when downgrading was taken into account. For people who had moved out of steel, there was no significant difference in long-term unemployment rates at interview between those who retained their previous grade and those who did not. For people who stayed in steel, however, there was a different story: those who downgraded when taking their first post-redundancy employment had a much lower chance (3 per cent as against 12 per cent) of being long-term unemployed at interview than those who retained their grade. Further analysis showed that this was due almost completely to the differences of experience among manual workers. The surest strategy for retaining employment for this group, especially the non-skilled, was to take lower level employment (almost certainly at lower wages) within the steel industry: no one who did this was long-term unemployed at interview. Where they managed to retain their grade within steel, or moved out of steel, then the probability of long-term unemployment was significantly higher than average. Economic insecurity meant not only long-term unemployment for many, and increased risk of further redundancy even for those who did find paid work again. It often also meant sacrificing the hard-won monetary and other advantages of experience in return for a greater chance of continuity of employment, despite remaining in the same industry where that experience had been acquired and presumably should have been of greatest market value.

While the late 1970s and early 1980s saw a general contraction in the hitherto traditional labour market opportunities for those whom we interviewed, there was also an expansion in certain other, non-traditional, areas. Two aspects of the labour force in particular began to change significantly across the country during this time (although change was more profound in subsequent years). Firstly, there was a major change in the proportions of part-time and full-time employees in the labour force, with the former increasing and the latter decreasing. Secondly, this was combined with changes in the sectoral distribution of the employed labour force where, broadly speaking, the size of the service sector (especially distribution, insurance, banking and finance and public sector services) increased while that of the manufacturing sector decreased, dramatically so in the case of traditional manufactures such as textiles, iron and steel and other 'heavy' industries. Thus many full-time jobs in manufacturing disappeared, while part-time employment in services increased. There was little if any evidence of the first of these trends affecting our informants: only 3 per cent of them were part-time workers at interview; and although 23 per cent of those employed were outside the manufacturing sector, they were not usually employed in the classic service sector jobs created during this time. This was not unexpected, since other evidence from employment history surveys (e.g. Halfpenny, Laite and Noble, 1985 and Noble et al., 1987) shows that the large majority of the new part-time jobs created during this period went either to people already in similar employment or to people outside the labour force altogether (often the spouse of someone already in full-time employment), and very rarely to an unemployed person.

There was also considerable discussion at the time of two other possible non-traditional employment activities that might be open to those made redundant, particularly when they were craftsmen with adaptable skills: self-employment and the 'black' economy. The early 1980s saw a major increase in the number of self-employed throughout the economy. However, such opportunites did not seem to exist for our informants: at interview only four of them were self-employed. Interest in the 'black' and informal economies began to increase in the mid 1970s, and it was suggested that with economic restructuring there might be a significant move underway from the formal economy of paid employment, where opportunites were becoming restricted, to an informal 'cash only' economy outside the regulation of state agencies such as the Inland Revenue, the Department of Employment and the DHSS. More sober analyses (e.g. Gershuny and Pahl, 1979 and Pahl, 1980) were reinforced by a large number of anecdotal reports that often seemed to owe more to folktale and fantasy than even journalistic licence (for impressionistic sketches concerning Sheffield at the time of our research see Beattie, 1986). However, empirical investigation by a number of often ingenious methods failed to produce hard evidence of either a major 'black' economy or a significant growth in that which actually did exist. Research *did* establish that one important reason why increased (and increased long-term) unemployment was unlikely to lead to a rise in 'black' activity by those exposed to it was that such work was, in any case, much more likely to be available to those still employed. It is the employed who enjoy access both to the resources (tools and raw materials) necessary to carry out such work, and to the social networks through which information about opportunities is obtained and arrangements are made to carry out the work. In addition, it is likely that the employed are subject to considerably less official surveillance on these matters than the unemployed. Pahl himself has suggested, as a direct result of testing hypothesized growth in informal economic activity, that the unemployed far from being *advantaged* in the informal economy are *disadvantaged* there as well as a direct consequence of their exclusion from paid employment (Pahl, 1984, Pahl and Wallace, 1986). It was clear that opportunities in the 'black' economy were either not available to those in our study or, if they were, those we interviewed were unable or unwilling to take advantage of them. Only 6 per cent reported being able to get any casual work or 'odd jobs' to supplement their incomes, and just two of those actually unemployed were working 'on the side' now and then, one in the building trade and the other as a nightclub bouncer. Where people did have extra jobs it was often the result of a hobby bringing in a little now and then, as no more than a small incidental bonus, or work done as a form of recreation rather than any manifestation of entrepreneurial initiative. Where employment 'on the side' was regular and businesslike it was, with the exception of the two cases mentioned, done by people already working full-time. It is possible that there was some level of concealment of 'black economy' work by our informants, but it is very unlikely that we are underestimating to a significant degree. Those interviewed were given general guarantees of confidentiality for the interview and specific ones about questions concerning work 'on the side'. Experiments elsewhere using randomized response methods (through which estimates for groups of interviewees are obtained without any possibility of identifying individual cases), which are generally successful in increasing positive responses to questions concerning participation in illegal or socially disapproved activity, have not shown any major increase in estimates of 'black economy' activity (Lee, 1984). For our informants, in or out of work, the booming black economy was a myth, as much a myth perhaps as the booming formal economy they heard about just as often.

COMMITMENT TO PAID EMPLOYMENT

One important issue in the study of people made redundant and facing economic insecurity is that of their levels of work involvement or commitment. This is a measure of the degree to which a person wants to be engaged in *paid employment*, their level of commitment to the labour market as such, rather than involvement in any one particular job. Social and occupational psychologists have researched this phenomenon thoroughly (see the review in Warr et al., 1979), producing multi-item attitude scales of good reliability which suggest that intrinsic work commitment is a common and persistent occurrence in Western-type industrial societies, and linking it (somewhat questionably, we believe) to Weber's concept of the 'Protestant Ethic'. We had two related interests in measuring the work commitment levels of our informants. Firstly, there was the question whether or not protracted unemployment, possibly combined with severely reduced prospects of any future re-employment, would act to *diminish* work commitment, perhaps through some mechanism of *post-hoc* rationalizing or psychological self-defence ('If I'm not allowed to work then I don't really want to'), perhaps through removal of the reinforcing factors of work discipline and collective experiences. Secondly, a number of studies (e.g. Jackson et al., 1983; Stafford et al., 1980; Warr, 1978) have shown the level of work commitment to be an important moderator of the relationship between employment position and levels of psychological well-being. In these studies, unemployed people usually showed significantly lower levels of well-being (or higher levels of distress) than people in employment, in retirement or otherwise withdrawn from the labour market. In addition, these levels were usually significantly lower again (or higher, in the case of distress levels) among those of the unemployed who had higher levels of work commitment. We deal with this second question of the interaction between commitment, unemployment and distress in the next section, after first discussing work commitment in general.

We measured work commitment by a scale drawn from responses to ten statements reproduced in Table 5.3, the majority of these statements being taken from Warr et al., 1979, with some later additions of our own design. The informants were each given a card with seven possible answers printed on it (ranging from 'No, I strongly disagree' to 'Yes, I strongly agree') and asked to give the answer that came nearest to how they felt about the statement when it was read to them. The first four items in the table were *negatively coded*, that is disagreeing with them was taken as showing a stronger level of work commitment than agreeing; while the remaining six were *positively coded*, so that agreement indicated commitment. On this basis, each individual item response was scored from 0 to 6 (the higher the score the higher the level of commitment indicated) and the scale obtained by summing the item scores. The usual measure of the reliability of such summated scales is Cronbach's

Table 5.3 Average scores for employment commitment scale and items by employment position at interview

Item	Working	Un-employed	Retired	Other	All
1 Work is necessary but rarely enjoyable	3.7	3.4	4.2	4.3	3.8
2 Having a job is not very important to me	5.5	4.7	4.6	4.8	5.0
3 I regard time spent at work as time taken away from the things I want to do.	4.1	4.5	4.3	4.4	4.3
4 Having a job is/was only important to me because it brings in money	3.6	3.0	3.2	3.4	3.4
5 Even if I won a great deal of money on the pools I'd carry on working	2.3	1.8	2.2	2.5	2.2
6 If unemployment benefit were really high I would still prefer to work	4.6	4.5	5.0	4.9	4.7
7 I would hate being on the dole	5.5	5.2	5.4	5.0	5.4
8 I would soon get bored if I did not go out to work	4.4	4.2	3.8	3.9	4.2
9 The most important things that have happened to me involved work	2.9	3.6	3.5	3.1	3.2
10 Any feelings I've had in the past of achieving something worthwhile have usually come through things I've done at work	3.7	4.1	3.8	3.6	3.8
Scale Scores:	40.3	38.7	39.9	39.9	39.8
(N)	(139)	(64)	(71)	(42)	(316)

(Alpha = .70)

coefficient alpha which in this case was .70, a satisfactory level.

The scale and item scores are shown in Table 5.3 by the informant's employment position at the time of interview. There were no significant differences on scale scores between any of the groups and, in particular, there was no evidence that long-term unemployment had eroded the 'will to work'. Although, as we shall see later in this chapter, a large number of the long-term unemployed had reduced their amount of job-searching or even abandoned it altogether, their commitment to work was as strong as when employed. What *had* been affected was their belief in their ability to obtain employment.

Certain aspects of work commitment shown in the answers to individual items are worth highlighting, in particular the high level of intrinsic worth attached to paid employment ('a job') and the highly negative evaluations of unemployment. Thus, the item with the highest average commitment score of all is agreeing with 'I would hate being on the dole', while the next highest is disagreeing with 'Having a job is not very important to me'. The heavily stigmatized nature of unemployment (and Unemployment Benefit) can be seen by comparing responses to the fifth and sixth items. For the large majority of our informants, a windfall, such as a pools win, would provide sufficient genuine reason for abandoning paid employment: the item dealing with this drew the lowest level of commitment of any. An almost equally large majority, however, were of the opinion that high levels of unemployment benefit would not affect their work commitment. Clearly, although people are bound to work primarily through a 'cash nexus' there is also, at the same time, a clear distinction made for the large majority between acceptable and non-acceptable sources of non-employment income: a point which displays, perhaps, the moral discipline of the capitalist labour process. It is also interesting to see which items drew significantly higher levels of work commitment from those unemployed compared to those employed: these items (the third and the final two items in the table) show clearly the importance attached by the unemployed to non-cash elements of paid employment, in particular the possibilities of achievement and fulfilment through work. These higher levels persisted even when former occupational class was controlled for, despite the routine and highly directed nature of their former work for the non-skilled when compared to the craftsmen (with their considerable levels of on-job autonomy) and the higher non-manual workers (many with quite wide-ranging technical or managerial responsibility and independence).

THE EXPERIENCE OF UNEMPLOYMENT

At the commencement of our research we proposed to define 'experiencing unemployment' in four separate ways, because we considered that each definition rested on factors that could mean a fundamentally distinct experience to the person affected. These four were as follows: firstly, having been unemployed at all during the time after redundancy; secondly, having experienced *long-term* unemployment in excess of either six months or a year; thirdly, having a relatively high total of unemployed time (without necessarily a single spell in excess of six months or a year); and fourthly, experiencing 'sub-employment', that is a succession of short term spells of employment and worklessness. In the event, we found that nearly all those unemployed at the time of interview had been so for over six months, over 90 per cent for more than a year, and three-quarters for more than two years. On average, they had been continuously unemployed for 28 months prior to interview. They were also the group with by far the highest level of unemployment over the whole period since redundancy, averaging 31 months or over four fifths of the full 38 months since then. In addition, there was little if any evidence of 'sub-employment' in the form of repeated spells of unemployment or of casual employment.

As we have already stressed, unemployment (taken here just in the official sense of registered unemployment) was a burden that was shared unequally between age and occupation groups. Table 5.4 gives a breakdown by age and former occupation of the number of months of unemployment experienced by those of our informants who had at least one spell of employment or unemployment after redundancy (thus excluding those who immediately became economically inactive and remained so until interview). The probability of unemployment increased directly with age, from an average of 7 months for the under-forties to 15 months for those over 55. The most vulnerable were those in the age group immediately below the 'official' retirement age. Over half (58 per cent) of those aged between 60 and 64 at the time of interview had not worked at all after the redundancy, compared to 13 per cent of those under 40, and 18 per cent of those aged between 40 and 55.

Within age-groups, the informants' former occupation exerted a strong influence, with the greatest contrasts found not along the manual/non-manual divide but between those with marketable skills and those without, the 'highest risk' group being those manual workers defined as non-skilled in their former occupation. They had an average of 18 months unemployment since redundancy, twice that for skilled

Table 5.4 Average number of months unemployed between redundancy and interview by age and former occupational class of informants

	Under 40	*40 to 59*	*60 to 64*	*65 and over*	*All*
Skilled Manual	5 (26)	7 (29)	15 (30)	12 (8)	9 (93)
Non-skilled Manual	16 (10)	17 (44)	21 (19)	17 (9)	18 (82)
Higher Non-manual	5 (22)	4 (19)	22 (8)	10 (4)	8 (53)
Routine Non-manual	7 (13)	11 (12)	13 (4)	—	10 (29)
All	7 (71)	11 (104)	17 (61)	14 (21)	12 (257)

Note

This table is for all informants with at least one spell either employed or unemployed between redundancy and interview. It therefore excludes all those who became economically inactive (e.g. retirement) immediately after redundancy and remained so until interview. There were missing data for a further 10 informants. Bracketed figures are the total number of informants for which each average is calculated.

manuals, a differential that applied roughly across the board irrespective of age. They were further disadvantaged by the length of time each individual spell of unemployment had lasted. We saw earlier that, when employed, there were no significant differences between different groups in the length of periods of employment; but this did not apply to unemployment. When we look only at those who had at least one spell of unemployment, we find that the average length of these spells for the non-skilled manual worker was 20 months, seven months greater than for any other group. This agrees with evidence from other studies (e.g. White, 1983, Moylan et al., 1984) that those previously in manual employment described as unskilled or semi-skilled are much more likely than any other groups to become unemployed, and when unemployed to stay so for longer periods.

In the eyes of the people who had experienced it, unemployment was seen almost invariably as unpleasant and sometimes highly distressing. Over half of those who had been unemployed at any time after redundancy described it as the worst thing they had ever experienced. The multi-faceted importance of paid employment in a modern industrial society, especially for middle-aged men, is shown in the diversity of distress that was reported. At a basic level, the unemployed experienced considerable financial problems: studies of unemployed working-class men suggest that at least two-thirds of them have a *household* income that is less than half of their previous employment incomes. Although we have no data for earnings prior to redundancy, comparisons between households' earnings at interview are much in line with this (see Chapter 4). The unemployed, quite understandably, feel severe restrictions on their freedom of action for financial reasons. All our unemployed informants reported having to cut down on various items of what they had previously considered essential expenditure, and having to withdraw savings to meet expenses. The longer someone was unemployed the more depleted their financial resources became, in terms of both their income and their savings; and the more vulnerable they felt themselves to be. Here we have a second aspect of the experience of unemployment: not only does unemployment bring a feeling of restriction, but there is also a perceived loss of the ability to respond to events. Things that would previously have been small problems, such as a larger than average gas bill during a cold winter, which would have been taken in one's stride (perhaps with a short-lived resolve to turn down the thermostat), become major crises to be dreaded. This is exacerbated by the much greater levels of uncertainty about the future that unemployed people experience: compared to those in paid employment they are more likely to see the world around them as capricious and potentially menacing, where an indeterminate 'something' is waiting to happen to them. Hence, following the general feeling of loss of control and increased vulnerability to the thousand natural shocks, there is an increased anxiety about some disastrous event that just might occur.

Moreover, the loss of employment income has further implications. In cases where the former employees are bread-winners, bringing in the main wage to their family household, there is firstly the loss of this socially valued role *per se*; in addition there is likely to be a succession of events during the period of unemployment which seem to demonstrate to them the loss of their ability, their *failure*, to live up to their obligations to other members of the household: Christmas and birthday presents, family holidays, everyday socializing and entertainment, can seem to be impossible to plan or provide for. The unemployed (and it seems to be especially *men* who feel this) see their own personal inability to obtain employment as increasing the insecurity and vulnerability of those around them. As one of our informants said: 'I felt I was letting them all down, like not being a proper husband or father . . . it was worse somehow when they were understanding . . . I felt I didn't deserve it.'

In addition, as we have seen, many if not most people, again especially men from a working-class background of secure employment (who were the large majority of our informants), see paid employment as good *in itself*. It is seen not only as an obligation to one's dependent family and to society ('A man just can't keep on taking out all his life, he's got to put something in, he's got to do something with himself not just sit around'), but also as the main means by which individuals are able to assert themselves, to achieve a recognisable social identity, to use their skills and talents in accomplishing definite goals. It is, therefore, to be expected that when comparisons are made between them and other groups on standard measures of psychological well-being, the unemployed show significantly higher levels of distress and lower levels of well-being: typically, the average distress scores for unemployed men are twice those for employed men. In our interviews we used two related (but independent) measures combined in the Bradburn Dual Affect Scale, where *Negative Affect* measures distress and *Positive Affect* well-being (Bradburn, 1967), the possible range of both being from 0 to 5. Unemployed informants had an average Negative Affect score of 2.4, more than three times that of the employed and significantly higher than all other economic activity groups. When the differences between the groups are expressed in odds, the unemployed were ten times as likely as the employed to have a negative affect score of two or more, 17 times as likely to score three or more. There were no significant differences in scores between the employed and other groups (the retired and the non-working). Our informants' former occupation appeared to make no difference to this, in the same way that general work commitment did not vary by occupational class. Neither did their age make any difference, although previous research has found that unemployment-related psychological strain is usually lower for those aged 60 and over. Positive feelings of well-being were also rarer amongst the unemployed, their Positive Affect scores being on average half those of the employed. An analysis of covariance, however, confirmed the ostensible moderating effect of work commitment. Where the informants were unemployed, those with higher levels of work commitment (usually the middle-aged between 40 and 60) showed significantly higher levels of distress and lower levels of positive feelings. It is important to stress, however, that more recent research (Payne, 1987) suggests strongly that other factors, in particular stable personality traits, may also have a major moderating role here.

Most of those who had been unemployed mentioned boredom and being forced to 'stay around the house all day' as among the worst things about the experience: 'Those long monotonous days sitting around the house with nothing to do', 'You let yourself go a bit . . . there's absolutely nothing to think about'. Many older men made particular mention of

having to 'sign on' or 'go down the Labour'. Several expressed feelings
of shame at having to claim social security benefits, their reactions
epitomized by a 63-year-old former stamper who said: 'I never thought
I'd have to do that, never . . . that was for those who weren't bothered to
try . . . scroungers . . . that sort, not for me . . . but in the end I had to go,
and *then* they told me I wasn't entitled because I'd put the redundancy
money in the building society and I'd have to spend that before they
could give me anything.' Where the financial penalties of unemployment
were mentioned (as they were in over half the cases where informants
had been unemployed), they were often seen as leading to a loss of
independence and status: 'I lost my self-respect . . . even children could
buy things I couldn't afford.' These accounts of the worst aspects of
unemployment were complemented sometimes by references to beneficial
effects, although less than a quarter of those who had been unemployed
could find any positive response to make to our questions on this. Those
who did were nearly all men aged 60 or over who had opted for early
retirement after an initial spell of unemployment after redundancy. For
many of these, enforced withdrawal from the world of work into the
household was less of a loss, indeed was something they felt ready for:
'After 50 years (of work) I thought I'd done enough.' For them,
registered unemployment was more a step on the way to full and well-
earned retirement; and it represented especially an opportunity to
establish closer domestic relations, one which might not be repeated. A
melting-shop worker who had just turned 60 at the time of redundancy
said: 'We'd seen so many people reaching the age of 60 and then dying. I
wanted to live longer with my wife.' Other than these older people there
were few who mentioned benefits of unemployment; where they did so it
was much more by way of what has been called 'resigned adaptation'
(Warr, 1987a) than any positive transformation.

PARTIAL WITHDRAWAL FROM THE LABOUR MARKET AND SOCIAL LIFE

This 'resigned adaptation' has been identified by previous researchers as
a common feature among people who have been unemployed for long
periods. We have outlined above the significantly greater scores on
measures of psychological distress that unemployed informants had
when compared with others, especially the employed. It is likely however
that these had *declined* from the scores that would have been recorded if
our interviews had taken place earlier than they did: as we have noted
several times, nearly all our unemployed informants had been so for over
six months (one possible definition of long-term unemployment), 91 per

cent for more than a year. Levels of well-being and distress usually reach a trough and a peak respectively during the first year of unemployment (often between three and six months after the unemployment begins). Thereafter the latter usually decline and stabilize (while remaining at relatively high levels) and the former may even improve slightly (Warr, 1987a). Where unemployed informants reported that 'things had been particularly bad for them' since redundancy, the crisis had almost without exception occurred during the first year of unemployment, and although quite often bothered subsequently by the same problems they now felt more able to cope: 'You just get used to things after a while. You can put up with it more.' This is 'resigned adaptation': a fatalistic acceptance of a predicament considered unimprovable which, however, also has the effect of reducing feelings of loss and depression. This is similar to the results of a process described by some sociologists as 'cooling the mark out' (Goffman, 1952), whereby the possibilities of violent reaction and counter-action to a perceived loss or failure (originally by the victim of a confidence trick) are reduced considerably. Warr has outlined the characteristics of this fatalism:

. . . job-seeking and all its associated problems often declines, as people conclude that the probability of success is too low to make it worthwhile . . . . Many people come to accept as normal their lack of influence on their environment, the atrophy of their skills and the fact that action is rarely required by external demands. They draw in on themselves, restrict their social contact and lower their aspirations. By wanting less, they achieve less and become less. (Warr, 1987b)

For a substantial number of our informants, their withdrawal from the labour market was complete and final. Some of these were able to take this course immediately after redundancy, but a significant number made initial attempts to stay in before taking an 'escape route'. (Their experiences are discussed in the next chapter.) It was clear, however, that long-term unemployment had discouraged job-seeking to a considerable degree, as we have noted earlier. Although two-thirds of informants had applied for jobs during their current spell of unemployment, less than half those who had more than one spell of unemployment had done so, and this was even lower amongst those whose second or subsequent spell of unemployment was longer than a year. Nearly 90 per cent of those unemployed at interview were applying less frequently than they had at the beginning of their current spell. The proportion was even greater among the older and non-skilled manual workers, who had received the most discouragement in the market. As one former furnace firer recalled: 'At one time I used to apply for everything . . . anything that looked at all possible. But you'd either hear nowt from them . . . or if you went in to see them it was . . . you know . . . "We've got nothing at all for people like you." And the girl at the Job Centre said the same after I'd been down a few times at the cards: "There's nothing for you there." . . . Well I thought, if there's nothing for me, what's the point of looking?'

There was also a more general withdrawal from social life, which was most acute among unemployed informants (that is, those so officially registered) but was by no means confined to them. Half (51 per cent) of those interviewed reported going out less than formerly to social events or pubs and clubs. This was most marked among those unemployed, where 71 per cent were less active socially; but 53 per cent of those in retirement, some 67 per cent of the non-working, and even 35 per cent of those in full-time employment, were also less active. The unemployed, however, were much more likely to give financial problems as the reason for their withdrawal, 85 per cent giving it as the sole reason and another 8 per cent as a contributory reason. A few felt that they could afford to go out more than they did but, as one informant put it, didn't '. . . like to be seen spending when I'm supposed to be on the dole. There's some might think I'm on the fiddle.' Finance was a problem that particularly affected the retired as well, especially those former manual workers who were by now dependent either solely on State Pensions and benefits or who received only limited supplement from an occupational pension. Sixty-six per cent of the less active retired mentioned finance as the sole reason for cutting down on entertainment, and another 13 per cent as a contributory reason. For the majority of the others, however, any reduction in social activity was much more likely to be ascribed to factors such as ageing, increases in family responsibilities, or losing touch with former work colleagues who had also been friends. Even then, over a third of those in employment who were less active socially gave finance as the sole reason for the change. All but two of these had either had to 'downgrade' in their post-redundancy employment and cited their reduced earnings, or had also had a spell of unemployment during which they had 'got out of the habit' of going out.

REDUNDANCY PAYMENTS AND THEIR USES

As the remarks quoted at the head of this chapter make clear, when our informants voiced their reactions to the announcement of the projected closure of the Forgings Division they were often concerned especially with the simultaneously announced redundancy payments scheme, designed to bring about the required shedding of employees on a formally voluntary basis. We have described the details of this scheme earlier (see Chapter 2). In its broad character it was similar to many other schemes to squeeze out labour during a period of economic recession and change. It was generally held in eras of full employment that rules of 'last in, first out' applied when redundancies were required, but it is clear that managements are much more likely to use redundancies where possible as a means of *restructuring* their work-forces, raising efficiency and productivity through 'buying out' less effective members of the workforce. Thus redundancy terms are almost always calculated to appeal more to older workers than to those of prime age; employees with long term sickness or injury problems are encouraged – with varying degrees of subtlety – to opt for severance; and there may often be a significant, even substantial, element of 'manufac-tured' redundancies. These latter occur when employees who are not initially eligible for the redundancy scheme are made so as a result of collaboration between unions and management, for example when older workers are able to transfer into an area of work where they become eligible for redundancy from one where they were not. Although there were rumours and anecdotes of large numbers of such redundancies among our sample, only a handful of informants (3 per cent) actually proved to have transferred to the Forgings Division specifically for the purpose of redundancy. In addition, there may be 'soft' (i.e. unresisted) redundancies, where union and even shop-floor opinion may encourage job losses among certain groups (especially older and part-time workers) to protect 'family-wage' workers (Callender, 1987). Under such conditions, older employees in particular may come under intense informal pressure to opt for redundancy as early retirement (Bytheway, 1987); and in such a context payments tied to years of service have a key role in both inducing and legitimizing redundancies, as years of service are transformed from a greater to a lesser claim to keeping a job, albeit with an enhanced entitlement to compensation. In such a context also, as Lee has stressed (Lee, 1987), the 'cooling out' functions of many redundancy arrangements are made manifest, whereby possible victims of a shift from a desirable status to a less desirable status are provided with the means of constructing an alternative, less stigmatized, less provoking, account of the transition: 'voluntary severance' rather than sacking, 'early retirement' rather than redundancy or unemployment.

As was clear from earlier analyses (see Chapter 2), redundancy payments reproduced the usual inequalities found in pay scales. The 'higher non-manual' (supervisory clerical, technical and managerial) workers were clearly the best off. The only exception to this was for those employees with between ten and 20 years of service, and here the larger amounts paid to skilled manual workers were either the result of their opting to draw out accumulated pension funds which were paid with redundancy payments in a single amount, or the result of additional payments in lieu of notice.

As has been noted already, we heard from several sources during the preparation for the research that there were numerous instances of redundant employees using large amounts of their redundancy payments for holidays, seemingly secure in the knowledge that work would be relatively easy to find on their return. We had several reasons for discounting these anecdotes: few of those interviewed actually mentioned a holiday of any significant period of time as their immediate intention on leaving (two possible exceptions being Moslems who used their payments to carry out a *haj*); only a handful of informants actually included a period of holiday longer than a month in their post-redundancy employment history, all of these aged under 30; and nearly all those who left the firm without alternative employment already arranged, but with the intention of continuing in paid employment, were concerned about their chances of getting another job. There was no evidence that our informants, even in this relatively early part of the recession, made light of the difficulties that lay before them in the labour market. What some of them did admit to underestimating, however, was the sheer difficulty of financial survival that they would face. For nearly all those we talked to, there was an element of a windfall about their redundancy money: they felt that perhaps the pleasant surprise of the payment was the good resulting from the sudden ill wind which had blown them out of work. Nearly a third (30 per cent) did use part of the money for a holiday, and a similar proportion replaced their car; over half (56 per cent) used part of the money either for home improvements of some kind (the installation of central heating and redecoration were most frequently mentioned) or to purchase consumer durables for the house.

The most usual use of the money, however, was simply saving: nearly three-quarters immediately put at least the major part of the money in building society or long-term bank deposit accounts. This was particularly the case for the older members of the sample, although there was an important contrast between those formerly in manual and those in non-manual (especially 'staff') jobs. The latter were more likely to withdraw from labour market activity early on, because many could already count on relatively bigger amounts from occupational pensions; and at the time of interview many of them still had substantial amounts of savings. When asked what their plans had been for using the payment, they clearly regarded the redundancy payments as a potential 'nest egg' for retirement; and they were almost invariably successful in retaining it for that purpose. Older manual workers showed a different picture, however, both in intentions and behaviour. Although they were just as concerned as higher grade non-manual workers to save the money from the beginning, they were much more likely to see the purpose as being to cushion the transition to the time when they would begin to receive the state pension. This was a realistic expectation: in fact, they often proved to have used all or almost all of the money in the interim between redundancy and interview to meet regular household bills, particularly once they had exhausted entitlement to unemployment benefit and so became dependent on Supplementary Benefit. But Supplementary Benefit was not available in this period to those with savings in excess of £1500; and so they found themselves having to run down their savings, on everyday expenses, to the point where they would become eligible for Supplementary Benefit. None of those who had been unemployed for longer than a year when interviewed (which means nearly all of those who had failed to find employment in the first six months after redundancy) had any savings income beyond a residual few pence a week: their redundancy money had all gone on managing the business of living.

The redundancy and its aftermath thus helped to ensure a transmission of inequalities beyond the world of work. Unemployment and retirement proved significantly different experiences in financial terms between people of differing occupational classes at the time of entry. Yet, because of the privatizing and atomized nature of the redundancy process, those of our informants on the less advantaged side seemed unaware of their disadvantage or of the causes behind it. Where informants were dissatisfied with the size of their redundancy payment – and over 25 per cent of those receiving a payment did express dissatisfaction – they amplified this not, save in a few exceptional cases, by reference to a relatively small level of compensation (just over £200 per year worked, on average), nor by references to the discrepancies between manual workers and higher non-manual workers in payments received by way of both redundancy money and the crucial arrangements for pensions; instead, they referred to the higher levels of redundancy payment gained by other steel workers in the same city, later in the recession, as a result of EEC support. It was the people who had fared worse who were much more likely to think that what they had experienced was typical of what had happened to the whole of the workforce; not that they had lost out compared to others. So the after-redundancy experience not only reinforced the pre-existing inequalities, it also seemed to conceal, at least partially, from those involved the very existence of the inequality and its underlying causes.

6

Retirement and Early Retirement

EARLY RETIREMENT: DEMAND PUSH OR SUPPLY PULL?

The majority (55 per cent) of those made redundant were older workers (55 years old or over when interviewed). When coupled with two further characteristics of our respondents – their concentration in the manual socio-economic groups, and their long service with the same company – this age bias makes them a particularly interesting group for the study of post-redundancy experiences and responses in a period of high unemployment and rapid economic and social change.

The preponderance of older workers in our study group was expected because of the relatively high median age of the workforce in the steel industry (Tolly, Creigh and Mingay, 1980) and the greater likelihood of older workers than younger ones being made redundant (Mukherjee, 1973; Daniel, 1974). The gender distribution also followed a predictable pattern: among those aged 55 and over, 90 per cent were men. This was unfortunate in view of the relative neglect of women in previous studies of redundancy (Daniel, 1972; Barron and Norris, 1978) and employment (Dex and Phillipson, 1986) among older workers, but there was nothing we could do to overcome this deficiency.

Interest in the labour market status of older workers has heightened recently as early retirement has come to be viewed widely as a means of reducing employment (see for example Bosanquet, 1987). This has led to the realization in some quarters that while labour market policy has been concentrated on young people, older workers constitute a significantly disadvantaged group in relation to employment. But previous research on early retirement has tended to focus on those in the higher socio-economic groups (McGoldrick and Cooper, 1980; Wood, 1980), and the finding there that the majority were satisfied with early retirement has encouraged the view that the attitudes of older workers towards early retirement have changed significantly (see for example,

House of Commons Social Services Committee, 1982). It was important, therefore, to compare this finding with the results of our study among contrasting socio-economic groups.

The After Redundancy study took place during a period when the level of economic activity among older people in general, and older men in particular, had been falling (Walker, 1980; Parker, 1982). The trend of declining economic activity among those over statutory retirement age is a long term one: in 1931, about 50 per cent of men aged 65 and over were in the labour force, in 1951 the figure was 31 per cent, and by 1983 it had fallen further to only 9 per cent. But since the mid 1970s, the decline in economic activity among men aged 65 and over has been extended quite dramatically into the age group immediately below pension age. Between 1975 and 1983 the proportion of men aged 60–4 who were economically active fell from 84 per cent to 63 per cent. Thus older people in the study were thrust into the labour market at precisely the time of the steepest fall in the economic activity rates of older workers at large. This growth in economic inactivity was almost wholly accounted for by the increasing trend towards early retirement among some groups in the 60–4 age group. Britain shares this changing pattern of retirement with other advanced industrial societies, although there has been no formal lowering of the statutory retirement ages here or in other countries (Tracy, 1979).

The processes of retirement and early retirement cannot be assessed in isolation from previous experiences in employment and the labour market, because these have an important bearing on decisions about retirement and, of course, on post-retirement standards of living and quality of life (Walker, 1981). With a cross-sectional data set it is not possible to make precise comparisons between changes in employment and economic activity over time. However, we did collect detailed information on the employment and labour market histories of respondents in the three years between redundancy and interview. The following analysis uses these post-redundancy histories as a guide to some of the influences on older workers when they came to decide whether or not to take early retirement. This suggests that early retirement is not simply a matter of individual decision-making on the supply-side, nor is it only one of labour demand. It involves rather the interaction of *both* supply and demand factors.

THE IMPACT OF REDUNDANCY ON EMPLOYMENT STATUS

Older respondents in this study were even less likely than older workers as a whole to be economically active. By the time they were interviewed in late 1982 and early 1983, some three years after being made redundant, they were divided almost equally between the economically active and inactive: 51 per cent and 49 per cent respectively. However, as we have already established, in common with some previous research (Sinfield, 1968; Norris, 1978; Townsend, 1979; Walker, 1982a) our data exposed the crude and unhelpful nature of the simplistic distinction commonly made between economic activity and inactivity. As we show in detail later, this dichotomy is particularly inappropriate with regard to older workers, many of whom do not choose to declare themselves as unemployed for personal reasons and so are counted as such only while entitled to unemployment benefit during at most the first year after redundancy.

Among those older workers in the study conventionally defined as economically inactive, nearly 70 per cent were retired (although only 18 per cent had retired at the normal pension age), 17 per cent were sick or injured and 4 per cent were looking after their families. As for the economically active, 56 per cent were employed full or part-time and 44 per cent were unemployed. Before they became redundant *all* of them had been economically active, in full-time and apparently secure employment. Figure 6.1 shows the employment status of older workers immediately after redundancy and three years later at the time of interview. The impact of redundancy on the employment status of older workers was remarkable, with only 17 per cent of all those aged 55 and over moving from employment with the steel company to a further spell of employment, and only 14 per cent to full-time work. Although these proportions altered subsequently, particularly among the 55–9 age group, after three years only 25 per cent of the whole group (excluding those who had retired at the normal pension ages) were in work. In contrast, almost 70 per cent of those under 40 at the time of interview, and some 60 per cent of the middle aged (40–54) were employed after three years. Nearly all of the former, and two in three of the latter, went straight into jobs after they were made redundant (see Figure 6.2). Both figures show the distribution of employment statuses at two points in time. If all of the statuses occupied in the intervening three years were included the picture would, of course, be a good deal more complicated.

Figure 1 also shows that there were important differences in post-redundancy employment status among older workers based on age, or more precisely, proximity to state pension age. Initially, the flow out of the labour force and into retirement was concentrated among men within three years of pension age. Three years after redundancy the picture had changed, with the level of employment rising among those still under pension age and the level of unemployment falling. But,

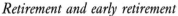

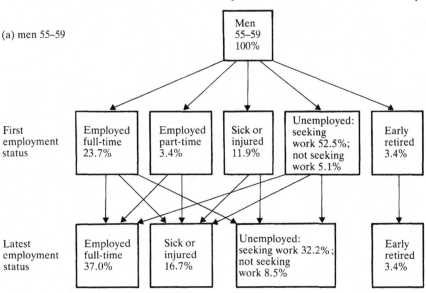

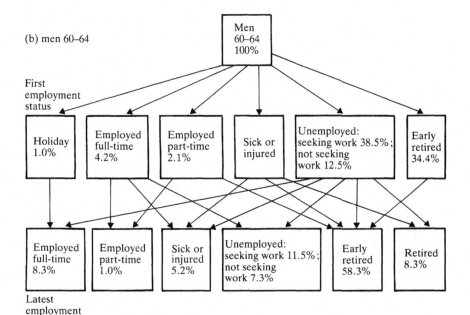

Figure 6.1   Employment status of older male workers following redundancy according to age at time of redundancy

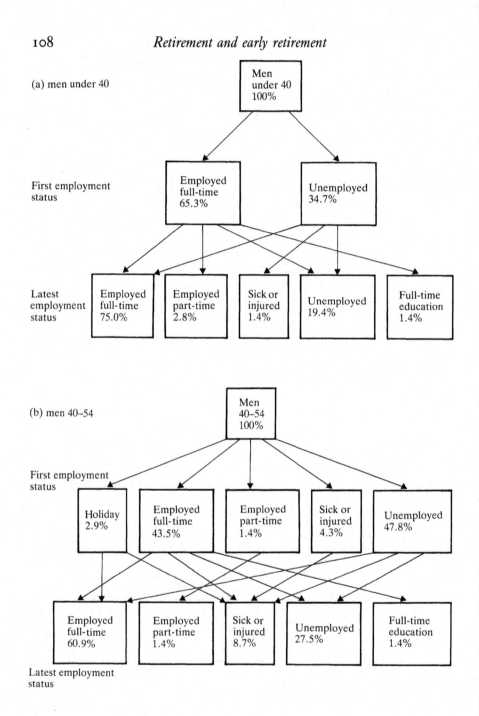

Figure 6.2 Employment status of younger and middle-aged male workers following redundancy according to age at time of redundancy

whereas for the 55–9 age group the fall in unemployment was compensated by an increase in employment (but an increase also in sickness and disability), for the 60–4 age group it was early retirement that increased more substantially than employment. Thus there is a clear difference in the direction of the flows, as indicated by the arrows in the figures, between those aged 60–4 at the time of redundancy and other older workers. The pattern of changes in status over the three years since redundancy is broadly similar for those aged 55–9, 40–54 and under 40 at the time of redundancy. But for those aged 60–4 the pattern is quite different: with the major flow of people being from unemployment into early retirement.

Although we are concerned in this chapter with exit from the labour market, it is worth noting that just over half of the 60–4 age-group remained 'economically active' for at least three years, together with the great bulk of the 55–9 age group. Just under 25 per cent of the former and just over 50 per cent of the latter were employed at the time of interview (for a detailed account of the post-redundancy experiences of all the older workers in the study see Walker, Noble and Westergaard, 1985).

NORMAL RETIREMENT: THOSE RETIRING AT 65

Before turning to the largest group among the retired – the early retired – it is worth noting a small group (8 per cent of the older people in our study, and 22 per cent of the retired) who retired at the usual pension age for men of 65. Did redundancy have any impact on the normal retirement process?

All of those who retired at the pension age were men. Most of them did so after redundancy, being either unemployed or sick or both, for periods between 3 months and 36 months before they became eligible for the state retirement pension. It is interesting that most of this small group chose to remain unemployed rather than declare themselves early retired. Although the numbers involved were small, our data suggest that those who waited for the pension age were more likely than the early retired to have wanted work. One 67-year-old, for example, said that he would have preferred to work: 'I didn't really want to leave my work, I enjoyed going there.' All of those who said that they wanted to retire referred to their own ill health as a factor or, in one case, for the need to care for a disabled wife.

There were two exceptions to this pattern of retirement at pension age. In both cases retirement took place at the same time as redundancy and both men had reached 65. In fact one was 68, and because he had worked beyond the normal retirement age did not qualify for a redundancy payment. The other was just a few months short of pension age when the redundancies were announced. He was refused voluntary redundancy and had to work on until he was 65 and accept retirement instead. Not surprisingly, he was 'very upset' because he had 'lost a lot of money'. So, redundancy had an immediate impact on the decision to retire at the normal pension age of the two people who were either very close to or over 65. The normative expectation concerning retirement at the state pension ages, and the practical barriers to continuing employment beyond them, are now so strong that only a minority of men and women work beyond 65 and 60 (Walker, 1980). But for those older workers who wanted to continue working beyond pension age, redundancy considerably reduced their chances of doing so. It added to the already powerful pressure in favour of withdrawal from the labour market at pension age at the very latest. Moreover, the financial penalty attached to those working beyond 65 would probably discourage this practice even more. In this context it is worth noting that when we interviewed them, there were only two men in the study group who were still working, although they were over the pension age. One was 66 and had worked full-time in his wife's retail business since being made redundant; the other was 67 and had been working full-time up to 12 months prior to the interview when he went part-time.

THE DECISION TO TAKE EARLY RETIREMENT

As Figure 1 shows, early retirement was the major route out of the labour market, from economic activity to inactivity. Over 75 per cent of those who were retired when they were interviewed had done so *before* pension age. Just over 50 per cent of those who retired prematurely did so at the same time as their redundancy. The rest retired at different points over the following three years.

There were four main characteristics which distinguished the early retired from other older people: age, state of health, financial circumstances and 'class'.

In the first place, age, or rather proximity to the state pension age, had an important bearing on early retirement. This relationship was also found by the national study of retirement and early retirement conducted in 1977 (Parker, 1980, p. 13). Answers to questions about their fellow workers' reactions when they heard the news of the planned redundancies suggested a difference in attitude between some of those who were close to pension age and had been with the company for long periods and other workers. The following comments were typical:

Some were very angry, they thought it would last for ever; yes a bit down in the dumps, especially the younger people, some old people looked forward to it.
(Man, 65, early retired)

The young ones were really upset, they didn't know whether they would get jobs. The older ones weren't really worried about it – same as myself.
(Man, 65, early retired)

Some my age weren't bothered, but the younger ones had decent jobs and didn't want to leave.
(Man, 66, unemployed then retired)

It just depends, some of them were laughing, they were pleased enough. Those that had any length of time in, they had a hand-out. Quite a few were very upset, they'd only 12 months to go – it was just like turning them out on the street.
(Man, 66, early retired)

Some were right happy, them that had been there ages, they put in for it and got a nice lump sum. But I had only been there six years and it wasn't much good to me.
(Man, 67, employed part-time)

The older ones were pleased because they would get a lot of money, the younger ones were upset because they were thinking about the future.
(Man, 68, early retired)

The division between those close to pension age and others suggested by these quotations was confirmed by analysis of other variables. For example, when asked whether or not they would describe their own redundancy as genuinely voluntary, the oldest group (those over 65 when interviewed) were much more likely than other groups to say 'yes' (83 per cent compared with 46 per cent of those aged 55–9 and 65 per cent of those aged 60–4). Furthermore, they were less likely to have applied to be taken on by the firm's main competitor, which took over its order book, or to look for another job before leaving the firm.

The oldest group of workers were much less likely than younger groups to say that they were angry or upset when they heard the news that the plant was going to close. The figures were 34 per cent, 54 per cent and 89 per cent for the 65 and over, 60–4 and 55–9 age-groups respectively. Moreover, even when length of service with the company was taken into account, those close to pension age were the least likely to be angry or upset.

Because we collected detailed record of economic activity statuses, it was possible to compare the proportion of time since being made redundant spent by each person in different statuses. If older workers are compared on the basis of their proximity to pension age when the redundancies took place, the proportion of the three years between redundancy and interview spent in retirement increased dramatically the closer they were to pension age. Thus the mean proportion of time spent retired by those within 4–6 years of pension age was 19 per cent, compared with 57 per cent of those within 3–4 years, and 84 per cent of those with 1–2 years to go before reaching pension age. In short, and not surprisingly, the closer to retirement age respondents were the more likely they were to retire early.

A second characteristic, health, was found by the study to be an important factor in the decision to retire early. However, it is not possible to say whether or not it was the over-riding factor. Certainly when asked directly why they had decided to take early retirement, ill-health was the single most frequently mentioned reason. This finding corresponds with research that has concentrated on early retirement (Parker, 1980; McGoldrick and Cooper, 1980; and in France, Cribier, 1981) and withdrawal from the labour market through the job release scheme (Makeham and Morgan, 1980, p. 14).

But we do not know how many of those older workers with poor health would have been fit enough to continue working if the plant had not closed. Some had been finding work a strain and early retirement came as a relief. Others were sick or disabled, yet still wanted paid employment (see Figure 1). In fact, the dividing lines were often difficult to draw between those formally described as sick and early retired. It appears that severity of illness or disability is likely to have been a critical variable, and in cases of severe disability health would have been an overriding consideration. But more commonly, it was ill-health in conjunction with other factors, such as proximity to retirement age, which determined propensity to retire early; and for some a poor state of health came to loom larger in their minds now that work was harder to find than it had been while they were still in a firm job. Ironically, there were some respondents who said that they would have preferred to have kept on working in order to remain healthy. In the words of one 66-year-old man, 'It keeps you fit and healthy, gives you something to occupy your mind and you don't get bored.'

A third and significant characteristic which emerged was financial circumstance. The After Redundancy study confirmed the finding of previous research (Friedman and Orbach, 1974; Parker, 1980; McGoldrick and Cooper, 1980) that the individual's or income unit's financial resources had an important bearing on the decision to retire early. Although those older workers in full-time employment were substantially better-off than other groups, the early retired were better-off than the rest – the unemployed and those who had pulled out of economic activity without formally retiring. They were more than three times as likely as the unemployed to be part of an income unit with an income of more than £100 per week (14 per cent and 4 per cent) and half as likely to have an income of less than £50 a week (19 per cent and 41 per cent).

Of course, the redundancy payment was an important source of capital for many older workers and, therefore, contributed to the decision about early retirement. Nearly 70 per cent of those aged 60 or over when interviewed had received a redundancy payment of £3000 or more. Those with the longer periods of service received higher payments than those with shorter periods and were more likely to have retired early. This was another way in which redundancy encouraged some older workers to take early retirement. As one 65-year-old man put it: 'The managing director said all those between 61 and 62½ years would get 1½ weeks salary for each year worked. That was the inducement to retire. It gave me security.' Some older workers feared that if they did not accept voluntary redundancy they would not receive any redundancy pay. When early retirement took place at the same time as redundancy, the fear of not getting financial compensation became a reason for taking early retirement. This is demonstrated by the following quotation from a 67-year-old man who said that the main reason he retired a year early was: 'If I had gone further I wouldn't have got any redundancy money.'

Differences in financial status between the early retired and other older workers were underpinned by a fourth characteristic – occupational class. Thus there was a clear division in the occupational class distribution of early retirement between the semi-skilled and unskilled, who were most likely to wait until the statutory pension ages (64 per cent of those retired had retired early), and the supervisory and managerial group, most of whom (95 per cent) had retired early. The proportion of retired skilled workers who did so prematurely was 79 per cent.

Differences of class are differences in access to resources, not least in retirement. We have shown earlier (in Chapter 4) how, in particular, the people from higher-grade non-manual work with the firm had levels of income in retirement distinctly better than others, while manual skill in past employment generally added no premium to the pensions of those who had been ordinary wage earners. The non-manual workers in the latter category were mainly women from routine-level office jobs, for whom 'retirement' into domestic activity could be more conventionally

acceptable than prolonged unemployment. But for manual workers –
and the skilled especially – early retirement was likely to entail a distinct
drop in income by comparison with employment earnings; and the
decision to make a definite break with the world of work was likely to be
the harder. It is this, no doubt, which found a reflection in the lower
propensity on the part of manual workers – especially the skilled –
compared with the non-manual people to take early retirement. The
point, moreover, is underlined by the fact that these class differences in
rates of early retirement showed up the more sharply the further people
were from normal retirement age.

Taking those within 1–2 years of the pension age first, non-manual
workers had spent nearly one third more time in retirement than skilled-
manual workers (85.7 per cent and 66.8 per cent respectively). For those
within 2–4 years of the pension age, the figures were 76.7 per cent and
59.3 per cent, and for those with 4–6 years before pension age, 37.9 per
cent compared with 7.7 per cent. These differences suggest very clearly
that those in the non-manual occupational groups were able to exercise
more effective freedom of choice about early retirement than skilled
manual workers.

PRESSURES ON OLDER WORKERS TO TAKE EARLY RETIREMENT

These are the main characteristics which distinguished the early retired
from other older workers: they were more likely than others to have been
close to pension age, to report ill-health, to be better-off financially; and
the higher their occupational class the more likely they were to be early
retired. On their own, however, these supply-side characteristics do not
explain fully why a significant proportion of older workers were early
retired. In order to do so it is necessary also to consider demand factors.

Frequently, early retirement is discussed purely in individual terms –
as if it were a matter simply of individual decision-making. In some
cases it is the result of a free choice on the part of the individual early
retirer, though these are concentrated in the higher social classes where
financial security is commonplace. Research which has suggested that
there has been an increase in voluntary early retirement has been based
on financially secure early retirees (see for example, McGoldrick and
Cooper, 1980; Heidbreder, 1972). More representative research, such
as that conducted by Parker (1980) in this country and Schwab (1976)
and her colleagues in the USA, found that voluntary early retirement
was relatively rare. But even research which has concentrated on the
decision to take voluntary early retirement by those who have been able

to exercise choice relatively freely, while still in employment, has noted external pressures on the individuals concerned. The occupational class differences in early retirement which we found point to divisions in the degree of choice available. The importance of ill-health, too, shows that there may be personal pressures on older workers to take early retirement. In addition, there are pressures on the demand side – the most important being changes in the demand for labour locally and nationally – which have been largely overlooked by previous research.

In the first place there is redundancy, which was undoubtedly the main spur to early retirement among those in the After Redundancy study. If the steel plant had not closed down, most of the early retired would probably have stayed in their jobs until the pension age. Although it is impossible to be certain, this assumption is supported by the overall length of service of the majority, by their attachment to the particular employer, as well as by answers to specific questions about redundancy and early retirement. For example, when asked whether they had ever thought seriously about early retirement before the prospect of redundancy was raised, less than 25 per cent had done so. In fact, those who retired prematurely were less likely than those who waited until pension age to have said that they had ever thought seriously about early retirement (24 per cent compared with 44 per cent in the group aged 60 and over).

If the plant had not closed, undoubtedly there would have been some older workers who would have retired prematurely in any case. But for the majority of those that eventually became early retired, redundancy appears to have been the deciding factor. This is true even where respondents reported ill-health or dissatisfaction with work, as is shown by the following responses to the question 'What were the reasons that made you decide to take early retirement?':

The firm were asking for volunteers. I have what is called nervous angina. I was finding it a strain.

(Man, 67)

The only reason was that they sent a letter round explaining redundancy at 63, I thought now's my chance because you seemed to be going on for ever.

(Man, 65)

The After Redundancy study did not find any evidence of widespread dissatisfaction among older workers with either their employment or their employer prior to plant closure. Indeed, they were much more likely than their younger counterparts to have expressed satisfaction with the firm and its management. For example, 75 per cent of the older respondents said that they would not have left the company to do the same job for a little more money, with another firm in Sheffield; this compares with 60 per cent of those under 40. Older workers were more than twice as likely as those under 40 to say that they had a great deal of respect for the top management at the firm (72 per cent). However, although only 5 per cent of those over the age of 55 reported that they were pleased about the plant closure, these few were concentrated almost entirely in the group who were within three years of pension age when the redundancies took place. So proximity to pension age had a significant impact on attitudes towards redundancy, and towards the end of working life which it signalled.

Secondly, there is the level of demand for labour locally and, particularly, the demand for older workers with specific skills. High and rising unemployment in Sheffield, and knowledge about the poor employment prospects of older workers, contributed to the decisions made about early retirement in two distinct ways.

On the one hand, it encouraged some people to retire at the same time as they were made redundant. As soon as the redundancies were announced, just over 50 per cent of those who retired before the pension age decided that they did not want to go through the process of trying to find work, in the face of widespread steel closures, rising unemployment and knowledge about their poor prospects of re-employment; or they had had enough of work and deserved a rest. Moreover, some indicated that they did not want to compete with younger people in the labour market. Thus, many older workers did not bother to search for alternative employment in the period between the announcement of the redundancies and the day they actually left the firm.

On the other hand, there was an only slightly smaller group of people, who ended up early retired, but at first had decided to remain economically active and, for the most part, to try to find jobs. The second group were more likely to be younger than the first. Although a minority succeeded in finding jobs, these did not last long and, like the rest of the group, who remained unemployed, they became frustrated and disillusioned by the difficulties they experienced in finding employment and the attitude of employers to older workers. As a result, they decided to change their status from either unemployment or sickness to early retirement. In early retirement, older workers have a socially acceptable alternative to the stigma of unemployment, which is not available to younger people (Bruche and Casey, 1982, p. 112), but first they must get close to pension age. Moreover, between 1981 and 1985, men aged 60–4 were able to secure a higher level of Supplementary Benefit than that paid to the unemployed, simply by declaring themselves early retired.

One critical aspect of the overall decline in the demand for labour was the discrimination that older workers believed employers exercised against them, in favour of younger ones. Objective evidence of employers' bias in recruitment was found by Jolly, Creigh and Mingay (1980). In our group, nearly all the unemployed men aged 60–4 mentioned the bias towards younger people in recruitment. The following comments are representative:

They have lost interest in me because of my age.

You're told they are looking for someone younger everywhere.

No one will employ me.

You lose interest and can see the situation as it is – you're not going to be set on, and who's going to set me on at 63?

Not surprisingly, job applications tended to be concentrated in the early stages of unemployment and ceased when older workers became discouraged from making further fruitless efforts.

Thirdly, official labour market intermediaries in the Job Centres are an important source of information about employment prospects and are, therefore, a crucial part of the process of discouraging older workers from searching for work and, indirectly, encouraging them to take early retirement. For many older people in the After Redundancy study, the process began as soon as they registered as unemployed: they were much less likely than younger people to be interviewed by Job Centre staff, and if interviewed, more likely to be told that their prospects of getting work were nil. The following comments were typical of those made by older men who tried to find employment but were discouraged by Job Centre staff. (They were all three years younger than the stated age when they were made redundant.)

When I went to the Job Centre they said they couldn't do anything for me at my age.

(Man, 63, early retired)

I've given up the idea of finding a job – since my wife was snubbed at the Job Centre – she was looking for a job for herself and asked the girl about one advertisement for a turner at Worksop. When she asked, the girl said it was too far away and anyway I was too old – it was a job for a younger man. I've not bothered since then, I felt very bad after that.

(Man, 62, unemployed)

The DHSS sent me to the Job Centre – when they knew how old I was, she said, "You won't be wanting a job at your age, will you?"

(Man, 67, early retired)

I went to the Job Centre, told them I was nearly 64 and he said, "You've been there (at the firm) a long time, I don't think we'll be bothering you." He took my card, put a tick by it and that's the last I've seen of it.

(Man, 66, early retired)

Finally, there is the economic and social policy context within which older workers come to a decision about whether or not to remain economically active. Attitudes towards employment, retirement and early retirement are not formed in a vacuum; and in addition to the long-term devaluation of the industrial worth of older people (Walker, 1980; Phillipson, 1982), the years since the late 1970s, including the periods leading up to and immediately after the redundancies under study took place, were marked by frequent references to the need for earlier retirement. These were accompanied, more importantly, by social policies aimed at encouraging early retirement – particularly the Job Release Scheme and the award of the higher rate of Supplementary Benefit to those men aged 60–4 shifting from unemployment to early retirement.

Together these policies and policy statements reflect an overwhelming official concern in the current period of high unemployment with the position of young people in the labour market and, conversely, a lack of interest in doing anything about improving the employment prospects of older workers. They reflect, in other words, an increasing tendency to discriminate against older people in favour of younger ones: a tendency to 'ageism' (Walker, 1982). In turn, this strong bias in policy and official interest affects the climate of opinion in society as a whole, but especially in the labour market, where it influences employers, personnel officers, Job Centre staff and other officials and, of course, older workers themselves. In December 1982 a Marplan public opinion poll found that 80 per cent of those questioned thought that early retirement was a desirable measure for alleviating unemployment. In the After Redundancy study, support for compulsory retirement at an earlier age was nearly as widespread, with over 30 per cent saying it would be very effective and 40 per cent saying it would be quite effective. Moreover, it was the group that were most likely to suffer long periods of unemployment and non-employment and for which early retirement was a realistic option, those aged 60–4, that was most likely to say that it would be very effective in dealing with unemployment: 46 per cent, compared with 34 per cent of the 55–9 age group, and 30 per cent of those under 30.

Statements by individuals in response to questions about early retirement also often reflected the dominant official concern. Not surprisingly, older workers themselves had apparently internalized the assumptions which underpin policy, including the priority to be given to young people. The terms respondents used to describe the advantages of early retirement, or to rationalize it in retrospect, often dwelt on the position of young people in the labour market. Although this was only rarely cited as a reason for taking early retirement, there is no doubt that there was an altruistic element in the early retirement of a significant proportion of older workers who believed – in line with government policy – that their withdrawal from the labour market would help unemployed young people. For example, one man who took early retirement at 61 because he had been made redundant thought, at the time, that the advantage of early retirement was '. . . the fact that there were so many young people out of work and I thought I'd done a lifetime's work and might as well leave it for the young ones.' Another, who took early retirement at 63, said that his reason for doing so was that '. . . It was more or less: no jobs available and I thought "I've had a good run, give somebody else a chance." There are lots of others with young ones to bring up, it's a greedy world.' Similar attitudes were reported by McGoldrick and Cooper (1980, p. 860) and Bytheway (1987).

So, the policy context within which the redundancies took place and the older workers experienced the labour market, often for the first time in 20 or more years, was indifferent if not actually antagonistic to their special needs. Official and public attitudes towards older workers – which to a large extent determine the extent of their inclusion in or exclusion from the labour force – rest primarily on the demand for labour. These attitudes are in marked contrast to those common in the period immediately after the Second World War, when people of retirement age were urged *not* to retire and 'sink into premature old age', but to work a little longer and, therefore, have 'a happier and healthier old age' (Phillipson, 1983, p. 33). At the same time, medical and social science research began to indicate that retirement had detrimental effects.

Today a formal lowering of the male retirement age to 60 has been rejected on grounds of cost, but high rates of unemployment among the 60–4 age group, together with official encouragement for unemployed men to leave the labour force, have amounted to an informal policy of increased early retirement for men. Unfortunately, while this policy may relieve the short-term burden of unemployment from some older men, the results of our study show that this burden was somewhat easier to bear for the group nearest retirement age. It was the majority of those in their mid and late fifties, who did not have the option of becoming early retired and faced the prospect of very long-term unemployment, who found the experience of unemployment very distressing (Walker, Noble and Westergaard, 1985). Moreover the possible long-term consequences of current policies, such as deeper poverty in advanced old age, have not been considered publicly (Walker, 1982, pp. 66–69).

SOCIAL EXCLUSION, DISCOURAGEMENT AND EARLY RETIREMENT

Which of these demand- and supply-related factors exerted a dominant influence on individual older workers in deciding whether or not to cease economic activity and become early retired? The After Redundancy study suggests that it was those on the demand side and, in the first instance, the redundancy. When presented with the alternative of long-term unemployment with no prospect of a job, some semi-skilled and unskilled older workers had no effective choice about early retirement. This conclusion is backed up by recent analysis of the discouraged worker effect in the national Labour Force Survey (Laczko, 1987). But if demand-related factors were dominant, they were not over-riding. There were still those in the skilled, supervisory and managerial groups who might have sought alternative employment and stood a better chance than the majority of finding it, but who chose instead to take early retirement. In these cases, financial security, reluctance to move to a new employer and proximity to the statutory pension age, coupled with a desire to do other things with their time or simply to stop working, led them to opt for early retirement. Also there were others who felt that they had to stop work because of their own or their spouse's ill health.

So, for the vast majority of older workers it was likely to be the interaction of the two sets of influences – individual characteristics and knowledge about the demand for labour and their chances of securing further employment of a similar kind – that determined their response to redundancy. However, in the absence of financial security, the option of early retirement rested primarily on proximity to pension age (see figure 1).

All of those who retired prematurely were forced by redundancy to make a decision about their future employment status. Half of those who retired at that point or subsequently were effectively forced into early retirement by ill health or the lack of job opportunities. Only 3 people among the whole group had worked since redundancy and only one of those did so for more than half of the time between redundancy and interview. So for the bulk of those who delayed a decision about early retirement, unemployment or sickness amounted to a similar status to early retirement: non-employment. But considerably more social stigma attaches to unemployment than early retirement. In addition, for those men aged 60–4 after November 1981, a simple change in the official label attached to their status would have resulted in an increase in their income by one-quarter. Thus the formal decision to retire prematurely, when it came later, was not simply a rationalization of the individual's situation, but a considerable improvement.

In sum, two approaches to early retirement may be distinguished. On the one hand, there were those who, once the prospect of redundancy had been raised, were reconciled to early retirement and to a greater or lesser extent relieved at leaving work, although they were attached to their employer and would not in all probability have left prematurely of their own volition. In the words of one 64-year-old man who took early retirement, it was '. . . due to the fact that I was made redundant, I'd been at (the firm) all those years and worked really hard and felt I could get through alright without working. I felt I'd done my duty.'

On the other hand, there were those who gave up work reluctantly and would have preferred to have kept on working, but for reasons of health or lack of alternative employment chose early retirement. As one put it: 'I was accepting early retirement but psychologically I was being pushed out.'

The early retirers were split evenly between the first group who wanted to retire and the second who would have preferred to work (this compares, incidentally, with just over 25 per cent of those who retired at the normal pension ages who would have preferred to keep on working). With the exception of a few of the non-manual workers, concentrated in the first group, early retirement cannot be said to have been chosen from a position of strength – financial security, good health and the option of continued employment – by the vast majority of people.

Those in the latter group – the reluctant early retirers – conform directly to what are more readily described in the USA as 'discouraged workers' (Sorrentino, 1980, p. 168; see also Laczko, 1987). They are people who would like to work but believe no work is available, who lack the necessary schooling, training, skills or experience, whom employers think too young or too old, or who have other personal handicaps in finding a job. The small number of older (and younger) women who gave up paid employment following redundancy to become housewives may also be included in this group of discouraged workers. They had given up the idea of gaining paid employment and withdrawn, temporarily or permanently, from the labour force.

The discouraging effects of prolonged unemployment; experience in the labour market with employers and official intermediaries; public statements by political and economic commentators, politicians and employers about the future of employment: all these are part of a social process of exclusion, which probably began to set the agenda in the minds of individual older workers in our study even before the redundancy itself took place.

The process of exclusion in operation currently is an important part of the social construction of the definition and redefinition of the labour force, the economically active and inactive, the unemployed and retired, the productive and unproductive, and, therefore, of working age and old age (Walker, 1980; Phillipson, 1983). It is the process whereby society encourages and legitimates certain forms of dependency, such as unemployment and early retirement among men aged 60–4, while subjecting others not only to substantially lower incomes, but also to control procedures intended to ensure that they continue searching for work (Sinfield, 1981, p. 142).

ATTITUDES TOWARDS RETIREMENT

For most of those who eventually took it, early retirement then was not the end result of a long process of discussion and deliberation, nor something they had planned carefully over a long period, but rather it was prompted by redundancy or first-hand experience of the labour market thereafter. What did those who took the decision think about it, and how voluntary did they regard retirement? We asked all of the retired if they had wanted to retire or if they would have preferred to have kept on working. Answers to this question revealed important differences between the retired and the early retired in their attitude towards becoming retired. (However, some caution is required in interpreting these differences because the number of people in the study that had retired at the normal pension age – 16 – was so small.)

Just over half (51 per cent) of the early retired said that they wanted to retire and just under half that they would have preferred to keep on working. Those who retired at the statutory pension ages were much less likely than the early retired to say that they would have preferred to keep on working (37 per cent). This underlines not only the involuntary nature of many early retirements, but also the continuing importance attached to the pension ages as marking the legitimate end to working life. The point is further supported by the reasons that retired respondents gave for wanting to keep on working instead of retiring. The most common reason was financial, but this was followed closely by the expectation and desire to continue working until 'retirement age', and by enjoyment of work. In several cases these reasons were combined. Others felt it was better to be at work each day than at home, or they wanted to remain physically and mentally active. Overall, the reasons given for wanting to keep on working indicated that this group of older people believed that their working life had been cut short:

I'd everything going for me, to carry on to 65. I'd have a decent pension – working was security – a wage coming in.

(Man, 62, early retired at 60)

My health was good and I wanted to keep on until I was 65. I just decided in my own mind that 65 was the age.

(Man, 66, early retired at 63)

The involuntary and sudden nature of the majority of the early retirements was shown, as reported earlier, by the fact that only just under 25 per cent of the early retired had ever thought seriously about it before. In contrast, more than 40 per cent of the retired had done so. This difference is explained by the fact that the retired were older than the early retired. But what about the significant difference between the proportion of the early retired who said that they had never thought about early retirement before, and those who wanted to retire (76 per cent and 51 per cent)? It appears that although early retirement was unplanned by the majority and reluctantly taken by some, once they had been made redundant early retirement was seen as an acceptable alternative to unemployment, and where their finances were judged to be right or there were other demands on their time – such as the need to care for a spouse – as an acceptable alternative even to employment. This hypothesis is supported by answers to other questions on responses to retirement.

Respondents were asked whether, in the time immediately before they were retired, they were looking forward to it with pleasure, were rather unhappy about the prospect or had mixed feelings about it. The majority of the early retired (64 per cent) said that they had looked forward to retirement, while the remainder said their feelings were mixed. A similar division was found among the retired. The reasons given for looking forward to retirement dwelt mostly on the freedom it allowed to pursue hobbies, such as gardening, and the removal of the need to get up early in the morning (4.45 am for shift workers) and other unpleasant aspects of work. 'I like to get about, walk about, do a bit of fishing, get out in the country, a bit of gardening. I'd worked hard all my life and I was relieved of things – no bind in getting up early, no going through ice and snow in winter, no shift work or unsociable hours.' (Man, 72, retired at 68.) There were those, however, who were more ambiguous in their attitudes towards work and retirement and said that they looked forward to retirement even though they would have preferred to continue working. Again, once the decision had been made to retire early, people tended to point to its positive aspects.

Those with mixed feelings about retirement were more likely than those who looked forward to it, to say also that they would have preferred to keep on working. They tended to stress the uncertainty of retirement, financial worries and the loss of social contact:

I was apprehensive, whether I would settle to retirement after working all those years. I didn't think that I could occupy my time with enough things to do.

(Woman, 61, retired at 61)

I didn't really want to leave, yet in another way I did. When you have worked all your life there you get used to the people and the work. I might miss my friends at work.

(Man, 67, early retired at 64)

How far did the experience of retirement and early retirement match expectations? Respondents were asked in what ways, if any, retirement had been the same as, or different from, their expectations. Most of the retired said that it had been the same as they expected. Here the leisurely pace of retirement, freedom of choice about what to do each day, and the time freed to spend on hobbies, were the most frequently mentioned factors. The only negative aspect, reported by a few people, was boredom. The vast majority of people said that retirement was not different to what they had expected.

Those with negative expectations and experience reported boredom, shortage of money, the problem of adjusting to retirement and poor health. For example:

It took me a long time to adjust mentally after using my brain for so long, it took me a while to wind down.

(Man, 68, retired at 65)

When I first left I didn't know what to do with my time. Now I have to do things that my wife can't.

(Man, 67, early retired at 64)

Those with positive expectations and experiences indicated that these were being realised, except in a significant number of cases where the individuals' health had deteriorated or where they found they had more time on their hands or less money than they had expected. An example of those in the first group: 'I don't have to get up early in the morning – your time's your own – you don't have to worry about getting up and catching a bus. It's what you make it – I just carried on the same as before, I've more time though.' (Man, 66, early retired at 63.) And of the second: 'We used to go out every night, used to have holidays and now have no money. It's not turned out as well as we thought. We thought we'd live comfortably and we'd go places we'd not been to and we've not been able to do it.' (Man, 66 retired at 65.)

As well as asking about the relationship between experience and expectation, we sought information about whether retirement had caused any particular problems. A large proportion of both the retired and early retired (68 per cent and 82 per cent) said that it had not. The main problem referred to by the remainder of both groups was lack of money.

When it came to the question of whether overall, in retrospect, retirement had been a good idea or a bad idea, an even larger proportion of both groups (75 per cent and 94 per cent), including nearly all of the early retired, said that it was a good idea. If individuals regretted their decision to retire early, or if it had not met with their expectations, they were not prepared to go so far as to say it was a bad idea. It may seem surprising that, on both scores, the early retired expressed with hindsight so little regret or worry, although their decisions to retire had often been reluctant. In the light of the findings reported earlier, this unanimity was likely to be based on the two different approaches to early retirement. On the one hand, there were those who wanted to retire and were, on the whole, happy with the result; and on the other, there were those who wanted to continue in employment but who knew that the prospect was bleak and saw early retirement as a preferable alternative to unemployment.

ATTITUDES TOWARDS RE-EMPLOYMENT

Most of the retired and early retired reported missing aspects of their work at the steel plant, particularly 'extrinsic' factors such as companionship and contact with workmates. Job satisfaction and daily routine were also mentioned frequently. In general, however, the majority of both groups indicated that once the die had been cast, they were not likely to re-enter the labour force. Although there was a significant minority who wanted to do some part-time work – 30 per cent of the early retired and 60 per cent of the retired – the majority did not want to take any paid work in the future even if it were available. Moreover, even those who expressed a desire to take part in paid work in the future thought it unlikely that they would ever work again.

The early retired were much more likely than the retired to express lack of interest in paid employment (74 per cent and 56 per cent), even when the prospect of a job with more money than they were receiving currently was proposed (only 20 per cent of the former and just over 40 per cent of the latter were tempted). Undoubtedly, crucial factors here were the element of choice in some early retirements and the greater likelihood of the early retired to suffer from sickness or disability and therefore be unable to contemplate a return to work.

However, when the question of being offered their old job back at the plant was raised hypothetically, a larger proportion of both groups (just under 50 per cent) said that they would take it. The main reasons given for not wanting their old job back were that the individual was now too old or ill (especially those who had subsequently passed pension age), was used to being at home or would have found the work too much of a strain. Those who wanted their job back again gave companionship, money and enjoyment of the work as the main reasons.

There were important differences between the manual and non-manual groups in their desire for part-time employment. Retired manual workers were more than twice as likely as non-manual workers to have said that they would like the opportunity to work on a part-time basis (58 per cent compared with 25 per cent). The figures for the early retired alone were 48 per cent and 26 per cent. Once again class differences, and the contrasts in access to resources that go with them, came to the fore. The decision which so many older people took to retire was one that, before their redundancy, few had thought they would need to take as early as they did; and many took it reluctantly even if they became reconciled to it later. It is not surprising that the people whose resources in retirement would be slimmest were also, by and large, those who found it hardest to make the decision to retire.

7

Voting and Defection from Labour

ECONOMIC EXPERIENCE VERSUS POLITICAL VIEWS: A DISJUNCTION?

Did economic adversity then make for political radicalism – or for more of it, among people who were already well inclined to the left before they were made redundant?

Certainly, economic adversity was their common experience, even if only briefly for some. To pull the threads together quickly, all the men and women we interviewed had lost a firm job in 1979: that, after all, was why we sought them out. All had worked full-time at those jobs, some two in every three of them with unbroken service over at least a decade. Many then found no regular work again during the three years and more that passed between their redundancy and our survey. At that point, in late 1982 or early 1983, nearly 60 per cent were without employment. True, these included a number who would not have wanted paid work then, even if they had been able to find it: those among the retired in particular who, though usually precipitated unexpectedly into retirement before their time, had found this on balance acceptable or even a relief. But most of the workless (well over 50 per cent, and up to about 65 per cent) had been ineluctably pressed into that state. So of the entire group originally made redundant, at the very least one third were without paid work three years later through no wish at all of their own, but simply because times had changed drastically for the worse. Twenty per cent were officially registered as unemployed, and had usually been so for a long time.

Moneywise, most were worse off than before their redundancy – as some 65 per cent told us. Of course, the formally unemployed had slipped furthest down the income scale. But with the partial exception only of one-time supervisors, managers and other 'staff', the retired too had generally lost out a good deal in terms of living standards, whether their retirement was willing, grudging or virtually enforced. Moreover, even the 40 per cent of the group who did have paid work three years after their 1979 redundancy were not immune from financial slippage: over a third of these relatively fortunate people seem to have found employment again in a lower grade of work – probably therefore also at a lower rate of pay – than they had before their old workplace collapsed. At least, however, they had still the sense of personal autonomy and self-respect that is – as our interviews underlined – commonly felt to go with paid employment, however routine and subordinate the job. And the retired, for all the new tightness of their belts, could often call on a sense of dignity to help keep up their spirits after long years of work. Not so the unemployed (taking the term in its conventional use), who had been most visibly thrown on the scrapheap while they were still able and willing to work for pay. For them, the sharpest shortage of money came together with common feelings of despair – and with a frequent though unwarranted sense of failure – to cause high personal distress.

This is to put in brief outline only what we have said in much more detail earlier. But the point of doing so now is to set in relief the contrast between all this – the common, if also very uneven, experience of economic adversity which hit this group of people on and after their redundancy – and such movement as there was in their ideas about the society around them. For while they had good cause to see themselves as innocent victims of that society and new changes in its character, the direction which any shift in their ideas about it took seemed rather the opposite to the one this might suggest.

Our respondents came to redundancy in 1979. In that year a government took office, in Britain, which was dedicated to freeing market forces and to a much higher priority for cutting back inflation than for keeping up jobs. In the years immediately thereafter, it was a steep rise in rates of industrial closure and unemployment that made so many of these people's search for other work devoid of hope. When we came to interview them, in late 1982 and early 1983, the next General Election was not far ahead, though neither our informants nor we could know quite how close it was to be. That election, in June 1983, returned the same government to power: triumphant, with a much increased majority in the House of Commons, even if with rather fewer votes in the country at large. It saw, moreover, a collapse of Labour Party support to only a few points above a quarter of the national poll, with the new Alliance of Liberals and Social Democrats hard at Labour's heels in voting numbers. Popular as well as elite political orientations in Britain seemed, then, to have moved dramatically to the right over the course of the four years 1979–83 – the years of our particular After

Redundancy record – and in the eyes of many commentators perhaps durably so.

But our record is a strictly local one – for one group of people in a city, Sheffield, which has traditionally been a bastion of labour movement radicalism, within a northern Britain still coloured pink or red with Labour loyalty more than most of the rest of the country. And while support for the party slipped in this city, too, in the general elections of 1979 and 1983 (by some 10 percentage points or a little more over the two events combined, to leave Labour in 1983 with not quite 45 per cent of the aggregate Sheffield poll, though still well ahead of its rivals), our respondent group in particular had come to feel the sharp end of Conservative-promoted economic 'restructuring' during just those years. Plausibly, they at least might have been expected to withstand the trend to the right – even to move against it, more solidly to the left – given this experience; given the degree of immunity from the new ideological currents which a local and regional culture of organized labour solidarity might be thought to offer them; given also the very abruptness of the change in Sheffield, from the late 1970s, which turned industrial 'affluence' and collective union strength into recession and market uncertainty. There had, locally, been no long slide into slump beforehand to dissipate the potential for collective resistance. So it could be tempting on this variety of grounds to anticipate, for the special microcosm of our respondent group, a polarization of political views and social attitudes towards the left – in contrast to that polarization towards the right which generally seemed to mark British public opinion around the turn of the 1980s.

In fact this did not happen. Party political support shifted rightwards in the group over the period of our record, in rough proportionate terms not much less than elsewhere; and it shifted the same way, to a degree, even among those people whose economic experience after redundancy was the hardest. The shift, moreover, appeared to be matched by a growth of distrust or scepticism of 'militancy' in trade union action: a turning of many backs on traditional means for bringing class solidarity to bear on industrial relations. In short, our respondents proved not to be immune from the drift of opinion elsewhere.

Yet – and the qualification deserves no less emphasis – neither of these trends can be taken to signal, at least for our respondents, a larger disavowal of labour movement values, a new and spreading endorsement of free-market prescriptions for the economy and society. Suspicion of union militancy was, in these people's expressions of opinion, shot through with an adherence to notions of common working-class interest and socio-economic equity quite out of line with the visions of the 'new right'. The internal tensions and ostensible contradictions within those expressions of opinion pointed to an uncertainty and changeability of political views – a potential for 'volatility', in fashionable jargon – though with little in them to suggest the future direction of any further change.

We aim in this and the next chapter to put some flesh on these bare bones of conclusion about, so to speak, the political aftermath of redundancy.

VOTING TRENDS

Our respondents were certainly typical – even 'over-typical' – of Sheffield citizens in, commonly, having long lent their support to Labour. Nearly 70 per cent said that they had always, or almost always, voted Labour in general elections up to 1979. Only 11 per cent had habitually voted for another party. And the rest – 20 per cent of the group – were people who had not then regularly supported any one party: whether because they had shifted from side to side; or, as often, because they had held back from 'politics'; or, as in a few cases, because they had simply not been of voting age long enough for a question about habitual support to make sense.

Massive as it was, this predominance of long-standing electoral loyalty to Labour varied markedly by 'class'. The ratio of habitual Labour support before 1979 to habitual support for another party – about 6:1 overall – was no less than 14:1 among those whose jobs before redundancy had been manual, with no difference to speak of between skilled and non-skilled. By contrast, it was just a little over 2:1 among the men and women from non-manual work, with routine-grade clerks and the like rather more Labour-inclined and 'staff proper' less so inclined. But the score for the latter group (where long-standing support for Labour up to 1979 was still nearly twice as high as loyalty to the parties usually regarded as the more natural political homes of people in supervisory and managerial work) was low only by comparison with the formidable near-solidity of habitual support for Labour among the manual workers. Clearly the class-line of political division was as sharp as elsewhere. But it was drawn here – in the context of a particular local climate of politics – at a level of much greater traditional Labour loyalty, class for class, than common nationally.

That broad contrast with the country as a whole remained true in 1979, and beyond then. Yet, just as Labour's fortunes dipped in the national polls in 1979 and slid a good deal further down still in 1983, so the trend over those years was similar for our group of respondents.

Among them, the 1979 General Election marked a slight dent in the solidity of Labour loyalty. Roughly 12 per cent of the people who had previously been regular voters for the party defected from it then, especially to the Conservatives. But as some others – formerly non-voters or 'floaters' – came in to vote Labour on that occasion, the net downward turn was small. So was the decline of the Labour vote as yet, in all Sheffield and in the country as a whole, where the Conservatives won the addition to their share of the poll at the expense of the Liberals and others more than of Labour. The main shift came in 1983: nationally and in Sheffield; and also among our respondents, if we go by the voting intentions they expressed to our interviewers over a survey period some three to nine months before the General Election of 1983 (see Table 7.1).

Table 7.1 Votes or vote intentions, 1979 and 1983: the UK, Sheffield and the After-Redundancy study group

Percentage of voters (or intending voters) supporting –	United Kingdom		Sheffield		Our respondents	
	1979	*1983*	*1979*	*1983*	*1979*	*1983*
Conservatives	44	42	34	30	17	15
Liberals (1979), Alliance (1983)	14	25	11	26	5	12
Labour	37	28	54	44	78	66
Others	5	5	1	—	—	7
All voters/intending voters	100	100	100	100	100	100

Notes

The UK figures are taken from Heath et al., 1985. The Sheffield figures, covering six constituencies, are calculated from returns reported in *The Times Guide to the House of Commons 1979* and in *The Times* following the 1983 election; boundary changes prevent exact comparison for Sheffield between 1979 and 1983, but their effect is probably very small.

The 1983 figures for our respondents represent voting intentions 'if a General Election were held tomorrow'. In that sense they are hypothetical and give, for example, an unrealistically high vote for 'others'. They exclude not only of course respondents intending to abstain (14 per cent of the entire group, slightly more than did abstain in 1979); but also 6 per cent of the group who did not know whether or which way to vote, or who gave no answer.

For all their direct experience of recession, our group showed quite a significant swing away from Labour between 1979 and the time of the survey. Taking for comparative purposes only those who expressed a definite and positive voting intention for the next election, overall support for the Labour Party dropped from 78 per cent to 66 per cent. This still gave a large majority for Labour; and the swing away from the party (some 12 percentage points down, compared with 10 or a little more for all Sheffield and 9 for the country as a whole) has to be seen against the fact that the 1979 baseline for our group was so very high. Calculated rather as a proportion of Labour's 1979 share of the poll, the drop in support for the party over the next four years or so was in fact less in the case of our respondents (about 15 per cent) than either in Sheffield across the board or in the country at large (around 20 and 25 per cent respectively). In such relative terms, the Labour vote held up rather better in Sheffield than nationally – an instance of a widening political gap between north and south, which has been shown (Heath et al., 1985) to reflect more than mere differences in regional class composition. It held up better, in the same terms, for our group of After Redundancy respondents even than in all Sheffield; and within our group itself, as we shall come to, the political division between classes tended to widen. Even so, all this happened as a set of variations around a general downward trend in Labour support, clearly visible among the people we chose to interview because they had fallen foul of recession, just as it was visible across the country.

We cannot be precise about this. We asked respondents about their intentions – hypothetically 'tomorrow', in respect of a General Election that in fact came to happen some three to nine months later. Some people may well have changed their minds between the survey and the actual event; others who were uncertain when interviewed may have made up their minds once they had the opportunity to vote; and we cannot know how respondents who in our survey expressed a hypothetical preference for a political line outside the trio of main parties would actually vote – if vote at all – should the real election offer no candidate to fit their preference. It could be that on balance, when the crunch came in June 1983, Labour managed to hold on to more support from its old loyalists than our figures suggest; but it might also have managed to hold on to less. Whatever the precise real outcome in our group, the incipient trend of reported defection already in 1979, and the growth of threatened defection thereafter, point at least to a sizeable spread of new hesitation over what had once been staunch support for Labour.

DEFECTIONS FROM LABOUR AND SOCIO-POLITICAL DIVISION

To repeat, nearly 70 per cent of our respondents had regularly backed Labour before 1979. But of these one-time party stalwarts, altogether just over a quarter withdrew their support then or later: either in 1979, with virtually none of these early defectors voicing any thought of returning to the fold the next time round; or, more usually, during the next few years as suggested by their voting intentions 'tomorrow'. We include here some people (about 20 per cent of all these defectors) who moved from habitual Labour support in the past to abstention (actual or intended) from voting; for their change of stance represented a real enough loss for their old party, though no positive gain for others. The rest split their new allegiances between the other main parties, with rather fewer moving to the Conservatives (usually in 1979) than to the Liberals or the Alliance (mainly after 1979). We do not include in this first measure of defection from Labour a fairly small number of one-time stalwarts who were uncertain about their intentions for an election 'tomorrow', though that uncertainty itself suggests some wavering of past Labour loyalty. If we put these people too into the count of defection, the drift away from the party among its once-regular supporters (again combining the smaller movement in 1979 with the larger threatened movement thereafter in the run-up to the election of 1983) rises from just over a quarter to a full third.

This is shown in Table 7.2 (lower half of sub-table 1). True enough, even the substantial drop in old Labour loyalty still left the party far ahead of others in the running for the General Election of 1983, with support from more than 50 per cent of all respondents in the group and from 66 per cent of those who expressed a definite voting intention (sub-table II). This was so for two reasons: because defection cut into what had been a very high level of support; and because some people – about 7 per cent of the entire group – who had not counted themselves as regular Labour supporters before 1979 joined in to back the party that year or by 1982–3, mainly after previous non-voting or 'floating'.

So, notwithstanding defection, the level of Labour support among our respondents remained very high by national standards; and this was so class by separate class. A major study of the 1983 General Election showed the Labour vote then across the country at 49 per cent among manual workers, broadly irrespective of skill; at 25 per cent among routine non-manual workers; and within a range from 26 per cent down to 14 per cent for the sort of mixture of supervisors, technical staff and managers that would correspond to our 'higher non-manual' sub-group (Heath et al., 1985, p. 20). Among our respondents, the roughly comparable figures in the run-up to the same General Election were 75, 56 and 44 per cent respectively (sub-table II of Table 7.2) – class-by-class levels of support for Labour which, for all the party's slippage even here, were still one-and-a-half times to twice as high as nationally. Of course, our informants were northerners; and most of the manual workers among them, at least, lived in working-class districts. To go by

Table 7.2 Party support and defection from Labour, by occupational level before redundancy

	Non-skilled manual	Skilled manual	Routine non-manual	Higher non-manual	All Respondents
I. LABOUR LOYALTY AND ITS DECLINE					
Regular supporters of Labour pre-1979 –					
(i) as % of all	75	83	53	52	69
(ii) as % of regular supporters of any one party	93	94	77	66	86
Percentage of regular pre-1979 Labour supporters who defected 1979/1982–3 –					
(i) lower estimate	18	30	46	34	27
(ii) higher estimate	21	38	46	42	33

II. VOTING INTENTIONS OF ALL RESPONDENTS 'TOMORROW', 1982/83

	% A	% B	% A	% B	% A	% B	% A	% B	% A	% B
Labour	63	79	58	68	44	56	34	44	53	66
Alliance	6	8	6	7	9	11	22	28	10	12
Conservatives	8	10	12	15	18	22	17	21	12	15
Other	3	3	8	10	9	11	5	7	6	7
Won't vote	12		12		18		14		13	
Don't know, no answer	8		4		2		8		6	
All respondents %	100	100	100	100	100	100	100	100	100	100
No.	113	90	106	89	45	36	73	57	350	285

Notes

The figures of defection from Labour among previous regular supporters, shown in the lower half of sub-table I, throughout include people who switched, or intended to switch, to abstention from voting. The first row (i) excludes previous regular supporters uncertain whether or which way to vote 'tomorrow', while the second row (ii) includes these as 'defectors'.

The % A columns in sub-table II show the voting intentions of all respondents, including those intending to abstain or uncertain whether or which way to vote. The % B columns (like the figures in Table 7.1) are confined to respondents expressing a positive intention to vote for a particular party.

The total of 'all respondents' (bottom right) includes some who, while giving sufficient information about their voting records and intentions, could not be classified by occupational level before redundancy.

the results of the national study just quoted, both these points – the latter in particular – could be expected to make for Labour support at levels above the country-wide average (Heath et al., 1985, pp. 76–8 and 83–4). Yet even making such allowances as we can for them, Labour's hold on people in our group seemed to remain stronger, and the

Conservatives' pulling power weaker, than likely just on those grounds. This microcosm made up of men and women who had lost their jobs with one particular steel company in Sheffield clearly *was* a special one in its continuing strong leaning to Labour.

But it was 'special' in that respect already *before* the redundancies; and the experience of redundancy and what followed did not prevent an overall slippage of Labour's hold on the loyalties of our respondents. Measured – as we think most tellingly – by defection from the party on the part of previous regular supporters, the slippage in 1979 and over the years thereafter was least among non-skilled manual workers, at around 20 per cent; and it was greatest among men and women from non-manual work – at an average around 40 per cent – though the still higher rate for routine-grade clerical workers in this general grouping has to be taken with a pinch of salt because the absolute numbers here are quite small (Table 7.2, lower half of sub-table I). By and large, therefore, class divisions in party support widened: steady backing for Labour dropped, but more so in its previously weaker social constituencies than in its stronger ones. Special though the 'sample' of the After Redundancy study is, its results are in line with national studies of the electoral trends of the period (see also Dunleavy and Husbands, 1985) in telling against fashionable notions that the drift to the right was also a drift towards class consensus in politics.

Among skilled manual workers, however, around a third of the one-time Labour loyalists defected in 1979 or up to 1982–3: fewer than in the case of our non-manual respondents, but more than in that of their non-skilled blue-collar mates. So a crack opened up within the manual group, which had not been there before 1979 (see Table 7.2 again, both sub-tables). Nor had such a crack been significantly visible nationally, in studies of voting behaviour up to at least the early 1970s (for a summary see e.g. Westergaard and Resler, 1975, pp. 361–2). How far one emerged later, in association especially with the countrywide collapse of the Labour vote in 1983, is a moot point that hangs much on the definition of 'skilled workers'. Analyses that have shown a distinctly larger national drop then in Labour support on the part of skilled than of semi-skilled and unskilled manual workers have relied, as did earlier studies, on classifications which include blue-collar supervisors, technicians and self-employed craftworkers among the 'skilled'. With these excluded, manual support for Labour in the country at large remained more or less uniform across the skill-line, though at lower overall levels in 1979 and especially in 1983 than earlier. (See particularly Heath et al., 1985, chapters 2 and 3.) The higher rate of defection for our skilled respondents (who had all been employees in their work before redundancy, and with no or only minimal supervisory duties) may therefore have been a 'quirk' in relation to the larger national pattern. But in other respects the trends in this localized After Redundancy group were, clearly, quite similar to those across the country: in showing both a general move away from Labour and a continuing – in some respects sharpened – social division of electoral opinion. They showed also, of course, the new appeal in 1982–3 of the Alliance of Liberals and Social Democrats – though, in our group, on a really sizeable scale only for supervisors, managers and the like.

SOCIO-ECONOMIC FACTORS IN DEFECTION FROM LABOUR

Of course, the non-skilled were hit very hard by redundancy, with unemployment high and rising for them over the years thereafter. By contrast, the skilled and the people from non-manual staff grades of work came out of their initial loss of employment on much better terms: not unscarred, but with more money to tide them over at least in the first instance, and distinctly greater opportunities of re-entry into paid work in both the short and the longer run. So the relative solidity of Labour loyalty among the former, and the higher rates of defection among the latter, might very plausibly reflect just that contrast in economic experience after redundancy.

This fairly simple assumption does not square too well with the pattern for routine-grade office workers. Generally speaking, redundancy dealt them as poor a hand of cards as it did the non-skilled, although they (mainly women) were more liable to drop out of the labour market altogether rather than formally register their non-employment. Yet these clerical workers, in contrast to the non-skilled, showed a high rate of defection from Labour. This could be a chance effect of their small absolute numbers, even if their shift to the right was on much the same scale, in relative terms, as that in the corresponding occupational group nationally. But there is more direct evidence from our survey to suggest that people's economic experience over the three years following redundancy had only a limited influence on their electoral choices and changes at this time.

Across the board, it is true, past loyalty to Labour held more steady among the workless than among the people who found employment again. The rate of defection was around a third for those who had paid work at the time of the survey; but a quarter or a little less, quite uniformly, for the registered unemployed, the retired and those who had pulled out of the labour market without formally retiring. Yet much of this difference, such as it was, reflected the uneven incidence of post-redundancy experience between the various occupational groups. Once 'class', in the sense of job level with the old firm, is taken into account, there is little visible left by way of direct effect from labour market experience after redundancy. Among non-manual workers, whether routine-grade or 'staff proper', one-time Labour loyalists defected at much the same rate (around 40 per cent) whatever their employment status at the time of the interview. And although the unemployed in either group of manual workers were rather less likely to defect than the employed, proportionately as many *un*employed skilled workers as *em*ployed non-skilled workers – over a quarter in each case – moved away from their old regular support for Labour. In short, experience of unemployment itself – even over all or most of the three-year period – did nothing to check the sizeable drift of staff and office workers away from Labour. And it did only a little to hold back the similar, though smaller, current of disaffection among blue-collar workers. It seemed to do more, only because unemployment was concentrated on the occupational group that in any case stayed most faithful to Labour: the non-skilled manual workers. 'Class' – an embodiment commonly of economic experience over many years – helped to shape the new patterns of electoral choice a good deal more than did the relatively short experience of the last three years or so.

Moreover, if the latter experience did have some effect on manual workers' political inclinations, clear adversity in the labour market was still not enough to stop a decline in support for Labour. Had it been so, hardly any of the unemployed among the party's blue-collar regulars should have left the fold; in fact about a quarter did so by our count, some non-skilled people as well as skilled. Absolute numbers became too small at this level of analysis for resounding declarations. But there are certainly no signs from our material that either the local climate of traditional Labour solidarity or the exposure of many of our respondents to the sharpest edge of recession were sufficient to keep the countryside swell of disaffection from the party fully at bay.

How far this current of disaffection went in our group varied, as we have shown, a good deal with 'class', but only little with recent labour market experience independently of that. What, then, of the influence of other factors commonly singled out for inspection in electoral studies? Among manual workers, the young and the middle-aged stayed rather more solid in their support for Labour than the older people: the party was *not* losing out disproportionately among 'tomorrow's voters' in its traditional social constituency. But age otherwise seems to have played no significant part by itself in defection. We could not explore any effect that gender might have had, because the quite small number of women in the group were mainly concentrated in one 'class', routine-grade office workers.

Union membership may have come into the picture at its margins – membership at the time of the survey, that is, because before redundancy it was near-universal among manual workers and only a little short of that among others. Three years later it had dropped drastically, to little more than a third over the entire group. This of course was in large part the effect of unemployment, retirement and other withdrawal from 'economic activity', though changes in type of employment among those still in paid work also played a part in reducing unionization. But it means that, class for class, only the skilled workers offer numbers even nearly large enough for analysis on this score. They, unlike others, often kept up union membership even when no longer employed; and among them, those who were still in a union were less inclined to defect from Labour than the current non-unionists among their former mates. The direction of the association is the same as in larger studies of voting behaviour; but there are different possible explanations of it. Continuing union membership may have helped to keep up something of an environmental bulwark against the general flow of change in political opinion. But those who stayed in membership in changed circumstances may also have done so just because they were the more steady in their loyalties to Labour.

There are similar problems in making sense of another, now standardly found, association with voting preferences: that of housing tenure. Class for class, our respondents were a little more likely to have been regular Labour supporters before 1979 if they were council tenants than if they owned, or were buying, their homes. And, again class for class, these one-time loyalists were on average only half as likely to defect if they were tenants than if they were owner-occupiers. But familiar as this sort of finding has now become, its interpretation is open still to dispute. It may be that home-owners are inclined, by their small stake in private property or by this in association with other opportunities for relatively privileged private consumption, to take a political stance further to the right than their employment circumstances by themselves would suggest. (See especially Dunleavy and Husbands, 1985, pp. 136–44.) If this were so – and if in addition, perhaps, council housing estates constitute a distinctive milieu conducive to support for Labour by contrast – there would be a direct causal connection from housing tenure to voting inclinations. But the chain of causation may be different.

One alternative possibility is that within each broad occupational class

– among, say, the non-skilled and again among skilled manual working-class households, each taken separately – there are differences of economic circumstance that, at one and the same time, *both* tend to tip the political preferences of the relatively better-off rightwards *and* allow them more opportunity to buy rather than rent their homes. This alternative may imply a more immediate as well as a more finely tuned relationship between household finances and electoral leanings than other evidence – from national studies or for that matter our own local survey – makes entirely plausible. But there is a third possibility: an element of self-selection may be at work, to the effect that – class for class – people who lean to the political right will be the more inclined also to choose owner-occupancy in preference to tenancy, within such opportunities as they have for choice in the matter. Indeed, all of these possibilities may be involved simultaneously. (Cf. Heath et al., 1985, chapter 4.) It is certainly too glib, both for these and other reasons, to read into the spread of home ownership an inexorable trend towards enduring right-wing electoral dominance.

In any case, the points we have discussed in the last few paragraphs bear only at most rather peripherally on the general drift of support away from Labour, a drift over only a few years; and they are no more than footnotes to the main point of difference in that drift, its uneven spread by 'class'. The question remains: why, as they saw the economic and political scene themselves, did quite a number of our respondents join the national bandwaggon away from a Labour Party they had long supported; and why so in particular, again as they saw it themselves, when the years that this bandwaggon rolled were just the years of a process of industrial decline which, hitting all of them in some way and many of them hard, might have been expected to bolster their old political loyalties?

REASONS FOR DEFECTION FROM LABOUR

For a start, it was certainly not the case that unemployment figured low on the defectors' lists of priorities for politicians to tackle. Asked what they thought should be the most important issue between the parties if there were a general election 'tomorrow', more than two in every three of the defectors from Labour – without any checklist to prompt them – said: 'unemployment', 'jobs', or other words to the same effect. In this they differed hardly at all from other respondents: unemployment was plainly the key issue. Nor were the defectors impressed with the record of the Conservative Government on that score. Even those who had moved from Labour across the spectrum to support the Tories commonly conceded that their new party had so far done little or nothing in office to hold back the spread of worklessness. Some, it is true, thought there was in fact little more the Government could do to improve matters on this front: Britain was caught up in a worldwide recession, or was facing the sharp edge of a process of international competition, to a degree that went beyond ready remedy by government action. Defectors held to this view a little more often than others. Yet even among them, such fatalism was a minority view. The majority, among the people who had parted company with Labour as well as among those who stayed loyal, believed that something could and should be done to bring down unemployment; and that as a matter of top priority.

Precisely what they thought could be done, to good effect, was in dispute to some degree: we shall come to that. By whom it could best be done was obviously in dispute. Some defectors from Labour, for all their apparent disillusion with the party on other scores, still thought Labour best equipped to tackle this particular issue – as did, of course, the party stalwarts in overwhelming numbers. Most defectors did not. Those who had gone over to the Tories, while unimpressed with the Government's record to date, often expressed a hope that better things might be expected from it in a second term of office. Those who had moved to the Alliance were uncertain which party would do best on the issue, at least as often as they voiced confidence in the ability of their own new party to do the trick. But overall, plainly, trust in Labour's competence to bring down unemployment was thin among the defectors. How much that says about what prompted them to defect, however, is a moot point: scepticism about Labour's capacity to build up jobs again may have followed from the decision to defect rather than have helped to cause it.

Probably, nevertheless, scepticism about Labour's political competence did play some part, even if this was directed more to the party's 'managerial' capacity overall than to its specific ability to tackle unemployment. Few defectors, it is true, put their views in exactly those terms, when our interviewers asked them why they had given up supporting Labour after such long previous backing for the party. But quite a number of them (upwards of one in three) either brought Labour's recent internal divisions into their explanations; or they described the Conservatives, by express or implied contrast, as sound, capable in office, 'good at housekeeping'; or they looked to the Alliance for 'good, middle-of-the-road sense'. The view that Labour were 'more concerned with arguing among themselves than getting on with the country's business', that they were 'pulling different ways and don't seem to know what they're doing', was certainly one significant strand in the comments made by defectors to account for their turning of coats. But it is hard to disentangle this from another and broader strand: a sense of disenchantment with Labour over its alleged 'extremism'.

'I'd always voted Labour before. They stood for the working man. But now they're a shambles, and they've gone too far to the left.' Comments to much this mixture of effects were routine from that quarter or more of previous Labour loyalists who drifted away from the party over the years of our record. The charge of an unwarranted shift to the left was certainly voiced often by defectors, in one way or another. But by itself it says little about their specific concerns: what matters more is the diversity of forms which that charge took – and did not take. It was, above all, a charge of encouragement for industrial militancy: far more that than a charge either of pursuit of traditional socialist economic policies or, for that matter, of some sort of 'seditious internationalism'.

To take the latter, negative point first, defectors on occasion spontaneously coupled an attack on Labour 'extremism' with sentiments of conventional nationalism or illiberal racism. The party then was said to be 'soft on the Russians'; or on defence; or on 'immigration' (the codeword here, as commonly, for attitudes to the coloured minorities in Britain). But if there was a thread of xenophobia so twined in, it was not one that marked the defectors from Labour off from others. Of the entire group of respondents – very largely white, in a city with only quite a small coloured population – more than a third, replying to a direct question, blamed unemployment in significant part on there being 'too many immigrants'; and much the same proportion thought 'repatriation' one effective way to bring it down. The volume of support for such views will seem alarmingly high in liberal eyes, even if there is consolation in the fact that more people explicitly opposed them than explicitly endorsed them. But more to the immediate point is the fact that the issue had little or no political salience. It was not a factor in defection. The people who drifted away from Labour were no more inclined than others to voice colour prejudice in these forms. Indeed, those who were more inclined to do so (with over half, for example, thinking 'too many immigrants' to be one main cause of unemployment) were also, as it happens, those least inclined to withdraw their support from Labour: the non-skilled and, by much the same token, the unemployed. Moreover, neither 'immigration' nor defence and foreign affairs – for all the attention these issues have sometimes received in commentary on electoral trends in the early 1980s – figured more than very occasionally and casually in the explanations given by 'our defectors' of their defection from Labour.

   The lack of 'salience' which we found to these issues could be thought to reflect the fact that we asked very few opinion questions directly about them: only two about 'immigration' and none about defence or foreign affairs. This explanation is improbable, however. Respondents were asked about their voting behaviour, intentions and motives at a fairly early stage of the interview – just after their accounts of the redundancies and their personal experiences immediately thereafter; well *before* the large number of questions concerning their opinions on industrial affairs, economic policies and issues of 'social justice', which might otherwise have influenced their expressed perceptions of priorities relevant to voting inclinations.

   Suspicion of economic policies conventionally seen as socialist did have some place in defectors' charges against Labour for left-wing 'extremism'; but still, it seems, only a limited place. A comprehensive analysis of the answers which respondents gave to the range of opinion questions we asked them about economic and other public affairs identified some particular issues on which defectors' views differed significantly, in a statistical sense, from the views of those who remained steady in their support for Labour. Among those issues were two of several 'left-wing prescriptions' for tackling unemployment – nationalization of North Sea oil with use of the revenues for general investment in industry, and giving employees 'a much greater say' in the running of companies – about whose effectiveness defectors were distinctly less hopeful than were the stalwarts. Differences in the same direction, though not large enough to qualify as 'significant', were visible between the two groups in respect also of such left-wing remedies as stopping the export of capital, and government take-over of 'the biggest companies and banks' in order to take charge of investment. Plainly, and not surprisingly, disenchantment with Labour was associated in some way with hostility or scepticism, relatively speaking, towards 'socialist' policies in macro-economic affairs.

   But interpretation of this needs caution. For one thing, as always, it is hard to know whether views on particular policies actually prompted, rather than just followed, individual decisions to defect. For another, the phrase 'relatively speaking' which we used a moment ago, has a substantial point to it. Though defectors were more sceptical than stalwarts about the efficacy of the prescriptions for employment-boosting singled out by this analysis, they were not consistently or uniformly opposed to them. Stopping overseas investment, for example, figured near the top of their lists of unemployment remedies, just as it did on the lists of other respondents. On a scale with a maximum score of 5 points for 'effectivity', the defectors on average gave this policy a score of 3.1 – less than the 3.4 recorded by Labour stalwarts, but still quite strong support. So, too, with nationalization of North Sea oil – a little lower down on the lists overall, but still quite popular even with the defectors: on this policy, their score was 2.9 compared with 3.6 for the loyalists. Giving employees 'more say' was a fair way further down the lists, and nationalization of the biggest companies and banks a very long way down; but this applied almost as much (not, as we have said, quite as much) to the people who maintained their old loyalty to Labour as to the people who had withdrawn their support from the party.

With this perspective added, the degree of similarity in priority-listing of remedies for unemployment was no less notable than the degree of difference. Overall, taking the views of all our respondents together, the top four policy prescriptions were all ones commonly thought of as 'left of centre', if not all distinctly left. Institution of import controls topped the list, with backing as effective in at least quite 'a big way' from 50 per cent of everyone. Then followed stopping investment abroad (44 per cent), a 'big programme of public spending' (40 per cent), and nationalization of North Sea oil (39 per cent) – the latter a hair's breadth away from the first 'right-wing' remedy to come somewhere near the top, 'repatriation' of recent immigrants (38 per cent). In fact, the defectors differed only moderately from others in their rankings. Import controls and public spending headed their lists; and though they thumbed down the more 'extreme' of the top left-of-centre prescriptions – stopping overseas investment and nationalizing North Sea oil – they did so only in a small way, to bring these to a par with or slightly below 'repatriation'. Withdrawal of once staunch support from Labour was certainly coupled with a measure of distrust towards left-wing economic policies, in relative terms; but, in absolute terms, without anything resembling a reversal of priorities in favour of some contrasting right-wing pattern of prescription. Keeping wages down and cutting unemployment benefits, for example, were low on everyone's list of effective remedies.

The defectors' common image of Labour as having moved 'too far left' seems, therefore, to have come less from opposition to particular economic policies – let alone from indifference to the issue of unemployment on which such policies would focus – than from other features of the 'extremism' which they now attributed to their old party. The point is confirmed by examination of the comments they made in direct reply to our questions about why they had changed political sides, or had moved to abstention in a mood of uncertainty or 'a plague on all your houses' cynicism. Very few then brought up Labour's commitments to public ownership and extended economic control as a thorn in their flesh – though it happened, as when one man (a middle-aged crane-driver, turned Conservative even though unemployed most of the time since his redundancy) vociferously condemned nationalization as a recipe for 'overmanning and the ruin of industry'. Nor, by the way, were the defectors exceptionally disaffected from politics at large, and on that score perhaps inclined to opt out, or switch sides 'just for a change' unlikely to make much difference anyway. Some did make comments of this sort – 'I don't think Labour will do what they say, so you might as well let the others have a go – for what it's worth.' But while 'electoral disillusion' was widespread (less than half the entire group of respondents said they felt 'it really matters who you vote for') the defectors were in fact just a little *more* convinced than others about the importance of voting.

Two things seem to have been uppermost in the minds of defectors when they explained their defection as a reaction to 'extremism' in Labour. One, as we have already noted, was a loss of practical grasp and momentum on the part of the party, brought about – as they quite often saw it – by the 'in-fighting' of recent years. The other, very frequently voiced, was resentment of a 'disruptive' militancy in industrial affairs, for which Labour was seen to share major blame with the trade unions.

This stood out time and time again in their comments. 'There are too many strikes, and that loses orders.' 'Union leaders are out of touch, and push conflict where there ought to be agreement.' 'There's a lot of greed around these days – the owners, too, as well as the unions – so trouble gets in the way of work.' 'There are too many unions and stewards setting themselves up as dictators and pressing wage claims.' Remarks of this sort were two a penny from the lips of people who had turned away from Labour; and the party clearly was identified in their eyes with the union militancy they found objectionable. Arthur Scargill – a 'hero' to quite a few stalwarts – topped *their* selection of people prominent in public life whom they felt 'most opposed to'; and Tony Benn came next. But, significantly, the duo of Norman Tebbit and Margaret Thatcher were not far behind. The latter – the Prime Minister especially – had their admirers, too. But more usually, overall, the defectors picked for praise somebody or other with an established 'moderate' image: David Steel, Shirley Williams, Edward Heath or – though a Labour spokesman – Denis Healey. Their hostility to militancy and 'the left' was a preference for the centre, for 'a middle way' in politics and for peacefully negotiated settlement between employers and workers, rather than an endorsement of the hard right – even when the Government was given credit for 'taking a firm line' and for 'good housekeeping'. Bosses were not held immune from criticism either – criticism for 'greed' or for 'inefficient management'. But at the end of the day, the prime target of the defectors' resentments were unions seen as too aggressive and too 'big for their boots'; and, by association, a Labour Party seen as too close to them in encouragement or tolerance of industrial unrest.

This came out in our comprehensive analysis of issues on which opinions differed significantly between those who had stayed with Labour and those who had abandoned it. As we shall show later, support was weak or limited among all respondents for either politically oriented industrial action or what, during just the period of our record, the Government managed to define and condemn as 'secondary' industrial action – strikes or picketing in sympathy with workers at another workplace. But such support was still, and significantly, weaker among defectors than among loyalists. The distinction here was not a matter of defectors trailing somewhat behind others in generally widespread endorsement of stances left-of-centre, as it was in the case of a number of policies for macro-economic management to boost employment. On this other score, it was rather a case of defectors spearheading a general swell of antagonism to trade union assertiveness, to industrial militancy at least in certain forms.

The qualification implied by the last phrase is, however, important. Fewer than a quarter of the defectors were prepared to endorse 'sympathy strikes' in principle, as against twice as many Labour stalwarts. Yet, to take another telling example, two in every three defectors agreed that 'If it wasn't for unions, bosses could do whatever they wanted to with their workers – and most of them would'. Still more of the loyalists agreed with that proposition: four in every five. But the point remains that hostility to 'aggressive' union action commonly went hand in hand with continued support for trade unionism as an essential means of self-protection for employees against employers. And the point applies in much the same way to defectors as to stalwarts, even though on either issue ('secondary action' on the one hand, principled support of unionism in collective self-defence on the other) the views of defectors ranged further to the right than did those of people who remained loyal to Labour. The apparent tension between principle and practice, between the general notion of labour solidarity and the means by which to pursue it, is a matter which needs more detailed exploration: we shall take it up in the next chapter. But briefly indicated already, it is in line with another point worth noting. In moving away from the Labour Party, the defectors in our group did not, at least for the most part, seem to be changing their 'class identifications'.

Our interview schedule, it is true, included no questions directly designed to explore respondents' perceptions of the class structure and their own places in it. It would, in our view, have taken more time and space than we could afford to carry such exploration further than a rather empty cataloguing of 'class tags' in common use. Yet, in fact, very many respondents brought class tags spontaneously into their comments. They did so, not least, when they talked about their political views and voting preferences. Why, for example, had the great majority of regular party supporters before 1979 voted Labour? A common part of the answers – familiar from much psephological research – was to the effect that Labour was the party of 'the working class', or 'working men' or 'ordinary people', like the respondents themselves: this from many non-manual as well as most manual Labour supporters, and from those who defected in or after 1979 as well as those who stayed faithful. When the defectors had changed party persuasion, however, it was not usually that they had come to see themselves as no longer 'working class' or the equivalent. Asked to say what they meant by 'people like me' (this following a question whether people like them had much or little 'say in how the country is run', to which the overwhelming majority answered 'little') the defectors, much like others, still used such terms as 'workers' or 'the working class', occasionally 'ordinary people' or 'the rank and file'; and this again not very much less frequently in the case of non-manual people than in the case of blue-collar workers. Their concerns in politics and voting, it was clear from their comments, were still in principle with the interests precisely of 'ordinary people' without influence or privilege. But they – a quarter or more of the one-time steady supporters of Labour – had evidently come to doubt the party's practical identity with those interests or its effectiveness in their pursuit: at least at that time.

8

Ambiguities of Socio-Political Orientation

There is, however, a risk of staring oneself blind at defection from Labour. We have looked at this in some detail because it represented a trend of the period of our record, more visible and more in line with the national trend of the time than could have been readily predicted from the special circumstances of the survey group. Yet the defectors from Labour were, for all that, a minority; and they were a smaller minority still among the party's traditional bedrock constituency, manual workers, than in the group as a whole. Concentration of attention on this minority, significant though it was, is liable to give a distorted picture in much the same manner that conventional voting research and commentary can tend to long-term imbalance of perspective, when it looks so closely at voters who at a given time seem open to inducement to switch party support that it comes to neglect the much larger numbers who – even in a period of considerable 'electoral volatility' – stay steadily on one political side or another.

The defectors from Labour could, it is true, be seen to mark out in sharp relief some wider currents of opinion at work also among other people, if without the same immediate repercussions on patterns of voting. Some of the evidence from our survey does indeed point to a groundswell of popular aversion to militant union activism, in forms that had come to receive much critical publicity over the years up to and around the turn of the 1980s, though with the defectors moving a step further than others by translating their aversion to militancy into withdrawal of support from Labour. The data set out in Table 8.1 go in part in this direction. Yet there are contrary signals too; and there is no simple one-directional inference to be drawn overall.

The statements for respondent-comment picked out in Table 8.1 are a limited selection from the full range of questions which we put to elicit

Table 8.1 Views on issues of industrial relations, by party-political support and by occupational level before redundancy

Proposition presented to respondents for agreement or disagreement	Per cent of respondents in each category below who gave a 'left-wing' response to the proposition:					
	All	Never usually Labour	Defectors from Labour	Labour stalwarts	Non-manual	Manual
A. Industry like football team: % disagree	4	6	3	4	3	4
B. Strikes caused by agitators or extremists: % disagree	21	22	16	23	20	21
C. Strike only over matters in own workplace: % disagree	22	22	20	23	21	24
D. Be prepared to strike in support of workers elsewhere: % agree	37	29	23	47	24	45
E. Most managements will try to put one over on their workforces: % agree	44	40	35	50	34	50
F. Teamwork impossible – employers and workers on opposite sides: % agree	47	44	42	51	42	50
G. Strike to support health workers: % agree	57	42	47	68	37	67
H. If it wasn't for unions, bosses would do whatever they wanted: % agree	68	52	65	81	48	79
I. Strikes caused by basic conflict: % agree	81	73	83	84	72	86

Notes

The full wording of these propositions was as follows:

A. Industry is like a football team, employers and workers are on the same side and success can only come if they co-operate.

B. Most major conflicts in industry are caused by agitators or extremists.

C. If you go on strike it should only be about matters that affect you directly in your own workplace.

D. A union member should be prepared to strike in support of other workers even if they don't work in the same place.

E. Given half the chance most managements will try to put one over on their workforces.

F. Teamwork in industry is usually impossible because in the end employers and workers are on opposite sides.

G. Recently various unions have been asking their members to take action, including strikes, to support the health workers' pay claim. If your union (had) asked you to strike for a day to support them, would you do (have done) so?

H. Most strikes result from the basic conflict of aims and interests between employers and labour.

The number of respondents from whom responses (including 'don't know, uncertain', etc.) were obtained to these propositions were, with small variations from one to nother, roughly as follows: all 335; those never usually Labour 102, Labour defectors 63, Labour stalwarts 159; non-manual 117, manual 205.

views on industrial relations and other matters of public affairs; and while overall, in putting propositions to informants for their agreement or disagreement, we sought a balance between right- and left-inclined statements, the list in Table 8.1 happens to include more of the latter slant than of the former. We start with this selection, however, for two reasons: first because, between them, the nine propositions give a good representation of the range of issues in industrial relations which we covered in the course of the interviews, often with several questions directed in different wording to much the same issue; second because, again between them, the nine statements show a pattern of response typical of the wider results of our exploration of opinions. This pattern involved, not least, a degree of ambiguity or even ostensible self-contradiction in the views people expressed, which the statements set out here will allow us to consider more closely.

The signs of a popular groundswell against industrial militancy are very marked, if we start from the top of Table 8.1. The virtual absence of opposition to the notion that success in industry is a matter of co-operative teamwork between employers and workers (well over 90 per cent of our respondents in all categories endorsed this statement, with very few undecided let alone against it) may say rather little by itself. The proposition – which has figured in earlier research at least since the 1960s (Goldthorpe et al., 1968/69) – has to it, probably, an aura of pious conventional wisdom likely to discourage its rejection by any but the most determined and stubbornly consistent people on the militant left. Even so, it says something about the climate of opinion that hardly anybody here found fault with the football team analogy.

It is more notable, because less readily predictable, that barely over 20 per cent of our respondents were willing to dismiss the propositions *either* that most strikes were caused by 'agitators' or 'extremists' *or* that, if workers take strike action, they should do so only over matters affecting themselves in their own patch. This latter notion in particular (strongly asserted by the Conservative Government at the time, and then in process of implementation through legislative measures against 'secondary action') goes in all logic, of course, straight against any idea of using strikes as a means – or even just a symbol – of class solidarity between workers otherwise separated by the contingencies of locality, workplace and day-to-day bread-and-butter issues. It is all the more remarkable, then, that rejection of a proposition so distinctly hostile to practical assertion of collective labour interests was just about as rare among Labour stalwarts and manual workers in our group as it was among defectors, among people who had never regularly supported Labour even before 1979, and among office and staff workers. On this evidence the trend of aversion to union militancy, with which electoral side-switching seems to have been coupled, had spread well beyond the ranks of those who actually pulled their votes away from the party.

FOR LABOUR SOLIDARITY

But this is still a fragment of the full picture; and the picture changes as we move further down the table. The very next proposition listed – which we put to respondents only a few questions later in the interview – points, by comparison with statement C, to a good deal more support for the notion of 'sympathy' strikes or 'secondary' action: substantial minority support now overall, at 37 per cent; and with enough support from Labour stalwarts and manual workers, at 45 per cent or a little more, in their case just to tip the scales against the 'anti-militants' when respondents without a clear view are discounted.

The seemingly paradoxical shift of opinion here, from one formulation of the same issue to another, might reflect an inclination on the part of some informants to prefer agreement to disagreement with whatever is put before them. Statement C took up the issue in 'right-wing' terms, statement D essentially the same issue in 'left-wing' terms. But if there was a tendency of this sort at work, it seems to have played only a small part by itself. A closer examination of apparent 'self-contradictions' in expressed opinions – to which we shall come – suggests that changes in question-wording uncovered genuine ambiguities of view among our informants, rather than merely triggering spurious response differences. In this particular instance, moreover, a third proposition on a closely related issue produced virtually the same pattern of response as statement D, despite formulation in 'right-wing' instead of 'left-wing' terms. This asked for comment on the idea that 'unions should not be allowed to stop people working when they want to.' The specific issue here was not 'secondary' action; but it was similarly concerned with labour solidarity in practice, and it advanced a familiar Conservative-promoted counter-notion of protection from union interference. A near-identity of response to this with response to statement D (a substantial 'left-wing' minority of 36 per cent overall, an approximate balance of 'left' and 'right' among respondents from Labour's 'core constituency') weighs against the hypothesis that informants, in any significant number, were prone just to tailor their answers to the varying ideological slants of the propositions incorporated in questions of opinion put to them.

So by themselves, the first three items in Table 8.1 suggest very widespread endorsement of a view of the industrial scene as essentially open to harmonious relations, if only 'agitators' and 'extremists' would leave it in peace and if only disputes could be left for settlement where they first arose, without outside union intervention. But both the next item and the parallel – while 'right-wing' slanted – question on individual freedom from union strike demands point to a much more complex and ambivalent diagnosis on the part of many respondents in our group. In the eyes of at least around half the manual workers, there was still a lot to be said both for strike action in solidarity with others outside one's own workplace, and for a right of unions to expect their members to support a strike call. Indeed, on the latter point (in answer to a question not listed in the table), some 75 per cent of manual workers – as against just under 50 per cent of our non-manual informants – said they would follow a union strike call even if they disagreed with it; and on the former point (see statement G in the table), 67 per cent of manual workers – as against little more than half as many of the non-manual people – said they would have followed a call for symbolic action in support of the health workers, whose protracted dispute over pay had been much in the news at the time with more favourable media treatment than usual in the common run of episodes of industrial unrest. No doubt, some here were voicing only reluctant or qualified agreement to toe a union line, conscious of a prospect of ostracism or worse if they were to hold out against a strike call; and a few made this plain in their comments. But comments at these and other points of the interviews far more commonly suggested a real and widespread sense of tension between, on the one hand, indiscriminate militancy and union pressures for action 'regardless'; and on the other, legitimate and inescapable demands of worker solidarity in defence against employers.

Considerations of the latter sort are evident not least from the responses to items in the lower part of Table 8.1. Near-universal acceptance of the analogy between industry and a football team did not imply corresponding trust in the goodwill of management, or indeed in teamwork as an effectively viable model of relations between them and their employees. Half the manual workers in our group (in practice a clear majority when those giving uncertain answers are discounted) agreed that management could usually be expected to 'try to put one over on their workforces'; and that employers and workers were so much 'on opposite sides' in the end as to rule out teamwork in industry (statements E and F). A substantial minority even of non-manual respondents – as well as of defectors from Labour and of people who had never regularly voted for the party – took the same views.

At this point of the table there is still a fairly fine balance; but with the last few items the scales tip 'leftwards'. It now appears that, notwith-standing aversion to heavy union activism, trade unions were widely regarded as essential to protect employees against 'bosses', who could otherwise 'do what they wanted with their workers (as) most of them would' (statement H); and that, whatever the part seen to be played by 'agitators' or 'extremists' in formulating industrial conflict, strikes were commonly agreed to arise out of a 'basic conflict of aims and interests between employers and labour' (statement I). Moreover, despite the uncertainties of view about class solidarity in 'sympathetic' strike action, the great majority endorsed at least the principle that 'working-class people have got to stand together and stick up for one another' (this from an item not listed in Table 8.1).

CONFLICTS OF 'CONVENTIONAL WISDOM'

These and many other statements which we put to respondents for their approval or rejection have a character to them of clichés: deliberately so, since our purpose was to explore complex matters of opinion through presentation of a range of alternative views couched in familiar, even hackneyed, terms. But it is too glib to dismiss responses to them as no more than off-the-cuff reactions of no significance. For one thing we rely, in our analysis and interpretation, on a series of different questions about the same or related issues; and on explanatory or qualifying comments accompanying the answers. For another, the responses even to clichés – taken together in this way – have something to say about the parameters of current or shifting conventional wisdom. The existence of some mood of common aspiration for co-operation in workday life is plainly suggested, for example, when nearly everybody goes along with the football team analogy – this across the class and political board – even though many, manual workers and Labour stalwarts especially, then move on in effect to put the aspiration aside as unviable because it is at odds with a reality of conflicting interests.

Recognition of those conflicting interests, again, is no less genuine because it is expressed in response to other clichés. It is indeed the more significant because, where our propositions for comment tended to mobilise 'left-wing' expressions of view, they generally also brought out quite marked differences of view between supporters and opponents of Labour – sometimes the defectors among the latter especially; and, above all, between manual and non-manual respondents. This is easy to see in Table 8.1 (from item D downwards), and from other questions on industrial relations which we have referred to without including them in

the table. The point is true also of answers in reply to the proposition
that 'working-class people have got to stand together. . .' – which manual
workers in the group endorsed almost unanimously (90 per cent), while
over 30 per cent of the non-manual respondents distanced themselves
from it. If there is a cliché character to that proposition, it is nonetheless
notable that it formed part of the common stock of thinking for our
survey's small slice of the 'traditional working class'. Yet it proved at
least contestable among 'traditionally middle-class' people, even to a
degree among those from routine-grade jobs in their former employment.
Conventional wisdom it may be, in a sense; but then within the working
class rather than across class lines.

Here and elsewhere in discussing 'class' differences in opinions we
have, for simplicity of presentation, generally omitted the distinctions by
skill among manual respondents and by grade among non-manual
respondents, because the main differences proved almost throughout to
follow the conventional line between 'blue collar' and 'white collar/white
blouse' people. Where there were differences within the manual group,
the skilled usually leaned a little more 'left' than the non-skilled. Within
the non-manual group, variations in opinion between the two grades
followed no consistent pattern.

As in respect of party political support, so also in respect of views on
industrial affairs: class remained a political divider of opinions, and the
class division that mattered here was the one long familiar in matters of
ideology and everyday culture. This was the line between manual and
non-manual workers, even though economic experiences after redundancy had pointed up a different line of division: that by which lower-
grade workers drew the shortest straws, whether they came from
shopfloor or office jobs; while skilled shopfloor workers fared much
better – in some respects almost as well as 'staff' – until, though not
beyond, retirement. From the evidence of our study, plainly, differences
of economic circumstances still made for differences of socio-political
outlook, for all the 1980s revival of the 1950s talk about an eclipse of
class. But the formative influence of economic circumstances on
opinions seems, again, to come far more from long-term experience and
prospects than from the shorter-term vicissitudes of the labour market,
however sharp.

This continuing imprint of class on ideology is one point that the
.analysis so far has underlined. Another is the tension between
commitments to labour solidarity and scepticism or hostility to its
pursuit in militant action. For the positives do not wipe out the
negatives; the two co-exist. In the minds of many of our respondents,
principled support for trade unionism and ideas of a common working-

class interest, it is clear, sat uneasily side by side with often strong reservations over union use of collective muscle. This tension itself was very much a matter of class, as a glance back at Table 8.1 will confirm. It was manual workers in particular who spanned the widest range in apparent 'self-contradiction', by simultaneous endorsement of 'left-wing' and 'right-wing' views. Large majorities of them went along both with standard Conservative vilification of strikes and 'secondary' action, and yet also with established class-defence arguments for worker solidarity. Non-manual workers, by contrast, while sharing this critique of union militancy in action, gave clear majority support only to one 'left-wing' premiss about industrial affairs. This was the proposition that strikes generally arise from a basic conflict of interests between employers and labour; even agreement with this, of course, would not necessarily signify support for labour rather than employers, though for manual workers it commonly did.

OSTENSIBLE INCONSISTENCIES OF OPINION

Such ambivalence of opinion comes out most plainly by direct comparison between the responses to particular pairs of questions that posed much the same issue in two alternative formulations. Different things may be involved when respondents in such cases give answers that seem mutually inconsistent (cf. Heath, 1986). Agreement with one proposition in a pair may, for example, be logically incompatible with agreement with the other. We would be close to that in the case of items C and D from Table 8.1: if workers should strike *only* over matters affecting them directly in their own workplaces, how might they properly be expected *also* to be prepared to strike in support of workers in other places? Even there, however, use of the phrase 'be prepared' – rather than, say, 'be willing' – may leave some doubt whether both statements are to the same full extent ethical injunctions and therefore entirely irreconcilable in logic. But they certainly are very hard to square with each other in any conventional reading of their sense.

So too, on the face of things, it is hard – if not entirely impossible in strict logic – to square statement A in Table 8.1 with statement F; statement B with statement I; and opposition to statement D with support for statement G. Again, since both statements E and H postulate that employers would pursue their own self-interests unless checked, the two might be expected – if precise wording mattered little – to evoke fairly similar patterns of answer. They do not; nor do the other pairs. In Table 8.2 we therefore look more closely at responses to all

Table 8.2 Consistencies and inconsistencies of view on issues of industrial relations, by party-political support and by occupational level before redundancy

Views expressed on each issue in response to two differently formulated propositions (propositions as listed in Table 8.1 above)		All respondents	Respondents who were –				
			Never usually Labour	Defectors from Labour	Labour stalwarts	Non-manual	Manual
		%	%	%	%	%	%
(i) Teamwork in industry (A and F)	Left	5	6	4	4	3	4
	'Inconsistent'	45	41	39	48	41	48
	Right	49	51	56	46	55	48
	Other	1	2	1	2	1	—
(ii) Main causes of strikes (B and I)	Left	27	25	28	27	26	27
	'Inconsistent'	56	52	58	58	49	61
	Right	16	20	14	14	21	10
	Other	1	3	—	1	4	2
(iii) Employers' self-interest (E and H)	Left	53	47	49	58	41	58
	'Inconsistent'	21	14	21	26	14	25
	Right	23	36	27	14	39	15
	Other	3	3	3	2	6	2

(iv) *Sympathy/secondary strikes* (C and D)	Left	20	19	12	24	17	23
	'Inconsistent'	19	13	14	25	10	23
	Right	53	58	61	47	62	49
	Other	8	10	13	4	11	5
(v) *Sympathy strikes/support for health workers* (D and G)	Left	46	38	31	59	30	56
	'Inconsistent'	17	11	20	18	12	18
	Right	31	41	44	21	46	23
	Other	6	10	5	2	12	3
Approximate total of respondents for each issue	%	100	100	100	100	100	100
	No.	335	102	63	159	117	205

Notes

Respondents are classified, in respect of each of the five issues, as:

Left if they either expressed a 'left-wing' view in response to both propositions (generally the more usual case) or (in general more rarely) expressed a 'left-wing' view in response to one but no clear view on the other;

'Inconsistent' if they expressed a 'right-wing' view in response to one proposition but a 'left-wing' view in response to the other;

Right if they either expressed a 'right-wing' view in response to both propositions (generally the more usual case) or (in general more rarely) expressed a 'right-wing' view in response to one but no clear view on the other;

Other if the views they expressed in response to the two propositions could not be so classified: in most cases because their response to both was 'neither agree nor disagree' or 'don't know/uncertain'; in some cases because, in the nature of the propositions posed, the particular combination of answers did not fit with the distinctions above (left, inconsistent, right) even though it was not 'consistently neutral'.

these five pairs, in order to pin down those juxtapositions of opinion which, while not of necessity logically inconsistent, are nevertheless distinctly puzzling at first sight.

The table, of course, repeats much of what could be seen already from the earlier one. Near-universal lip-service to an ideal of co-operative teamwork in industry (issue i), for example, is qualified by recognition of the opposition between 'two sides' so often that about half the respondents come out sitting on the fence with apparently inconsistent views; but hardly any – manual or non-manual, Labour or whatever – take a clear 'left' stance by dismissing the notion entirely. Yet with the idea that employers are essentially self-interested and so have to be checked (issue iii), the balance goes the other way: 'left-wing' distrust of management prevails; fence-sitting is less common; and only among non-manual workers and people never attached to the Labour fold does 'right-wing' confidence in employers' goodwill get as high even as 35–40 per cent. On the principle of strike action in 'sympathy' (issue iv), the overall pattern is just the reverse: clear opposition outweighs clear support by 2:1 or more, even among manual workers and Labour stalwarts, while around 20 per cent of respondents are torn. Yet when it comes to practice in a particular instance, with the possibility of action in sympathy with the health workers brought into the picture (issue v), the pendulum swings to the left; and especially so for manual workers and Labour stalwarts. Strikes clearly are a thorny issue, and diagnosis of their causes particularly thorny. On that matter (issue ii), 'structural' diagnosis in left-wing fashion has the lead over 'conspiracy' diagnosis in right-wing fashion; but well over half the respondents try to have it both ways.

Generally, of course, manual workers and Labour stalwarts are to the left of others. Still more noteworthy, though – if again a confirmation of what we have already said – is the point that manual workers are also more often internally torn than others. It is they (and so also usually the Labour stalwarts) who on each of the five issues show the highest percentage of 'inconsistent' responses, though the percentage naturally varies a great deal with the issue to which the two propositions compared are directed. It could have been that defectors from Labour would also show a high incidence of 'fence-sitting': of ambivalence between views they might still hold from their Labour past and views associated more with their new party-political resting-places. But that is so in respect only of two issues (ii and v), on which their degree of 'inconsistency' is on a par with that of Labour stalwarts and manual workers. Otherwise they lean towards – or even exceed – non-manual workers and people who were never behind Labour, in showing both a 'right-wing' trend of views and a relatively limited frequency of 'inconsistency'. Whether defectors were to the right even before they changed political sides, or shifted views and votes more or less at the same time, or adapted their views to their votes after crossing the party line, by the time our interviewers talked to them their outlook on industrial relations was now, on the whole, pretty well in line with that of others on the non-Labour side of the political fence.

Might a number of the Labour stalwarts go the same way in time? It was they, and the manual workers that made up their great majority, who most often proved divided in their minds when presented with left- and right-wing propositions on the same issue. That ambivalence was not just muddle-headedness. It reflected – as we have already suggested, and shall say more about shortly – a set of tensions between rival conceptions of the workday world of industry: conceptions on the one hand with their source in the traditional labour movement; conceptions on the other hand with their source in 'establishment ideology', recently promoted in strident form by a government of the radical right and long promoted by the bulk of the popular press. It is hardly surprising that manual workers – the traditional core constituency of the union movement and the Labour Party – should prove especially exposed to the cross-fire between these conflicting conceptions of industrial affairs; and so should be especially liable to vacillate between them. Such vacillation could lead to further defection – though it might equally, in other circumstances, be resolved by a consolidation of still strong leftward strands of opinion.

VARIETIES OF 'INCONSISTENCY'

In order to explore these questions further, we looked closely at the sorts of comments and explanations that manual workers most evidently caught in the crossfire (those who expressed 'inconsistent' views on at least three of the issues set out in Table 8.2) gave in elaboration of their opinions. It seemed clear that virtually all had in some part of their minds an image of an ideal state of affairs in industry, where co-operation across the board would be the order of the day; and for quite a lot of them, their old firm had come reasonably close to this most of the time, at least until the take-over. Just as clearly, virtually none of them could be described from their comments as 'trigger-happy' about strikes: whatever their views on the case for strike action, they saw a price to be paid for striking – a price for workers in lost pay and sacrifice of easy relations, as well as a price for management. But if industrial peace was the ideal, it was acknowledged to be hard to achieve in practice. Management and workforce were 'on different sides' and their interests and priorities were at odds.

Some thought that this divide, while a fact of current life, was unnecessary or wider than it might be. They felt that workers 'greedy' for more pay, or union leaders who had 'set themelves up to boss others around' and 'blow petty little grievances up into big disputes', kept up conflict and disruption to self-serving purposes. Alternatively, there were 'faults on both sides' and a lack of communication all round – too little 'coming together' between managers and workers, too little of 'the talking' that with goodwill could settle most disputes: 'There's usually a way round if they'll just sit round a table and work it out.' The 'fence-sitters' who took one or the other of these lines – either blaming 'their own side' for industrial division, or hoping for a mutual understanding that they thought within reach – saw, as one might expect, little or no real purpose to strikes except, at most, as a last resort in rare circumstances: 'Going on strike never does anyone any good.' Some of these people were not, or no longer, Labour supporters. Most still were; but it seems easy to imagine that industrial militancy in the future might turn more of them away from the party, if their views otherwise were to stay as they were.

Yet that may well be to oversimplify. These were people whose 'inconsistencies' of opinion on matters of industrial relations proved, on a closer look, to lean 'centre and right'. But there were things pulling them the other way too. Most, for example, firmly shared the view common among the manual workers that management could not be relied on 'always to know best'. So if there was a way forward through more readiness to 'talk', this would require '*real* give-and-take' on the other side too. Management was not just a matter for managers, as certainly the hard right would have it. Most also leaned to the left in their views of British society at large, in answer to questions we shall take up later; and that could well work to maintain their normal loyalties to Labour – which they, like so many others, still mostly saw as 'the working man's party', the only party for 'people like themselves'. In any case this cluster of 'fence-sitters', tipping centre-right in industrial relations, were rather thinner on the ground than those who seemed to tip the other way.

There are no very hard and fast lines to be drawn between this and that category of 'inconsistent' respondents: ambiguity of outlook is the essence of their 'inconsistency'. But rather than blaming industrial division on 'their own side', or on ultimately surmountable obstacles to communication and negotiated settlement, the manual workers we picked out as regularly falling between two stools in their answers to questions about working life more commonly put the weight of blame for conflict on management or on 'the system' at large. This did not preclude some recognition of 'cussedness' on the part of workers or unions as well. But the emphasis, often strongly articulated, was on employers' self-interest, preoccupation with profit and unwillingness to give as well as take: 'Yes, it's right that we should co-operate and put in a good day's work for a good day's pay. But it depends on the managers, and they often don't do their bit. Then *we* get the blame.' 'The gap's growing. The owners aren't bothered. They take a lot out of industry but they're not putting enough back in to keep things up.' 'Money goes to money, that's the trouble.' 'They don't seem to realise how ordinary workers have to manage on a pittance while the top bosses get fantastic salaries.' 'Those in charge don't care – you're just a number to them.' 'Managers go round in big cars while we stand in queues for the buses.'

Comments of this sort generally went with more positive views of strike action. Pay was usually seen as the key issue in most strikes; and from this perspective legitimately so, rather than out of wage-earner 'greed' or trade union aggression. In any case, strikes were necessary sometimes in sheer self-defence, 'or management would just impose unbearable conditions': 'There are times when you've got to show guts and stand up for your rights.' But there was no pleasure or glory to be found in strikes, and there was scepticism among these people, too, about what they could achieve: 'It's a poor weapon but it's the only one you've got in the end.'

Rather more manual 'fence-sitters' proved to lean leftwards in the sense illustrated by the comments we have just quoted, than proved to lean centre and right in the sense we discussed earlier. And the left-leaners were generally solid Labour supporters: distinctly unlikely, it would seem, to leave the fold – unless either they were to change their spots, or the party were to do so leaving them with no effective political home. Yet they shared some of the reservations about industrial militancy voiced more stridently by those who leaned 'centre and right'. True, in their eyes workers were necessarily at odds with employers: over 'money', they usually said – the division between wages, salaries and profits in the first instance; but also over the place of profit in the running of industry: 'The owners can close down a firm when it pays them, and just start up again somewhere else. But when you lose your job, that's the end of it.' For all that, they could still see some mindless militants 'out there', 'agitators' or 'extremists' who might stir up more trouble than it was worth: they quite often, as we just noted, had reservations about the efficacy of strikes.

It was, of course, for just such apparent 'inconsistencies' of view – conventionally unexpected juxtapositions of opinion perhaps, but not necessarily logical self-contradictions – that we picked the interviews with them out for a closer look. Plainly enough, however, much as they too hankered after some sort of ideal of co-operation in industry, by the nature of their diagnosis of the causes of conflict it would take more than mere 'goodwill on both sides' for the ideal to become reality. So, of course, even more in the case of the many of our respondents – manual workers especially – who were less ambiguously inclined to the left.

SOURCES OF 'ANTI-MILITANCY'

Qualms about industrial militancy were to be found among the latter, too, though less extensively; and that finding is generally in line with the evidence from national opinion polls of the same period, though we tried to probe a good way deeper than is possible in snap day-to-day polling. But our respondent group might still have been atypical on this score – readier to take a jaundiced view of assertive union activism than, perhaps, the general run of workers in Sheffield – for two reasons in particular.

First, the firm from which they had been made redundant had a record of peaceful industrial relations and a reputation for 'paternalistic' management. When so many of them now expressed sympathy – however qualified in practice – for an ideal of industrial co-operation, they may have taken their own experience of the firm as some sort of model: the more so perhaps because, at least until the take-over by a multinational corporation, the management there implemented 'co-operation' by keeping a distance from shopfloor activity while staying in close touch with the unions through conveners and stewards. Our respondents might then have brought to their responses in the interviews a set of attitudes more friendly and 'deferential' to management than is common.

Second, their qualms about industrial militancy might have been accentuated by what they had seen, read or heard about the firm's involvement – after their own redundancy, but before the final closure – in the national public sector steel strike of 1980 (for an account of which, see Hartley et al., 1983). The events of that dispute included some fairly tempestuous and highly publicized clashes at the firm's gates, when pickets tried to induce workers still employed there to come out 'in sympathy'.

We cannot be sure about either possibility. But the first, at least, looks unlikely. Widespread rejection of the idea that managers 'always know best' is not incompatible with friendliness but suggests little deference. That point, however, relies on only one of the several questions we asked to explore attitudes to managerial authority. So we worked out an index of 'deference', taking in the whole series of relevant questions. (For a more detailed discussion of the construction and results of this index of 'deference', and of the index of 'labour solidarity' referred to below, see Noble, 1987.) For lack of adequate comparative information, we could not use the results to say whether our respondents showed more or less 'deference' to management than workers elsewhere. But the 'internal' comparisons we could make told against the notion that personal experience at their old firm had nurtured, among our respondents, a distinctive set of attitudes likely to favour 'co-operation' and decry 'militancy'.

If that had been so, one would expect the longest-serving people – exposed over many years to the particular 'sub-culture' of the firm – to show the most 'deference'. They did not: length of service with the firm made for no significant difference among our respondents in their overall attitudes to managerial authority. Nor did the longest serving people prove any weaker than others in their general commitments to trade unionism and collective self-defence on the part of labour, according to an index of 'labour solidarity' which we constructed from a series of other questions relevant also in this connection. Only 'class' made for significant differences on the latter score with, as is clear from much of what we have already said, manual workers distinctly more committed to 'labour solidarity' than office and staff workers. And only age made for significant differences on the former score, with the younger people, irrespective of length of service, less deferential to managerial authority than the older ones. Deference, then, did not seem to be 'the mood of the future'. Nor were there signs that it had been successfully cultivated through peculiarities in the climate of everyday work relations at the firm.

In respect of the second possibility, few respondents actually brought the steel strike picketing scenes into their comments. Those events could perhaps still have helped, with others widely publicized, to encourage negative images of militancy in the minds of the people we interviewed. Certainly, such images were not the product of our informants' own direct experiences from work in their former workplace, where such disputes as arose had usually been handled in low key. Most had no criticisms to make of their own unions there; and the minority who did had generally been put off, not by militancy on the part of the unions, but by the opposite: 'a bit too cosy a set-up' between management and conveners. So if they thought there was excessive militancy around, officials and stewards who would 'blow the whistle over ridiculous things' or 'to get more pay when what matters nowadays is just to keep people in jobs', this was apparently in *other* places and at the hands of *other* people's unions. Aversion to militancy, it seems clear, came from second-hand sources. How much from family, friends and neighbours, how much from remoter voices like those of the media, we can only guess: we did not ask. But our respondents rarely referred to acquaintances' experiences, let alone their own, when they criticized trigger-happy unionism; and their collective knowledge from the firm covered quite a range of different unions. It seems likely, therefore, that the image of militant unionism that aroused their suspicion or hostility was one of which they knew little from their own personal circles of experience.

VIEWS OF BRITISH SOCIETY

Yet whatever its sources, a mood of 'counter-insurgency' had plainly spread far among our respondents. It was substantially qualified, however, by equally widespread endorsement of the general values and premises of labour solidarity. And to that in turn has to be added a commonly held sense in our group that British society is scarred by inequalities of wealth and influence. When it came to questions about the social shape of the country, the people we interviewed held quite firmly to the left. Ideas of right-wing inspiration had much less hold with them; and especially so in the case of ideas associated with the 'new right'.

Table 8.3 does not include all the questions we asked about matters of this sort; but those listed are representative of the larger range, in terms both of their character and of the general pattern of response which they produced. There is a notable difference between this pattern and the one which came out of answers to questions about industrial relations. There the full catalogue, if re-arranged in order of overall agreement with the variety of statements posed for comment, would have been led by propositions of a 'right-wing' orientation: in support of co-operation in industry, in hostility or scepticism to militancy of this or that kind. Only a few of the rival 'left-wing' propositions from the full range asked would have appeared quite so high on the list. But with questions about the larger social order in Britain today, the balance shifts leftwards.

That is illustrated in Table 8.3. Here – where the order from top to bottom runs from high agreement to low agreement – 'left-wing' propositions very clearly head the list, and show widespread recognition of a picture of British society as skewed through concentration of wealth and power. Only in fourth place on the table does a 'right-wing' proposition turn up; and that complacent 'cliché' about individual opportunity attracts far less support, albeit from a majority of both non-manual and manual respondents, than the critical 'clichés' about influence and wealth which come before it. 'Radical right' views of the poor and the unemployed, as deserving no better than they get, almost come off the list, so small is the support they find. Perhaps this is not surprising for our group of respondents, many of whom knew only too well what poverty and worklessness were about; but it is notable nonetheless, perhaps especially since the near-consensus against these particular ideas ranged across the 'classes'.

Manual workers clearly felt most strongly, leaning more evidently to the left, on issues that directly concern 'class' in the sense that has to do with economic and political interests. An overwhelming majority of them agreed that wealth was too concentrated, 'public school influence' excessive, the country run with little say from people like themselves – even though a great many office and staff workers felt the same (propositions 1–3). Quite notably, too, a near-majority of the blue-collar respondents lent their support to the notion – a radical one if it were to be implemented – that income tailored to needs should replace earnings according to job (proposition 7). That support, however, came a good deal more from the non-skilled than from the skilled (54 and 33 per cent in favour respectively); and a still more radical proposition (which we do not list) to the effect that 'Parliament should share out all the money in Britain equally', found very few takers overall – though even so, some 20 per cent from the non-skilled group and 10 per cent from the skilled.

There was one issue on which, taken together, manual workers' views tipped further to the right than those of non-manual people: the contention that 'immigration' had a large part in making for unemployment (proposition 6). Out of line as this was with our respondents' other perceptions of unemployment, the contrast between manual and non-manual groups is in any case misleading at this particular point. Both support for the proposition, and opposition to it, in fact crossed the blue-collar/white-collar line. The majority of skilled workers and 'staff' more or less alike opposed it, with only around 25 per cent in favour; but support for it was roughly twice as high, around 50 per cent, among the two sub-groups that had proved most vulnerable in the labour market after redundancy: the non-skilled and the routine-grade office workers.

At that time and in that place, this fragmentary sign of 'proletarian

Table 8.3 Ideas about British society, by occupational level before redundancy

Proposition (in rank order of % agreement)	Per cent of all respondents who –			Per cent expressing 'left-wing' view among –	
	Agreed	Disagreed	Gave other answer	Non-manual	Manual
1 People like me have little say in how the country is run	86	8	6	78	91
2 In Britain today wealth is concentrated in the hands of too few people	85	8	7	75	91
3 People from wealthy families who have been to public schools have too much influence and power in Britain	75	12	13	65	81
4 In Britain today anyone with brains and initiative can get to the top regardless of who their father was	54	35	11	33	36
5 Politicians are all the same. No matter which party they belong to they're only interested in themselves and not in people like you or me	48	35	17	43	51

6 The main reason for unemployment at the minute is that there are too many immigrants in the country	39	45	16	51	40
7 It would be more fair if people in Britain today were paid by how much they needed to live decently rather than by the jobs they do	38	49	13	26	44
8 The poor have only themselves to blame for their problems	14	72	14	72	72
9 The majority of the unemployed are people who are too lazy to look for work	11	77	12	77	77

Notes

Agreement with propositions 1, 2, 3, 5 and 7 is taken as 'left-wing' for the purpose of the last two columns; so is disagreement with propositions 4, 6, 8 and 9.

The total numbers of respondents vary a little from one proposition to another but are roughly the same as in tables 8.1 and 8.2.

illiberalism', while disturbing, seems to have had little or no political salience. We have noted this point earlier, though to do so is not to make a forecast for the future. By contrast, the issues of inequality of wealth, power and influence, on which above all the manual workers among our respondents stood firmly to the left, have long been staples on the agenda of labour movement politics, however muted their effective expression. The evidence from this local survey – in respect of ideas on matters of economic life as well as on the bare facts of economic life in their everyday impact on 'ordinary people' – gives good reason why such issues should still claim central attention in political contest.

Promoted to a high place in public ideological controversy of the period, trade union activism in its more militant contemporary forms had certainly become a target of substantial hostility or suspicion from many of the people we interviewed. This seemed to sit oddly with their own recent experience of adversity in the labour market – brief or enduring, surmountable or harsh, but at all events outside their own individual control; and it seemed to sit oddly with the traditions of a local culture that might have been expected to offer more protection against the prevailing national political wind. Yet the trend of aversion to militancy was counterposed by uncertainties and ambiguities of opinion; and it represented, just on this score and among the 'working class' majority especially, no trend of aversion either to general ideals of wage-earner solidarity or to the labour movement's long-standing premiss that the society around it is injust. On our survey's findings, whether about plain facts or about less plain opinions, 'class' had not gone away.

9

Conclusions

THE SURVEY AS A CASE STUDY

This has been just one case study in the impact of that uneven dissipation of 'affluence' which came to mark the economic and political scene in Britain from the late 1970s. The boundaries of the project are limited: in space, to one northern industrial city; in time, to the years from 1979 to 1983; in scope, to what happened over those years among fewer than 400 people who had lost their jobs with one private sector steel firm in the city at the outset of the period.

These and related limitations of the study, however, have their advantages too. We have been able to follow up this group of men and women from their common experience of a single event of crisis to a diversity of experience that followed for them during the next three years or so. The fact that most had been with the firm for a long time before they found themselves redundant made the transition of our respondents from security to uncertainty a distinctly abrupt one; but the dissipation of 'affluence', around the turn of the 1980s, was little less abrupt in the industrial areas of Sheffield generally or in many other places in Britain. The fact that, just because they had usually served long with the company, most were middle-aged or older when they lost their jobs, skewed their age profile by comparison with that of the working population at large; but it brought into focus for study people at points of the life cycle that have otherwise figured rather little in research and debate about the impact of recession. The fact that Sheffield has long been a prominent bastion of the labour movement makes the locale distinctive; but it also turns the project into a small test case for exploration of some of the currents of opinion involved in the electoral landslip of the years around 1980.

UNEMPLOYMENT AND NON-EMPLOYMENT

Controversy about the trends and balance of employment and unemployment was centre-stage in those years; so too in the later 1980s, even if the sheer persistence of widespread worklessness – still at high rates despite a downward slope of the figures on public record from 1986 – had then somewhat dulled political sensitivities to the issue. One prominent result of our survey is to underline the inadequacy of conventional categorization for capturing the reality of the impact of new stringencies in the labour market. We are not the first to make the point; but it stands out very clearly from our findings: officially registered unemployment shades into unregistered non-employment, with no sharp line between them.

More than three years after their redundancy, nearly 60 per cent of the people we followed up had no paid work. Classified in conventional terms, they comprised two categories. Twenty per cent were unemployed, in the sense then used for official accounting: that is, they were registered and 'available for employment' if it could be found. About 40 per cent, while also jobless, were not on the books as such: they had ostensibly withdrawn from market economic activity. Sometimes this was an apt enough description: reaching retirement age, falling ill, having more things to do at home – such normal changes in personal circumstances would have led a number of people to leave the world of paid work anyway, never mind the change of economic climate. But very often the decision to pull out of the labour market was prompted, precipitated, accelerated or forced by redundancy in the context of recession. Most of the many who retired did so 'before their time'; and whether they retired more or less immediately on redundancy or only after struggling to get another job – whether also they eventually found retirement a relief, a matter for regret, or a mixture of both – most had had no thought of retiring early before redundancy came. So too with a good many others who left the labour market: when new employment proved hard to find, taking care of the home could look more attractive, or poor health more of a hindrance to carrying on, than it had done before. The pressures of the labour market changed the ways in which people made up their personal balance sheets for the future.

Probably at least a third to a half of those among our respondents who were out of 'economic activity' by the time of the survey would have stayed in it had employment prospects not crumbled around them. If so, the overall three-year effect of the redundancies – in circumstances of deepening recession – was to push almost as many people out of work as there were people in the group who did find employment again. But the point at issue does not hang on precise figures. Those reflect in part particularities of the respondent group – not least its age profile – which prevent unadjusted generalization beyond this one survey. Precision, moreover, is in any case difficult, just because the distinction between 'voluntary' and 'involuntary' joblessness is a contingent one: in practice, people's concern to look for paid work – even to think about it – depends in good part on the prospects they see of actually getting it. That is the point which needs underlining – and its corollary, that recession has a double effect. It forces some of its victims onto the dole; it discourages others from engagement in the labour market altogether. The balance between the two will vary with local circumstances; it will also vary with official policy.

People on the dole are counted; people eased out of the market in discouragement are not. So one part of policy – the art of counting – can be to try to shift numbers from the former to the latter category. At least one government measure to this outcome affected some of our respondents: the Supplementary Benefit incentive introduced to encourage older men without jobs to retire early. Measures that came later would no doubt have affected others, if our record had gone beyond early 1983. To jump to 1986–7, for example, steps taken then to shake out from the unemployment register people deemed not o be 'genuinely' looking for work could have moved a number of the long-term unemployed in the respondent group into the category of 'economically inactive' – unless, of course, they had by now already done so themselves through 'retirement'. For though they wanted employment when we interviewed them, they had often more or less given up looking for it: what else, when neither they nor the Job Centre had been able to find any over months and years? Maybe then a fresh late effort, a 'Restart' prod, would uncover a few new job openings; but hardly many, in a market which had still eased only a little overall and less for the likes of these people at its fringe. With their re-classification as outside the market, the count of unemployment would improve. The realities of job shortage would be much the same.

DIVISIONS OF ECONOMIC EXPERIENCE

Individual economic experience after redundancy differed widely. But this diversity was patterned, not random. It followed the contours of socio-economic structure: contours in the main very familiar, though sharpened by recession and perhaps changing somewhat in the process.

Outstanding, first, were the divisions of the labour market which our respondents were to encounter when they looked for new jobs after losing their old ones. Many had not been 'in' the labour market, in an effective sense of the term, for a long time before the plant closure, because they had been with the one firm for many years. All except those who pulled out of 'economic activity' at once had now to find their way in that market – and at a time when, locally and nationally, it had set into cumulative decline. They were to do so to very different outcomes.

Age, of course, made a difference. It was easier for the younger than the older to regain a foothold in the world of paid work; and the older men, together with a number of women, were those who most often were eased, through discouragement, out of the market altogether into retirement or seclusion in domestic activities. But for people still some way from normal retirement, it was not age that made the main difference; it was what they seemed to have to offer by virtue of the kind of work they had done earlier.

Categorized by 'class' or 'credentials' in this sense, two groups found new job slots fairly ready to come by: skilled workers from the shopfloor of the old firm, and a mixed lot of supervisors, managers and technical or commercial staff. Two other groups found the doors far more often closed: non-skilled (in fact usually 'semi-skilled') workers from the shopfloor; and routine-grade office workers, mainly women. The gap in outcome between the first two and the second two was marked from the outset; and it widened. After three years and more, among young and middle-aged pretty much alike, most of the 'better credentialled' had paid work; only half as many (just over 40 per cent) of the 'poorer credentialled' did so. The gap, moreover, was plainly a product of the market; not significantly of differences in individual initiative. True, the non-skilled had tended to make a later start on job-hunting than their better qualified former colleagues, and to rely more on Job Centre advice in the process: in part, no doubt, just because there were not many doors open to them. But in the end the non-skilled were equally badly off, whether they had made an early start or not. It was their corners of the market, in particular, that were closing off.

This division in the labour market differed from the line, familiar from much conventional class analysis, between manual and non-manual work. The latter is in any case outmoded for many purposes of economic differentiation, in assigning routine-grade office employees to the relatively privileged side; and the reality of their subordinate and potentially insecure place in working life was underlined – even to a degree more than one might have expected – in our findings. But the survey results on the same score pointed up a very wide gap in labour market outcome within the blue-collar group: between non-skilled and skilled, the latter neck-and-neck in re-employment success with former 'staff'. This could be taken as a sign of new labour market divisions that might come, in turn, to break up an older mould of class structure. We have discussed scenarios of this kind in Chapter 1: scenarios according to which a gulf is widening, in the late twentieth century, to separate a body of employees secure in their conditions and tenure of employment from a growing group of people able to find paid work, if at all, only at low rates, in unprotected conditions and in an intermittent manner, 'in and out' as the vagaries of market demand might require.

Our findings can be seen to fit in with prognosis to that broad effect on one score: in showing skilled manual workers to have had a hold in the hardening labour market on a par with former 'staff', and a much firmer hold than either blue-collar or white-blouse people who were short on employment credentials. But that is about as far as evidence from this survey goes in support of the new-style scenarios. Unlike a good many steel-workers made redundant by British Steel in South Wales at much the same time (Harris, 1987), few of our respondents found places after redundancy in a new 'semi-detached' labour force available for hire, on-and-off, through sub-contractors. By and large, they either found new places in regular and full-time employment; or they were out altogether, long-term unemployed or disengaged from the market. To note that is not to deny trends towards the growth of a peripheral labour force elsewhere, or for that matter in Sheffield. It is to say only that our respondents – former employees of a relatively small private company that soon closed entirely – took no part in such trends.

On some other scores, however, our findings can throw at least a little light on the debate; and this to the effect of entering a cautionary note or two against some of the inferences for future class structure that it has become fashionable to draw. When the skilled blue-collar workers in our group so often did find employment again, it was with no guarantee of their former status: a third or more took up jobs of lower grade. The credentials – maybe also a degree of market know-how – which these people took with them into redundancy helped them find other places in employment; but far from always places that were likely to let them carry forward an equivalent advantage next time round. Indeed, in general, enforced acceptance of occupational downgrading proved a means to regain some form of re-employment after redundancy in a declining labour market. But that benefit was then bought at the price of lower pay, poorer conditions, and probably less security over longer years ahead. The point underlines the importance of patterns and frequencies of occupational mobility. There has, at least until the recent past, been a good deal of movement in the course of working life between skilled and non-skilled manual jobs (Goldthorpe, 1980; Payne, 1987; Westergaard and Resler, 1985): up *and* down though more down than up, probably, after middle age and, plainly, in recession. This sort of mobility has made for a degree of communality of economic experience among manual-wage earners, across distinctions of skill that are attributes of jobs rather than people. The forecasts of a sharply increased segmentation of the labour market between regular and peripheral employees imply, if this is to become a segmentation of distinct classes, much reduced mobility between the two sorts of position. This may happen. But it has yet to be shown to happen; and one effect of an insecure labour market, in the longer run, is to blur the line of distinction between skill and non-skill by forcing people downwards across the line.

Former 'staff', too, often moved down the occupational scale when they found employment again. So they were not, on that count again, very different from the workers from skilled shopfloor jobs whose immediate market advantages they shared by contrast with the 'poorly credentialled'. Yet they were distinct in other respects. If they had been long with the firm, they took a fair amount more away with them in redundancy pay than their skilled counterparts: this as part of a more general and conventionally accepted pattern that the highest earners get most when the crunch comes, though it is they who are likely to need it least in place of income from re-employment. Former 'staff', moreover, could rely on distinctly better pensions than the skilled if they retired: by no means in grand figures, for these were generally people only from the low to middling rungs of management; but with enough of a premium from salaried careers to make their qualified privilege stand out. By contrast the skilled, if they retired, could expect no more than the non-skilled: low incomes by any standards. Small wonder that, while older members of the former 'staff' were often fairly happy to retire, manual workers of the same age group – and the skilled among them especially – showed much more reluctance to do so.

So, in summary, redundancy and recession threw into sharp relief divisions in respect of immediate experience in the labour market that could suggest new contours to the map of economic class. But in longer perspective, with account taken of people's prospects in the market beyond the first few years and out of the market into retirement, the more familiar contours came into view again. From the evidence of our survey, the contrast is then still clear between the circumstances of wage-earning life on the one hand, irrespective of job skill or the line between shopfloor and office; and the circumstances of salaried life on the other, even for people on quite modest career paths. Reaches of the class structure above that level – in particular those circles of the population in which the guiding assumptions of policy are formed, transformed and turned into action and inaction affecting many millions – are not, of course, directly represented in this survey. Only the impact of their influence on the lives of one group of fairly ordinary people is visible.

THE NEED FOR AN EMPLOYMENT POLICY

Much in the climate of policy that affects the lives of ordinary people involves no new and active decision-making; only a routine acceptance, in practical politics and everyday management, of most things more or less as they are. That goes for fundamental features of the class inequality which was imprinted on the experiences of our respondents after redundancy – quite possibly too in their selection for redundancy, though the circumstances of the survey prevented us from looking into this. But the fact that these people were made redundant, and that the labour market into which they were thus pitched was to be a market in accelerating decline, was in large part an outcome of policies in far more tangible form. It was a result – one of many across the country – not just of a turn to recession in the world economy; but also, and significantly, of specific government responses: first of a gradual shift in priorities away from former commitments to 'full employment'; then of very definite decision-making by the government newly elected in 1979, to sharpen the trend by measures both of action and inaction: to deflate the economy, and to leave a vacuum where there might otherwise have been a policy for employment. It is beyond our scope in this book to discuss alternatives to continuing routine acceptance of class inequality at large. But we still need to discuss, as a matter more immediately in the arena of current practical politics, alternatives to these specific decisions – mixing as they did intervention with non-intervention – in respect of the labour market.

The final closure of the private steel company that had employed our informants, and the larger decline around it of Sheffield as a world-renowned centre of steel manufacture, are symbols of a process of 'de-industrialization' that became very fast in Britain at the turn of the 1980s. It will be said, of course, that they mark a long-term shift in the facts of world economic life, to the effect that Britain can no longer sustain large-scale manufacturing industry; that, however much the experience and skill of people like our respondents had made British industry what it was, their know-how is now redundant. They and others must adapt, and the labour market acquire 'flexibility', in response to changing demands. This sort of reasoning, with its refrain of finding fault with the victims, has been a commonplace of government rhetoric since 1979. For example, when in 1985 the first White Paper on Employment Policy was issued since the famous 'full employment' White Paper of 1944, it asserted that 'the biggest single cause of our high unemployment is the failure of our jobs market, the weak link in our economy' (Department of Employment, 1985, p. 13). This is not, however, a diagnosis easy to square with the evidence.

It does not square with the rapidity and steepness of the rise in unemployment after 1979: as officially recorded, from a little over 5 per cent in that year and under 7 per cent even in the next, to more than 12 per cent in 1982 and on an upward curve still for the following three to four years. What did happen in that period was an adoption of policies explicitly aimed to deflate domestic demand; and a definitive abandonment of the commitments to 'full employment' which had – if with increasing reservations in small print and practice – been proclaimed by governments of either main party from the 1940s to the 1970s. When so many of our respondents found it hard or impossible to get paid work again after their redundancy in the second half of 1979, this was not because there was little call for their particular skills or experience, while there were new opportunities opening up if only they could adapt themselves to them. It was because demand for labour overall was dropping drastically, and in major part as a plain consequence of deliberate government policy.

The people we followed up were the worse placed in the shrinking labour market because, on the whole, they were middle-aged or older. How far their age profile might in any case have told against them is a moot point; that it did so was certainly in line with official policy. The government had, and has, no positive employment policy: no programme for reducing unemployment by job creation on a significant scale. That, by and large, was to be left to 'the market'. But the labour market was to be made more 'flexible'. The discipline of job shortage was to be one means to that end, though this form of shock treatment turned out to be long and blunt rather than short and sharp. Another means was to be training schemes to increase marketable skills. These have been aimed primarily at young people, among whom lack of job training has been argued to be a major cause of long-term unemployment.

So government policy on this front – a labour market policy, or rather part of one, but not an employment policy – has been largely confined to a series of training measures for the young; and more official attention appears to have been paid, even here, to reducing the numbers counted as unemployed than to creating long-term employment (Taylor, 1987).

Older workers, with experience and skills often assumed to be redundant, have figured very little – except, in the case of those at the tail end of middle age, as targets for encouragement to resign from economic activity. That could be seen as a way of making more room in the market for younger workers; and this was certainly how many of the older people in our respondent group, sensitive to the pressures in the new climate, in part rationalized their decisions to retire early. It also again, helped to reduce the formal count of unemployment.

Once demand had been deflated, official sights have thus been set on supply-side adjustments to the market. There are implications to that, which policy-makers and policy-analysts committed to this line of government priorities have been reluctant to take on board. Above all, of course, it means a continuation of widespread unemployment – whether officially so recorded or not – with all the enormous costs that this entails, human and financial. Of course most of these costs – poverty, deprivation, insecurity, mental stress or ill health, the full range of hardship and distress illustrated by our findings – are borne with full weight only by the individuals and families concerned, less directly by the local communities where they live. But the country as a whole also bears a high cost.

In crude terms of drain on the national purse – direct public expenditure on benefit payments, loss of revenue from taxes and national insurance contributions – the current cost to the exchequer alone has been estimated at over £21 billion a year (Taylor, 1987). To this has to be added the increased service costs borne by local authorities, the health and personal social services, the Manpower Services Commission in running its training and other schemes; and no account even then, of course, is taken of the way in which society can be said to be diminished by the existence of mass unemployment (Sinfield, 1980). It has often been argued, further, that widespread worklessness triggers popular unrest and 'inner city' violence; in some eyes this has appeared to make the prime case for a restoration of full employment. We do not share that view. No doubt chronic unemployment is often an ingredient in the mix of concentrated deprivation that can lead to urban rioting. But, as our findings have underlined, the general impact of redundancy and labour market insecurity on people once in steady employment is more liable to be politically fragmenting and socially isolating than to prompt even inchoate opposition to authority and the current order. Moreover, the case for urgent action against unemployment does not have to rest on fears about the stability of that order or on aspirations to preserve it. In our eyes the case rests firmly on the demonstrable costs – personal, social and economic, costs in human adversity and indignity as well as in pounds and pence – of continuing high unemployment and insecurity in the labour market.

What form might a positive policy for employment take? We can make points here only towards a sketch of its parameters; and the first point is that there is a long way to go. The problem has grown so large in scale now as to defy very easy and very rapid solution. The central purpose of a new policy must be to boost overall demand for labour; but the gap to be filled is probably equivalent to some 4 million full-time jobs – a gap that would take 30 years to eliminate entirely at the slow rate of 'market-driven' job creation prevailing when officially recorded unemployment flattened out and turned slowly down in 1985–6 (Taylor, 1987). So long a time perspective is intolerable. But a concerted programme to add, say, the equivalent of 750,000 full-time jobs per year to the stock of regular employment opportunities, at a steady pace and without allowance for possible acceleration through multiplier effects, would still take nearly five years to reduce unemployment to about 500,000.

All the more reason, then, that economic policy be addressed squarely to job creation. One promising notion for the purpose may be that of 'employment-centred growth' (Jenkins and Miller, 1987). According to this, first priority would go to support and stimulate – through a variety of means including tax incentives – those industries and services likely to offer wide employment opportunities, not least for the lower skilled. There were related possibilities suggested already in the early 1980s by the House of Lords Select Committee on Unemployment (1982). This, in a very modest programme, looked to a combination of investment-led job creation, expansion of public and voluntary sector service employment, encouragement of job-splitting for older workers and award of the higher rate of Supplementary Benefit to older workers out of employment, to reduce unemployment by over 500,000 at a gross cost then of some £3 billion. Not all of this would have gone to boost demand; some would have gone to reduce supply. But it gave at least some pointers – ignored by the government – towards a positive and targetted policy of job creation.

It was a central feature of 'social reconstruction' in the 1940s that employment policy – the commitment to maintain 'full employment' – was seen as indispensable to social policy. The link between the two was severed sharply at the turn of the 1980s. It now urgently needs to be restored, and the concept re-established that it is a prime function of 'the welfare state' to secure its citizens the degree of independence and self-sufficiency that regular employment can offer. As a matter even of minimum rights, in short, the production of welfare must again be seen to include the provision of employment (Walker, 1985). But more is needed than just an adequate number and range of jobs, at fair levels of pay by contemporary standards. A disturbingly large group of our respondents, for example, gave up economic activity in part because of ill health. The quality of life – in work and outside it – must be a matter for economic and social policy no less than the sheer quantity of work. That requires more positive action to enhance opportunities for leisure. It also, and not least, requires measures to make working conditions less dispiriting, less arduous and less disabling than they often are; and to make working hours more flexible and adaptable to personal circumstances: all this without the reduction of security which is currently a frequent price of 'flexibility'.

There is a good deal else to go into a positive employment policy, seen as a central strand to welfare provision. Older workers have been encouraged to leave the labour market, and discouraged from returning to it, with very little official knowledge or concern about the long-term impact of early retirement on individual access to resources in old age (Walker, 1982). Poverty of the kind to which former wage-earners are often exposed when they come to the end of their working lives may well be spreading in consequence of these politically expedient measures and exhortations: we need to know whether and how far, as a matter of urgency, before the wheel is given any further turns in this direction. Moreover, when older workers and others are discouraged from staying on jobless in the labour market, the effect is to take them out of the politically sensitive 'headline count' of the unemployed. But they receive no recognition and little if any reward for that, or for the contribution they may make to the economy in 'making way for others' and in joining the conscript army supposed to be needed in 'the battle against inflation'. They certainly deserve the right, at the very least, to be counted; and official policy is in any case blind to its own consequences so long as there is no reasonably accurate, continuing and socially responsible count of all the non-employed – currently unregistered as well as registered. Finally – even in the absence of wider and larger benefit changes to compensate the jobless more adequately for the costs thrust upon them in consequence of economic 'restructuring' – one very specific injustice cries out for remedy: the fact that the younger and middle-aged unemployed are denied the long-term rate of Supplementary Benefit, no matter how long they are unemployed.

That may seem a small point on which to end this discussion of current policy and alternatives to it. It is one, nevertheless, that illustrates the way in which, since the turn of the 1980s, official thinking has turned to 'blaming the victims', even with effects in hard cash; and has stripped social policy of its former concern with employment. If people like our respondents – redundant, unemployed, discouraged, or now in work again but without the security of an effective right to regular work – are to have citizenship in a meaningful sense, development of a positive and wide-ranging employment policy is a matter of urgency.

TRENDS AND DIVISIONS OF POLITICAL OPINION

The history of political prognosis is littered with forecasts which events have proved false. Marxist prophecy, of course, is an example on the grand scale: over 100 years after the founding father's death, there has still been no successful revolution, socialist or working-class, anywhere in the capitalist heartlands of the West; nor are there signs of one coming round the corner. But there are other examples, and to other effect. In the 1950s and early 1960s, conventional wisdom across the board triumphantly proclaimed an end to 'ideology' in Western countries and an accelerating conversion of wage earners, through 'affluence', to middle-class political quiescence and social conformity. That prognosis foundered in the following years, when new turbulence came at the hands of students in many places, black people in the USA, others here and there; and, more tellingly, when industrial militancy in older forms re-emerged at the hands of organized labour. This was not revolution, for all the heady talk about it – glowing expectations on the left, nervous forebodings on the right. But the realities of the political and industrial stage into the 1970s looked little like the standard prophecies that had gone before. 'Affluence', still growing if less certainly than before, seemed to have launched not a spread of social complacency but a wave of rising expectations and an undercurrent of popular iconoclasm.

It took an evaporation of that 'affluence' – first at a creeping pace, then rapidly – to give the wheel another turn. We have discussed in Chapter 1 the shift in mood of 'establishment opinion' that gave free-market prescriptions for the economy a new lease of life in a curious coupling with entrenchment of state authority. With hindsight at least, this is not too hard to explain, seen as a shift in the framework of assumptions that policy-makers brought to the business of making policy. It is a good deal harder to explain why popular electoral opinion moved the same way – if less massively than suggested by the turnover in parliamentary representation, then enough to put into office in 1979 a government wedded to the formula of a 'smaller but stronger state'; and to keep it in office in 1983 and 1987. Few professional social commentators can honestly claim to have predicted, well before it began to loom large, that spread in popular appeal – acceptability at least – of what has come to be known as Thatcherism. From a vantage point around the turn of the 1970s, it could seem more plausible to anticipate that, if a steep rise in unemployment were to puncture the 'affluence' that had given the labour movement new confidence in its ability to pull muscle, the result might be to spread disaffection from the system of wage-earner dependence on capital, and to give industrial militancy a sharp edge of political radicalism that it had previously lacked. Certainly one of us committed that sort of scenario to paper then (Westergaard, 1970).

'Prophecy' in this vein failed in part because it took too little account of the effects of recession in both dividing labour and depleting its resources of organization and morale. Those effects – familiar enough from the inter-war years – have been written large in the history of British industrial relations since the late 1970s. The abortive strikes in steel (1980) and coal (1984–5) are among the most dramatic episodes in that history; a general re-jigging of the labour market, in forms whose outline we discussed in Chapter 1, has had still wider if less eye-catching impact. Our After Redundancy study has illustrated some of the same effects in miniature.

The workforce and their union branches did not resist the plant closure: in part, perhaps, because they had no tradition of sharp opposition to management; but, above all, because they could see nothing to do which might stop the closure, and because they were divided about the individual consequences of redundancy for them. Once they became redundant, moreover, they were scattered; their fortunes differed widely; and those who fared worst – jobless without even the dignity and pension rights of retirement – were cut off from one another and from much of their previous circle of contacts, by lack of money and lack of self-confidence. There was little in their experience to make for active political mobilization: they were 'privatized' far more out of work than they had ever been when in work. Nor was there much to mobilizing effect in the experience of those who fared better: whether they found work again, or retired, they could – and quite often explicitly did – count themselves lucky to have escaped the worst consequences of redundancy in a world that had lost its familiar security.

But lack of inducement and resources to 'go marching' is one thing; tuning inward sets of mind to listen more attentively to voices from the political right is another. Yet a number of our respondents seemed to have done just that. Most had long been stalwart supporters of the Labour Party up until the late 1970s. The special imprint of Sheffield's political tradition was visible in the voting records of nearly all the manual workers, and a majority even of the non-manual workers. Their experience of redundancy, and often of hardship thereafter, might have been expected at least to keep *their* Labour loyalties intact, even while popular opinion in the country at large was shifting away from the party. Not so: a quarter or more joined the national drift of disaffection from Labour from 1979 to 1982–3; and the defectors included some, though not quite as many, of the people hardest hit after redundancy.

This might seem to add weight to the common line of argument which holds that now, in the 1980s at last, Labour really is a spent force and political alignment in the old mould of class is definitively on the wane. So might the reasons, as they appeared from our respondents' expressions of opinion, why the party had lost some of its former hold on their support, for all the ostensible odds against slippage of that sort in their particular circumstances. For those reasons seemed to turn mostly on Labour's association with trade unions regarded as too aggressive, and too readily led into indiscriminate militancy by leaders and activists out of touch with ordinary members. Suspicion or hostility to industrial militancy spread beyond the ranks of party defectors in our group; and its targets included, perhaps especially, action outside union members' own workplaces – just the sort of action, in larger sympathy or solidarity between workers here and workers there, which must figure centrally in any direction of union organization to 'class' objectives; and just the sort of action, by the same token, which the government at the time was particularly concerned to stop.

Yet, taken in the round, the results of the survey do not lend themselves to this or any other sort of simple interpretation. Our respondents asserted distaste for militancy in one breath, the need for union vigilance against self-seeking employers in the next; opposition to 'secondary' action in general at one moment, support for it in particular circumstances at another; dismissal of union activism for 'political' ends in reply to some questions, endorsement of labour solidarity as a matter of common class interest in reply to others. They also voiced firm views to the effect that Britain is an unfair society; and, notably, they gave little shrift to alternative views from the 'new right' that the poor and the unemployed have themselves largely to blame for their misfortune.

One conclusion, which might be thought to follow, does not: that 'you can get people to say anything you like by manipulating the questions you ask'. Certainly our results underline the importance of question formulation and context. But where our use of different formulations and contexts brought out ostensible contradictions of opinion, closer examination showed that these commonly reflected genuine ambiguities and uncertainties of view. Two further points need emphasis in that connection. First, it was the manual workers among respondents who were most inclined to ambiguity of opinion; and that especially on the issues of industrial relations and union action which seem to have been politically central. Second, but close behind the first point, uncertainty of opinion points to a potential for change of opinion. Views had shifted, in political effect, to the right. They could do so further; but there was still plenty of class-oriented ballast that could pull them leftwards again.

There is fair sociological sense to the observation that manual workers especially were internally torn in their attitudes to industrial relations. For one thing, it is broadly in line with research on 'social imagery', going well back into the days of 'affluence' and labour self-confidence, which showed a distinctly two-faced or even 'fragmentary' character to class consciousness, and particularly so in the industrial working class (see e.g., within a considerable literature, Bulmer, 1975; Mann, 1970 and 1973; Roberts et al., 1977). This could be taken to reflect, in one way and another, an exposure of wage-earning people above all to conflicting influences on their perceptions of the world around them: influences from the conventions and assumptions of established society-as-it-is; influences from the organized labour movement and from the routines and necessities of everyday life in and out of work (see e.g. Parkin, 1971). The first set of influences on the whole prescribe conformity; the second set prescribe, not the converse, but a mixture – in itself ambiguous – of opposition to the status quo, pragmatic self-defence and equally pragmatic accommodation to things-as-they-are (see e.g. Westergaard and Resler, 1975). So, for example, even when the labour market was firm enough to give unions and shopfloor organization some real collective muscle, it was commonplace for workers to endorse *both* teamwork co-operation with management *and* rejection of the premiss of common interest required to sustain such co-operation (e.g. Goldthorpe et al., 1968–9). Our respondents, interviewed in recession, were no different on that score.

For another thing, the climate had changed by the 1980s, politically as well as economically. Public controversy over industrial relations, not least, had accelerated; and the voices in 'establishment opinion' that identified labour indiscipline as the prime cause of the 'British economic disease' had grown louder – from governments of either main party as well as from the media. When our interviewees castigated mindless militancy, not from their own direct experience but as something that had led other people's unions astray, they must be seen as responding to that shift in the balance of rival influences on their outlook. Moreover, labour militancy – 'mindless' or not – could with some reason be regarded as having rather little to show in the end for its efforts: neither any significant progressive redistribution of incomes, whether through the market or through 'corporatist' policies; nor prevention of a slide into recession.

Union activism had been pursued, by and large, in a sectionally divided fashion, which the eruptions of the 'winter of discontent' in 1978–9 made starkly plain. Such sectionalism in action may match the historical development of union organization in Britain; and, ironically, it matched the thread in our respondents' views that defined union action as properly concerned only with members' interests in their own immediate workplaces. But whatever its sources, sectionalism in any case undercut any part that union action might perhaps have had otherwise in holding off industrial decline; and recession, when it came full-blast, served to highlight the element of rhetorical gesturing associated with militancy. On all these counts, if with hindsight, there is cause to be found why the balance of influences on workers' perceptions of labour relations – even in a group such as the one of our survey – should have shifted against high profile union activism.

The point stands, however, that this shift involved no rejection of general principles of labour solidarity and common interest; no suspension of disbelief in establishment rhetoric of social unity across class divisions; no endorsement of recipes for economic competition that leave the devil to take the hindmost. On all these matters, manual workers especially held firmly to views left of centre and well in the labour movement's tradition. Issues of class were still high on their political agendas; and class was still a potent divider of opinions.

Here the prominent line of division was the old one between blue-collar and white-collar workers: between the labour movement's traditional core constituency and other people. Class was no less a potent divider of access to resources for livelihood. On the latter score, one line of division, in respect of shorter-run opportunities in a declining labour market after redundancy, sets the better credentialled apart from the poorer credentialled, regardless of colour of collar. But in longer-term perspective, another line of division loomed large: the divide between the world of wage-earning life, shopfloor or office; and the world of salaried careers, even in quite modest trajectories. There was, then, less simplicity to the shape of class shown up by the After Redundancy study than would satisfy the crudest uses of the concept, or would allow very easy extrapolation from economic divisions to political alignments. But the continuing reality of class fissure, as a basic matter of both economics and politics, was beyond all doubt from the evidence of the survey. The clarity of that conclusion stands out against the ambiguities of some others; and it tells strongly against those proclamations of the final eclipse of class that have once again swung into fashion.

Appendix 1   Response to the Survey

A Names and addresses available for inclusion in survey		Number
Total on list supplied by company		606
Not available for following reasons:		
Marked 'do not visit' (serious illness, etc)	12	
Address untraceable	12	
Address beyond reasonable travelling distance	12	
Used for pilot interviews to prepare/test schedule	16	
Named individual had died	21	73
Leaving as available for inclusion in survey		533

B Response	Number	%
Interviewed (including some interviews too in-complete, usually through illness or infirmity of respondent, for consistent inclusion in analysis)	378	71
Refused	53	10
No contact for following reasons:		
Address demolished, individual untraceable 17		
Other movers, untraceable 65		
Other no contact after repeated calls 20	102	19
Total available for inclusion (as in A)	533	100

C Alternative calculation of response rate		
Deduct from total 'available' shown in A:	21	
Demolished addresses as effectively out of scope	17	
Estimate of deceased among 'non-contacts'	4	
Leaving as effectively in scope: 533 − 21 = 512 (estimated)		
Interviewed	378	74%

Note See chapter 2 for discussion of the effects of shortfall in response.

Appendix 2   Summary of the Interview Schedule

The sequence is as in the full schedule, the numbers to the left being those of the questions (which were usually subdivided, with one or more consequential questions following a first question under each number). Factual questions are summarised only briefly, but the wording of most opinion questions is given in full. Pre-codes were provided for most questions; but these are indicated below only for opinion questions. Open-ended opinion questions are marked * (though questions asking 'why/why not' are not so marked, though they were almost always open-ended). Subheadings have been added to help the reader to get an overview. These did not appear in the original schedule; but transitions from one main subject to another were marked by appropriate explanatory comment from the interviewers.

Personal and household information

1–2   Personal details of respondent and other household members: age, sex, marital status, employment status, relationship to respondent.
3–4   Housing tenure.
5   Length of residence at address and in South Yorkshire; if moved to South Yorkshire, from where and why?
6–8   Length of employment with firm; immediately preceding employment if any; any previous experience of redundancy?
9–10   First, last and main jobs with the firm; duration of last job; any training relevant to main job, and where received; transfer to Forgings Division for voluntary redundancy under extension of scheme?
11   Full-time education, any qualifications then or since.

The redundancy

12–13   News of closure of Forgings Division: time, source and personal reactions.
14   Recollections of fellow-workers' reactions and of effects in 'uniting or dividing' workforce.
15–16   Own redundancy 'voluntary' or 'compulsory' (with probes)? Appli-

cation for transfer to other company under special scheme (why yes or no; outcome if yes)?

17–19   Other applications or search for new jobs around time of redundancy? Timing, means, and outcome.

20   Intentions/plans on redundancy and their outcome.

21   Worries if jobless on redundancy? Registration as unemployed? If so: when; reactions to registration and any interviews with officials. Other job search then?

22   Redundancy payment (if none, why?): total amount, in lump sum or instalments; inclusion of any repayment of pension contributions?

23–26   Redundancy payment: initial placement; plans for use and actual use; satisfaction/dissatisfaction with size of sum; any regrets/second thoughts about actual use?

27–28   Any pension from firm, now or in future? If now, from what time and how much?

Voting and membership of organizations

29–33   Vote at general elections of 1979 and 1983; 'usual' vote if any before 1979; vote intention if general election 'tomorrow'; reasons for any changes, for vote intention 'tomorrow', for not voting.

34   *What are most and next most important issues at general election 'tomorrow'; which party has 'the best policies' on each of these issues?

35   Present or past membership of any political party; activity in, and duration of, membership; if withdrawn, why?

36–38   Membership of other organizations (tenants'/residents' associations, pressure groups/campaigns, social/working men's clubs) and church attendance.

39–40   Membership and activity in a trade union, when with firm and now; payment/non-payment of political levy; changes and reasons why (or why not union member); eligibility for membership if retired or unemployed.

Experience since redundancy

41   Any time when respondent felt 'things had become particularly difficult for you'? If yes: when, over what ('worst problem'), recurrence and frequency of worries since then.

42   Detailed record of employment, unemployment, etc. since redundancy: time and duration of each job or status; reasons for each change; occupation and industry for each job; 'odd jobs'; receipt of benefits and/or use of savings in each period; employment or non-employment of spouse in each period. (The record was compiled by working backwards in time from the respondent's current situation to the time of redundancy.)

43–48   Retired respondents only. Time of retirement (at or before 60–5);

reasons, preferences and expectations at time; any previous thoughts
about retirement; comparison of feelings now with expectations then;
any 'particular problems', and which most difficult; interest in paid
work again if it were available – with former firm or elsewhere, on
what terms; anything missed about former job; expectations and experience in respect of money.

49   All respondents again. Views on age of retirement. Should people be
'allowed to carry on working for as long as they are able . . .'? Is it better
'to work full-time up to retirement age or to reduce gradually the hours
worked'? Should the 60–5 difference in normal retirement age
between men and women be changed or stay? Reasons for views.

50–51   Changes in recreation and expenditure since redundancy.

Views of former firm (first part)

52   *Views on conditions of work: in general, sources of particular satis-
faction/dissatisfaction.

Views on 'certain aspects of work and society in Britain today'

53   *How far agree/disagree with view 'that the main conflicts in Britain
today are between those who own or direct industry and the workforce
employed by them'.
Agree/disagree (five-point scale from strong agreement to strong disagreement) with following statements:

(a)   Industry is like a football team, employers and workers are on the
same side and success can only come if they co-operate.

(b)   Working-class people have got to stand together and stick up for
one another.

(c)   Good employees are loyal to their firms even if it means putting
themselves out quite a bit.

(d)   Teamwork in industry is usually impossible because in the end
employers and workers are on opposite sides.

(e)   Most managers have the welfare of their workers at heart.

(f)   It's no use relying on other workers to help you, you've got to
stand up for yourself and get things done on your own.

(g)   Obedience to management and a respect for their authority are
the most important characteristics of a good worker.

(h)   Given half a chance most managements will try and put one over
on their workforces.

(i)   Workers in private sector steel industry stand to gain more by co-
operating with their managements than by taking action with
steel workers in the public sector.

54   Agree/disagree (on five-point scale) with (a) to (g) below:

(a)   If a union I was a member of called on me to strike I'd do so even
if I disagreed with the decision.

(b) Most major conflicts in industry are caused by agitators or extremists.

(c) Unions should not be allowed to stop people working when they want to.

(d) If you go on strike it should only be about matters that affect you directly in your own workplace.

(e) Most strikes result from the basic conflict of aims and interests between employers and labour.

(f) There should be a law to stop people joining pickets outside places where they don't work themselves.

(g) A union member should be prepared to strike in support of other workers even if they don't work in the same place.

(h) 'Recently various unions have been asking their members to take action, including strikes, to support the health workers' pay claim. If your union (had) asked you to strike for a day to support them would you do (have done) so?' (Yes/No/Don't know.)

*(i) 'Finally, what do you think are the *main* causes of strikes in Britain today?'

Views of former firm (resumed) and related matters

55–56 Anything 'special or distinctive' about working for firm? *Particular advantages/disadvantages? Would respondent have accepted offer of same job 'for a little more money' at another firm? Any effects of take-over by multi-national corporation on respondent's working life?

57 'In the past many firms and factories were run directly by the people or families who owned them and lived in the same area. In contrast today most factories are run by large companies with many share-holders and from a central place such as London. Overall. . .a good thing or a bad thing?' Why?

58–59 Respondents who were union members at the time of redundancy, *only. General satisfaction/dissatisfaction with union; satisfaction/ dissatisfaction with union's handling of redundancies; should it have done something more/else? and did it do something it shouldn't have done? Respondent's view of main aims of a good union; was own union at firm good or not in those terms?

Views on 'some matters to do with the managing of firms and factories'

60 *View of proposition (a) 'that managers know what's best for a firm and because of this the employees should do exactly what they're told'. Agree/disagree (five-point scale) with following:

(b) You've got to pay top managers a lot more than others. It's the only way to get the right people for the jobs.

(c) People in top management should not be paid as much as they are. They don't deserve to be paid a lot more than the other people in the workforce.

(d)   Giving workers more say in running a firm would only make things worse.

(e)   Unions only get in the way of good relations in industry.

(f)   When I was at [the firm] the management there treated the employees like numbers rather than as people.

(g)   If I've got a problem at work I'd rather talk it out with the boss myself than rely on the union to deal with it for me.

(h)   If it wasn't for unions bosses could do whatever they wanted with their workers, and most of them would.

(i)   When I was at [the firm] I had a great deal of respect for the top management there.

(k)   A good manager is one who is prepared to work on the shop floor from time to time.

Views on unemployment

61   *Views of main reason for current unemployment in general and for redundancies at firm; of role if any of multi-national take-over in redundancies; and who should have main responsibility for finding work for people made redundant (latter pre-coded: employer, self, government, local council, other).

62   *Views of (a) priority government should give to reducing unemployment (running prompt, from 'not at all important' to 'the most important') and (b) of government's success in reducing unemployment; whether companies 'only start making people redundant as a last resort';

      – and on following statements (agree/disagree on five-point scale).

(c)   Redundancies are the result of people pricing themselves out of a job through pay claims.

(d)   If you really want a job you can always find one, even if it means earning a little less than before.

(e)   The only way to tackle unemployment is for the workers to take over control of industry for themselves.

(f)   There's nothing the government can do to get people back to work that it isn't doing already. It's just a matter of waiting for things to pick up in the economy.

(g)   Most redundancies are the result of mistakes by managers.

(h)   If management ask for voluntary redundancies people in that firm ought to take them. (Why/why not?)

63   Views on how effective the following might be in reducing unemployment (five-point scale from 'not at all effective' to 'very effective').

(a)   Compulsory retirement at an earlier age than now.

(b) The government taking over the biggest companies and banks and investing their money for them.

(c) Cutting unemployment benefits.

(d) Nationalizing North Sea oil and using the money to build up British industry.

(e) Holding down wages.

(f) A big programme of public spending by the government on things such as railways, roads and housing.

(g) Job sharing between people so that two people work part-time to do a job that would normally be done by one person working full-time, and share the wages or salary between them.

(h) Import controls, that is setting limits to the amount of goods that can be brought into this country from abroad to be sold here.

(i) Making it easier for people to move around the country to find jobs.

(j) Stopping people and companies investing their money abroad.

(k) More training schemes for young people, such as the Youth Opportunities Programme (YOP).

(l) Leaving the Common Market.

(m) More retraining schemes for older workers such as TOPS.

(n) Giving employees a much greater say in the way companies are run.

(o) Compulsory national service for school-leavers and other young people.

(p) Discouraging the employment of married women.

(q) Sending recent immigrants to Britain back to their countries of origin.

(r) Making money available to fund workers' co-operatives.

(Which of these *most* effective?)

Views on other political and social questions (first part)

64 List on card of 'people who are active in public life today': which if any is closest in policies or ideas to respondent's; and to which if any does respondent feel most opposed? Why?

65 Agree/disagree with view 'that it doesn't really matter who you vote for, in the end things go on much the same no matter which party is in power'. Why?

Agree/disagree (five-point scale) with the following statements:

(a) In Britain today wealth is concentrated in the hands of too few people.

(b) In Britain today anyone with brains and initiative can get to the top regardless of who their father was.

(c) People from wealthy families who have been to public schools have too much influence and power in Britain today.

(d) The poor have only themselves to blame for their problems.

(e)   Politicians are all the same. No matter which party they belong to they're only interested in themselves and not in people like you or me.

(f)   The majority of the unemployed are people who are too lazy to look for work.

(g)   Trade unions don't have enough power. It's time they started to take a tougher stand against the employers and the government.

(h)   The main reason for unemployment at the minute is that there are too many immigrants in the country.

(i)   What Britain needs now is a strong leader who can unite the people in a common effort.

(j)   Parliamentary action by the TUC and the Labour Party has failed, it's now time to take more direct measures to stop unemployment.

(k)   People like me have little say in how the country is run.

This was followed by the question:

*What do you understand by the phrase 'people like me'?

66   *Respondent's knowledge and views about City Council's and local labour movement's activities in respect of unemployment.

Experience of unemployment

67   *Respondents with any period of registered unemployment since redundancy. Feelings about experience; worst things and any benefits of experience; any different from expectations?

68–70 Currently unemployed only. Assessment of chances of finding a job; importance of finding a job; job applications during current period of unemployment – number, whether as many now as at start of period, kinds of job applied for most recently; any offers turned down and why?

71   All respondents. Feelings at any time during past few weeks of: pleasure at accomplishing something; restlessness; 'things going your way'; boredom; pride on being complimented for something done; depression or being 'very unhappy'; excitement or interest in something; loneliness or remoteness from other people; being 'on top of the world'; very upset after criticism.

Economic activity 'on the side'

(Interviewers instructed to stress confidentiality of information)

72   Is respondent 'ever able to get any odd jobs or occasional work, including any work you may do for friends or here at home (including work such as cleaning, baby-sitting or running a mail order catalogue)'? If yes: what sort(s); which most often in past year; when last; as self-employed or working for someone; starting before or after redundancy;

how found; purpose – 'to bring in a little extra money' or for other reasons?

73　　Any 'occasional income from selling things you may make or grow yourself, such as craftwork or garden or allotment produce'? If yes: what; to whom sold (friends or more widely); carry on making/growing 'even if you weren't selling some of them from time to time'?

Work commitment

74　　Agree/disagree (five-point scale) with following statements concerning *paid* work, 'without limiting yourself to your present circumstances':
　　(a)　Even if I won a great deal of money on the pools, I'd carry on working.
　　(b)　Work is necessary but rarely enjoyable.
　　(c)　I (would) hate being on the dole.
　　(d)　Having a job is very important to me.
　　(e)　I would very soon get bored if I did not go out to work.
　　(f)　I regard time spent at work as time taken away from that available to do the things I *want* to do.
　　(g)　The most important things that have happened to me involved work.
　　(h)　If unemployment benefit were really high I would still prefer to work.
　　(i)　Having a job is (was) only important to me because it brings (brought) in money.
　　(j)　Someone without a job can lose the respect of those around them.
　　(k)　The main reason I have worked in the past has been for the company of the people I've worked with.
　　(l)　Any feelings I've had in the past of achieving something worthwhile have usually come from things I've done at work.
　　Followed by question about sources of friendship outside immediate family: 'nearly all' to 'hardly any at all' through work?

Views on other political and social questions (resumed)

75　　Agree/disagree (five-point scale) with following statements about what is 'fair or unfair about some common events or situations in everyday life':
　　(a)　It's fair that rich people who can pay their fines can stay out of gaol while poor people may have to go to gaol for the same crime.
　　(b)　It's unfair that people in some occupations get much more respect from others than people in other occupations.
　　(c)　Landlords should be allowed to turn away prospective tenants even if they do it for racial reasons.

(d)   It would be more fair if people in Britain were paid by how much they needed to live decently rather than by the jobs they do.

(e)   It would be a good thing if Parliament decided to distribute all the money in Britain equally among the population.

*Followed by: 'Is there anything about the state of Britain today that you think is particularly unfair?' (If yes, what?)

Current income of respondent and spouse

(Interviewers instructed to stress confidentiality of information)

76–83   Comprehensive record of income (gross and net) from all sources including regular and occasional paid work, with overtime, bonuses and commissions; state benefits (in detail and with prompting about different types); rent; interest; other sources outside household; and members of household other than respondent and spouse.

84   Assessment of household income now compared with when at work in firm: better off, about same, or worse off? Reasons for any change.

Knowledge of former colleagues

85   Does respondent think own experience after redundancy 'reasonably typical'? Does he/she know how others have done; and in how many cases?

References

Allen, S., Waton, A., Purcell, K., and Wood, S., 1986 (eds): *The Experience of Unemployment*. Macmillan.

Bakke, E.W. 1933: *The Unemployed Man*. Nisbet.

Barron, R.D. and Norris, G.M., 1978: Sexual divisions in the dual labour market. In Barker D. and Allen S. (eds), *Dependence and Exploitation in Work and Marriage*. Longman.

Bauman, Z., 1982: *Memories of Class: the Pre-History and After-Life of Class*. Routledge and Kegan Paul.

Beattie, G., 1986: *Steel City Survivors*. Allen and Unwin.

Bonney, N. 1987–8: Gender, household and social class. *British Journal of Sociology*, forthcoming.

Bosanquet, N., 1987: *Public Policy Towards the 55–65 Age Group*. Centre for Public Policy.

Bradburn, N.M., 1969: *The Structure of Psychological Well-Being*. Aldine, Chicago.

Brittan, S., 1977: *The Economic Contradictions of Democracy*. Temple Smith.

Brittan, S., 1978: Inflation and democracy. In Hirsch, F. and Goldthorpe, J.H. (eds), *The Political Economy of Inflation*. Martin Robertson.

Bruche, G. and Casey, B., 1982: *Work or Retirement*. Berlin International Institute of Management.

Bulmer, M., 1975 (ed.): *Working Class Images of Society*. Routledge and Kegan Paul (with Social Science Research Council).

Byrne, D., 1987: Rich and poor: the growing divide. In Walker, A., and Walker, C., 1987.

Bytheway, B., 1987: Redundancy and the older worker. In Lee, R.M., 1987, (ed.).

Callender, C., 1987: Women and the redundancy process: a case study. In Lee, R.M., 1987, (ed.).

Colledge, M. and Bartholomew, R., 1980: *A Study of the Long-Term Unemployed*. Manpower Services Commission. (Summarized in *Employment Gazette*, January 1980, pp. 9–12.)

Corrigan, P., Kowarzik, U., Taylor, D., Townsend, P. and Convery, P., 1987: *Hidden Unemployment: the True Measure of Unemployment in London* (Survey of

Londoners' Living Standards report no. 2). Unemployment Unit.

Craig, C. et al., 1985: Economic, social and political factors in the operation of the labour market. In Roberts, B. et al., 1985 (eds).

Cribier, F., 1981: Changing retirement patterns of the seventies: the example of a generation of Parisian salaried workers. *Ageing and Society*, 1.

Crompton, R. and Mann, M., 1986 (eds): *Gender and Stratification*. Polity Press.

Crona, G., 1981: Partial retirement in Sweden. Paper presented to the XII International Congress of Gerontology, Hamburg, 12–17 July.

Crouch, C., 1977: *Class Conflict and the Industrial Relations Crisis: Compromise and Corporatism in the Policies of the British State*. Heinemann.

Curran, J., 1984 (ed.): *The Future of the Left*. Polity Press and New Socialist.

Curtice, J., 1986: Political partisanship. In Jowell, R., Witherspoon, S. and Brook, L. (eds), *British Social Attitudes: the 1986 Report*. Gower and Social and Community Planning Research.

Daniel, W.W., 1972: *Whatever Happened to the Workers in Woolwich?* Political and Economic Planning.

Daniel, W.W., 1974: *National Survey of the Unemployed*. Political and Economic Planning.

Daniel, W.W. 1981: *The Unemployed Flow*. Policy Studies Institute.

Deacon, A., 1981: Unemployment and politics in Britain since 1945. In Showler, B., and Sinfield, A., 1981 (eds).

Department of Employment, 1983: *Employment Gazette*, 91, (November).

Department of Employment, 1985: *Employment: The Challenge for the Nation*. Cmnd 9474, HMSO.

Department of Health and Social Security, 1981: *Growing Older*. Cmnd 8173, HMSO.

Dex, S. and Phillipson, C., 1986: Social policy and the older worker. In Phillipson, C., and Walker, A., 1986 (eds).

Dunleavy, P. and Husbands, C.T., 1985: *British Democracy at the Crossroads: Voting and Party Competition in the 1980s*. Allen and Unwin.

Fagin, L. and Little, M., 1984: *The Forsaken Families*. Penguin.

Fevre, R., 1987: Redundancy and the labour market: the role of 'readaptation benefits'. In Lee, R.M., 1987 (ed.).

Fraser, C., Marsh, C. and Jobling, R., 1985: Political responses to unemployment. In Roberts, B. et al., 1985 (eds).

Friedmann, E.A. and Orbach, H.L., 1974: Adjustment to retirement. In Arieti, S. (ed.), *American Handbook of Psychiatry*, vol. 1. New York, Basic Books.

Fryer, D., and Ullah, P., 1986 (eds): *The Experience of Unemployment*. Open University Press.

Gamble, A., 1979: The free economy and the strong state. In Miliband, R. and Saville, J. (eds): *The Socialist Register 1979*. Merlin Press.

Gamble, A., 1981: *Britain in Decline: Economic Policy, Political Strategy and the British State*. Macmillan.

Gershuny, J.I., and Pahl, R.E., 1979: Work outside employment, *New Universities Quarterly*, 34 (1).

Goffman, E., 1952: On cooling the mark out: some aspects of adaptation to failure, *Psychiatry*, 15.

Goldthorpe, J.H., with Llewellyn, C. and Payne, C., 1980: *Social Mobility and Class Structure in Modern Britain*. Clarendon Press.

Goldthorpe, J.H., 1983: Women and class analysis. *Sociology*, 17; followed by debate with contributions from M. Stanworth, A. Heath and N. Britten, R. Eriksson, and a rejoinder by Goldthorpe, *Sociology*, 18 (1984).

Goldthorpe, J.H., 1985: The end of convergence: corporatist and dualist tendencies in modern western societies. In Roberts, B. et al., 1985 (eds).

Goldthorpe, J.H., and Hope, K., 1974: *The social grading of occupations*. Oxford University Press.

Goldthorpe, J.H., Lockwood, D., Bechhofer, F. and Platt, J., 1968–9: *The Affluent Worker*. Cambridge University Press.

Gorz, A., 1982: *Farewell to the Working Class: an Essay on Post-Industrial Socialism*. Pluto Press.

Halfpenny, P.J., Laite, A.J., and Noble, I.A., 1985: *The Blackburn and Darwen Labour Market*. Centre for Applied Social Research, University of Manchester.

Halsey, A.H., 1978: *Change in British Society*. Oxford University Press.

Halsey, A.H., Heath, A.F. and Ridge, J.M., 1980: *Origins and Destinations: Family, Class and Education in Modern Britain*. Clarendon Press.

Harris, C.C., 1987: Redundancy and class analysis. In Lee, R.M., 1987 (ed.).

Harris, C.C., Lee, R.M. and Morris, L.D., 1985: Redundancy in steel: labour market behaviour, local social networks and domestic organisation. In Roberts, B. et al., 1985 (eds).

Hartley, J., Kelly, J. and Nicholson, N., 1983: *Steel Strike: a Case Study in Industrial Relations*. Batsford.

Haveman, R.H. and Wolfe, B.L., 1981: *Have Disability Transfers Caused the Decline in Older Male Labour Force Participation?* Institute for Research on Poverty, University of Wisconsin-Madison.

Heath, A., 1986: Do people have consistent attitudes? In Jowell, R., Witherspoon, S. and Brook, L. (eds), *British Social Attitudes: the 1986 Report*. Gower and Social and Community Planning Research.

Heath, A., Jowell, R. and Curtice, J., 1985: *How Britain Votes*. Pergamon Press.

Heidbreder, E.M., 1972: Factors in retirement adjustment: white collar/blue collar experience. *Industrial Gerontology*, 12.

Hill, M.J., Harrison, R.M., Sargeant, A.V. and Talbot, V., 1973: *Men Out of Work*. Cambridge University Press.

Hills, J., 1987: What happened to spending on the welfare state? In Walker, A., and Walker, C., 1987 (eds).

Himmelweit, H., Humphreys, P. and Jaeger, M., 1985: *How Voters Decide*. Open University Press.

Hobsbawm, E.J. et al., 1981: *The Forward March of Labour Halted*. Verso.

House of Commons Select Committee on Social Services, 1982: *Age of Retirement*. HC 26, HMSO.

House of Lords Select Committee on Unemployment, 1982: *Volume 1: Report.* HL 142, HMSO.

Jackson, P.R., Stafford, E.M., Banks, M.H., and Warr, P.B., 1983: Unemployment and psychological distress in young people: the moderating role of employment commitment. *Journal of Applied Psychology*, 54.

Jahoda, M. et al., 1972: *Marienthal: The Sociography of an Unemployed Community.* London.

Jenkins, M.C. and Miller, S.M., 1987: The next American welfare state. In Evers, A., Nowotny, H. and Wintersberger, H. (eds), *The Changing Face of Welfare.* Gower.

Jenkins, R., 1985: Black workers in the labour market: the price of recession. In Roberts, B. et al., 1985 (eds).

Jolly, J., Creigh, S. and Mignay, A., 1980: *Age as a Factor in Employment.* Department of Employment.

Jowell, R., Witherspoon, S. and Brook, L., 1986 (eds): *British Social Attitudes: the 1986 Report.* Gower and Social and Community Planning Research.

Laczko, F., 1987: Older workers, unemployment, and the discouraged worker effect. In Di Gregorio, S. (ed.): *Social Geronotology: New Directions.* Croom Helm.

Laite, A.J. and Noble, I.A., 1986: Caring and sharing: factors affecting the domestic division of labour. In Fryer, D., and Ullah, P., 1986 (eds).

Lane, T. and Roberts, K., 1971: *Strike at Pilkington's.* Fontana.

Lee, R.M. 1984: Dejeopardizing techniques for asking questions on surveys: applications from the study of the 'black' economy. Paper from Department of Sociology and Anthropology, University of Swansea.

Lee, R.M., 1987: 'Introduction', in Lee, R.M. 1987 (ed.).

Lee, R.M., 1987 (ed.): *Redundancy, Layoffs and Plant Closures: their Character, Causes and Consequences.* Croom Helm.

Lockwood, D., 1966: Sources of variation in working class images of society. *Sociological Review*, 14.

Lockwood, D., 1981: The weakest link in the chain? Some comments on the Marxist theory of action. *Research in the Sociology of Work*, 1.

Makeham, P. and Margan, P., 1980: *Evaluation of the Job Release Scheme.* Department of Employment.

Mann, M., 1970: The social cohesion of liberal democracy. *American Sociological Review*, 35.

Mann, M., 1973: *Consciousness and Action among the Western Working Class.* Macmillan.

Marsden, D., 1982: *Workless: an Exploration of the Social Contract between Society and the Worker.* Croom Helm.

Marshall, T.H., 1950: Citizenship and social class. In Marshall, T.H., 1950: *Citizenship and Social Class and other essays.* Cambridge University Press.

Martin, R. and Fryer, R.H., 1973: *Redundancy and Paternalist Capitalism.* London.

McGoldrick, A. and Cooper, C., 1980: Voluntary early retirement – taking the decision. *Employment Gazette*, August 1980.

McKee, L. and Bell, C., 1985: Marital and family relations in times of male unemployment. In Roberts, B. et al., 1985 (eds).

Mckennell, A.C., 1977: Attitude scale construction. In O'Muircheartaigh, C.A., and Payne, C. (eds): *The Analysis of Survey Data*. Wiley.

Middlemas, K., 1979: *Politics in Industrial Society: the Experience of the British System since 1911*. Andre Deutsch.

Morris, L.D., 1985: Re-negotiation of the domestic division of labour in the context of male redundancy. In Roberts, B. et al., 1985 (eds).

Moylan, S., Millar, J. and Davies, R., 1984: *For Richer, for Poorer? DHSS Cohort Study of Unemployed Men*. Department of Health and Social Security, Research Report No. 11. HMSO.

Mukherjee, S., 1973: *Through No Fault of Their Own*. Macdonald/Political and Economic Planning.

Newby, H., 1977: *The Deferential Worker*. Penguin.

Newby, H., Vogler, C., Rose, D. and Marshall, G., 1985: From class structure to class action: British working class politics in the 1980s. In Roberts, B. et al., 1985 (eds).

Nichols, T., 1986: *The British Worker Question: a New Look at Workers and Productivity in Manufacturing*. Routledge and Kegan Paul.

Noble, I.A., 1987: Unemployment after redundancy and political attitudes: some empirical evidence. In Lee, R.M., 1984.

Noble, I.A., Thomas, C.J., Walker, A., and Westergaard, J.H., *Economic Experiences Project Working Paper 1: Households and employment*. Department of Sociological Studies, University of Sheffield.

Noble, I., Walker, A., and Westergaard, J.H., 1984: Paying the price of the shake-out. *The Guardian*, 20 June 1984.

Norris, G., 1978: Unemployment, subemployment and personal characteristics. *Sociological Review*, 26, pp. 89–103, 327–47.

Office of Population Censuses and Surveys, 1982: *Labour Force Survey 1979*. HMSO.

Office of Population Censuses and Surveys, 1983: *General Household Survey 1981*. HMSO.

Panitch, L., 1980: Recent theorisations of corporatism. *British Journal of Sociology*, 31.

Panitch, L., 1981: The limits of corporatism. *New Left Review*, no. 125.

Pahl, R.E., 1980: Employment, work and the domestic division of labour. *International Journal of Urban and Regional Research*, 4 (1).

Pahl, R.E., 1984: *Divisions of Labour*. Blackwell.

Pahl, R.E. and Wallace, C., 1984: Household work strategies in economic recession. In Redclift, N. and Mingione, E. (eds): *Beyond Employment: Household, Gender and Subsistence*. Blackwell.

Pahl, R.E. and Wallace, C.D., 1986: Polarisation, unemployment and all forms of work. In Allen, S. et al., 1986 (eds).

Parker, S., 1980: *Older Workers and Retirement*. HMSO.

Parker, S., 1982: *Work and Retirement*. Allen & Unwin.

Parkin, F., 1971: *Class Inequality and Political Order*. MacGibbon and Kee.

Parkin, F., 1979: *Marxism and Class Theory: a Bourgeois Critique.* Tavistock Publications.

Payne, G., 1987: *Employment and Opportunity.* Macmillan. (A companion volume to Payne, G., 1987: *Mobility and Change in Modern Society.*)

Payne, R. et al., 1983: Social class and the experience of unemployment. *SAPU Memo* 549, Social and Applied Psychology Unit, University of Sheffield.

Payne, R.L., 1987: A longitudinal study of the psychological well-being of unemployed men and the mediating effect of neuroticism. *Human Factors*, 1987.

Phillipson, C., 1983: *Capitalism and the Construction of Old Age.* Macmillan.

Phillipson, C. and Walker, A. 1986 (eds): *Ageing and Social Policy.* Gower.

Pollard, S., 1959: *A History of Labour in Sheffield.* Liverpool University Press.

Pollard, S. and Holmes, C., 1976 (eds): *Essays in the Economic and Social History of South Yorkshire.* South Yorkshire County Council.

Roberts, B., Finnegan, R. and Gallie, D., 1985 (eds): *New Approaches to Economic Life.* Manchester University Press.

Roberts, K., Cook., F.G., Clark, S.C. and Semeonoff, E., 1977: *The Fragmentary Class Structure.* Heinemann.

Sarlvik, B. and Crewe, I., 1983: *Decade of Dealignment: The Conservative Victory of 1979 and Electoral Trends in the 1970s.* Cambridge University Press.

Schwab, K., 1976: Early labour-force withdrawal of men: participants and non-participants aged 58–63. In Irelan L.M. et al., *Almost 65: Baseline Data from the Retirement History Study.* DHEW. Washington D.C.

Showler, B., 1981: Political economy and unemployment. In Showler, B., and Sinfield, A., 1981 (eds).

Showler, B. and Sinfield, A., 1981 (eds): *The Workless State: Studies in Unemployment.* Martin Robertson.

Sinfield, A., 1968: *The Long-Term Unemployed.* Paris, OECD.

Sinfield, A., 1980: The blunt facts of unemployment. *New Universities Quarterly*, Winter 1980.

Sinfield, A., 1981a: *What Unemployment Means.* Martin Robertson.

Sinfield, A., 1981b: Unemployment in an unequal society. In Showler, B., and Sinfield, A., 1981 (eds).

Smith, D., 1982: *Conflict and Compromise. Class Formation in English Society 1830–1914: a Comparative Study of Birmingham and Sheffield.* Routledge and Kegan Paul.

Sorrentino, C., 1981: Unemployment in international perspective. In Showler, B., and Sinfield, A., 1981 (eds).

Stafford, E.M., Jackson, P.R., and Banks, M.H., 1980: Employment, work involvement and mental health in less qualified young people. *Journal of Occupational Psychology*, 53.

Taylor, D., 1985: Unemployment, White Papers and Budgets. *Unemployment Bulletin*, 16.

Taylor, D., 1987: Living with unemployment. In Walker, A. and Walker, C., 1987 (eds).

Townsend, P., 1979: *Poverty in the United Kingdom*. Allen Lane and Penguin Books.

Tracy, M., 1979: *Retirement Age Practices in Ten Industrial Societies, 1960–1976*. Geneva, ISSA.

Unemployment Unit, 1986: Creative counting. *Unemployment Bulletin*, 20.

Urry, J., 1985: The class structure. In Coates, D., Johnston, G. and Bush, R. (eds): *A Socialist Anatomy of Britain*. Polity Press.

Verba, S. and Scholozman, K.L., 1979: *Injury to Insult*. Harvard University Press.

Walker, A., 1980: The social creation of poverty and dependency in old age. *Journal of Social Policy*, 9.

Walker, A., 1981a: South Yorkshire: the economic and social impact of unemployment. In Crick, B. (ed.), *Unemployment*. Methuen.

Walker, A., 1981b: Towards a political economy of old age. *Ageing and Society*, 1.

Walker, A., 1982a: *Unqualified and Underemployed*. Macmillan.

Walker, A., 1982b: The social consequences of early retirement. *Political Quarterly*, 53.

Walker, A., 1985a: Early retirement: release or refuge from the labour market? *Quarterly Journal of Social Affairs*, 1.

Walker, A., 1985b: Policies for sharing the job shortage: reducing or redistributing unemployment? In Klein, R. and O'Higgins, M. (eds): *The Future of Welfare*. Blackwell.

Walker, A., and Laczko, F., 1982: Early retirement and flexible retirement. In Social Services Committee, *Age of Retirement*. HC 26–II, HMSO.

Walker, A., Noble, I. and Westergaard, J.H., 1985: From secure employment to labour market insecurity: the impact of redundancy on older workers in the steel industry. In Roberts, B. et al., 1985 (eds).

Walker, A. and Walker, C., 1987 (eds): *The Growing Divide: a Social Audit 1979–1987*. Child Poverty Action Group.

Warr, P.B., 1978: A study of psychological well-being. *British Journal of Psychology*, 69.

Warr, P., 1983: Economic recession and mental health. *SAPU Memo 609*, Social and Applied Psychology Unit, University of Sheffield.

Warr, P., 1985: Twelve questions about unemployment and health. In Roberts, B. et al., 1985 (eds).

Warr, P., 1987a: *Work, Unemployment and Mental Health*. Oxford University Press.

Warr, P., 1987b: This unhappy breed. *New Society*, 10th July 1987.

Warr, P., Cook, J. and Wall, T., 1979: Scales for the measurement of some work attitudes and aspects of psychological well-being. *Journal of Occupational Psychology*, 52.

Warr, P., and Jackson, P.R., 1983: Men without jobs: some correlates of age and length of unemployment. *SAPU Memo 593*, Social and Applied Psychology Unit, University of Sheffield.

Westergaard, J.H., 1970: The rediscovery of the cash nexus? In Miliband, R. and Saville, J., (eds): *The Socialist Register 1970*. Merlin Press.

Westergaard, J.H., 1977: Class, inequality and corporatism. In Hunt, A. (ed.): *Class and Class Structure*. Lawrence and Wishart.

Westergaard, J.H., 1983: Income, wealth and the welfare state. In Coates, D. and Johnson, G. (eds): *Socialist Arguments*. Martin Robertson.

Westergaard, J.H., Noble, I. and Walker, A., 1987: After redundancy: economic experience and political outlook among former steel employees in Sheffield. In Rose, D. (ed.): *Social Stratification and Economic Decline*. Hutchinson.

Westergaard, J.H., and Resler, H., 1975: *Class in a Capitalist Society*. Heinemann (Penguin Books, 1976).

White, M., 1983: *Long-term Unemployment and Labour Markets*. Policy Studies Institute.

Wiener, M.J., 1981: *English Culture and the Decline of the Industrial Spirit*. Cambridge University Press.

Winkler, J.T., 1975: Law, state and economy: the Industry Act 1975 in context. *British Journal of Law and Society*. Winter 1975.

Winkler, J.T., 1976: Corporatism. *European Journal of Sociology*, 17.

Winkler, J.T., 1977: The corporate economy. In Scase, R. (ed.): *Industrial Society: Class, Cleavage and Control*. Allen and Unwin.

Wood, D., 1982: *The DHSS Cohort Study of Unemployed Men*. Department of Health and Social Security.

Wood, S., 1980: Managerial reactions to job redundancy through early retirement. *Sociological Review*, 28.

Index

age differences in experience and
    reactions
  first reactions, 40, 41
  political and social attitudes, 137,
    163
  redundancy payments, 42–4, 48
  withdrawal from labour market,
    39–40, 59–68, 105–12, 183
  work search and re-employment,
    59–60, 62–3, 67–8, 85–6
  see also retirement
Alliance, Liberals and Social
    Democrats, 24, 128, 131, 133,
    136, 140

'black economy', 14–15, 61, 89–90

careers, as distinct from jobs, 23, 70,
    80, 174, 184
class, general features
  changes and continuities of pattern,
    18–25, 68–75, 79–80, 172–5,
    184
  consciousness, 23–5, 35–6, 145–6,
    150–68, 180–4
  electoral and political divisions, 24–
    5, 130–9, 145–6
  and labour market insecurity, 18–
    23, 68–75, 79–80, 103, 172–4,
    177, 179
class differences in experience and
    reactions
  first reactions, 32–3, 35–6
  incomes at interview, 76–80, 112–
    13, 174
  pensions, 69–70, 112–14, 174
  political and social attitudes, 130–
    9, 145–6, 148–68, 182–4
  redundancy payments, 42–5, 47–8,
    101–2, 174
  withdrawal from labour market, 50,
    67–8, 113–14, 120, 126
  work search and re-employment,
    44–5, 51–3, 55–6, 63–75, 85–
    6, 171–5
colour prejudice *see* 'immigration'
Conservative Party
  electoral support, 24, 128, 131, 133
  governments and policies, 10–13,
    21–2, 24, 139–40, 144, 150,
    175–7
corporatism, 9–12, 24

'deference', 162–3
'de-industrialization', 21, 26, 175–6
downgrading on re-employment, 69,
    79, 87–8, 173–4

early retirement *see* retirement
elections and electoral support
  among respondents, 130–46, 181–2
  in Sheffield, 28, 129, 131
  in UK, 24–5, 128–9, 131

employment *see* 'black economy',
    downgrading on re-employment,
    labour market, unemployment,
    work

health, as influence on withdrawal
    from labour market, 112, 179
holidays on redundancy, 49, 102
housing tenure, 45, 138–9

'immigration', attitudes to, 141–2,
    165–8
incomes at interview, 75–80
    see also class differences,
    retirement, unemployment
industrial relations *see* 'deference',
    labour market, strikes, trade
    unions

labour market and labour relations
    conditions in and around 1960s, 8,
    12
    conditions from late 1970s, 12, 14,
    16, 19–23, 84, 173
    economic theory, 13
    policies, 7–15, 118–20, 175–80
    relations in company, 33, 35–6, 40,
    162–3
    segmentation, 21–3, 70, 74, 79, 84,
    172–4
    views on labour relations and
    strikes, 144–5, 148–64, 183–4
Labour Party
    electoral support in Sheffield or
    UK, 24–5, 28, 128–9, 131–2,
    135–6, 138–9
    electoral support and defection
    among respondents, 129–46,
    148–9, 156–9, 181–2
    governments and policies, 9–13

multinational corporation take-over,
    33–4, 37–8

new right, 9–13, 17–18

    see also Conservative Party
'non-employment' *see* retirement,
    unemployment

racism *see* 'immigration'
redundancy
    composition of redundant
    workforce, 1, 30–2, 104
    lack of resistance, 34–40, 181
    notification, 33
    payments, 41–5, 113
    previous experience, 31
    reactions of workforce, 30, 32–40,
    49–50, 81–2, 104
    scheme, 39–45, 101
    secondary redundancy, 86–8
    selection for, 5, 101
    use of payments, 47–8, 102–3
    views of payments, 45–8, 103
retirement
    attitudes and reactions to, 118–19,
    121–6
    class differences in propensity to
    retire, 67–71, 113–15, 120, 126
    incomes in retirement, 41, 69–70,
    76–7, 79–80, 100, 112–13, 122,
    124–5, 174
    inducements and pressures to
    retire, 40, 43, 59–61, 67–8, 70–
    1, 83, 109–26, 170, 176–7
    trends, 105

search for work *see* work
secondary redundancy, 86–8
self-employment, 89
Sheffield
    general, 25–9
    politics and voting, 27–9, 131–2
    steel industry, 25–7, 86–8
strikes: steel strike 1980, 162–3
    see also labour market

trade unions
    in companies, 33, 35–6, 40, 162–3
    membership, 33, 138

in UK, 8, 12, 18, 184
see also labour market

'under-class', 22–3, 173–4
unemployment
  economic theory, 13
  images, 14–16, 18
  incidence in respondent group, 59–75, 82–90, 94–5, 106–9, 170–1
  incomes and expenditure, 75–7, 93, 95–6, 98, 100, 103
  long-term, 19–20, 63, 74, 83–4
  national costs, 177–8
  policies, 7–10, 13–18, 118–19, 175–80
  political reactions to experience, 136–7, 181–2
  as private experience, 81–2, 100, 103, 181
  psychological reactions to experience, 81–2, 94–100
  recorded rates in Sheffield, 26–7, 67

recorded rates in UK, 7–8, 11, 16–17, 19, 176, 178
recorded versus unrecorded incidence, 14–18, 56–7, 59–62, 106, 170–1, 179
registration, 56–8
remedies seen by respondents, 142–3
uneven incidence and effects in UK, 19–20

voting *see* elections

women's experience of and after redundancy, 1, 30, 42, 59–60, 67, 71, 77–8
work
  commitment and 'work ethic', 15, 49–50, 55, 67–8, 90–3, 97, 125–6
  search for, 50–6, 58, 69, 99–100, 116–18, 171

Lightning Source UK Ltd.
Milton Keynes UK
UKOW01n0050070318
318986UK00002B/39/P